CREATED FOR Joy

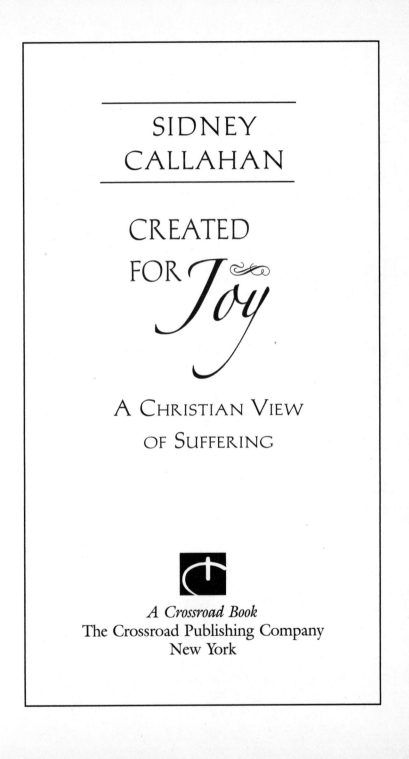

SIDNEY
CALLAHAN

CREATED
FOR *Joy*

A CHRISTIAN VIEW
OF SUFFERING

A Crossroad Book
The Crossroad Publishing Company
New York

The Crossroad Publishing Company
16 Penn Plaza – 481 Eighth Avenue, Suite 1550
New York, NY 10001

Printed in the United States of America on acid-free paper

The text of this book is set in 11/15 Galliard.

Library of Congress Cataloging-in-Publication Data
Callahan, Sidney Cornelia.
    Created for joy : a Christian view of suffering / Sidney Callahan.
       p.   cm.
    Includes bibliographical references and index.
    ISBN-13: 978-0-8245-2566-8 (alk. paper)
    ISBN-10: 0-8245-2566-3 (alk. paper)
    1. Suffering – Religious aspects – Christianity.   I. Title.
    BT732.7.C33 2007
    231'.8 – dc22
                                                   2007003649

1 2 3 4 5 6 7 8 9 10   12 11 10 09 08 07

For Thomas Hawkins Callahan
January 18, 1961–March 6, 1961

and

Perry Ann Turnbull Callahan
born March 6, 1996

CONTENTS

– One –

SUFFERING

❧

I N AN EXCESS of confidence, the eighteenth-century poet William Blake proclaims,

> Man was made for Joy and Woe;
> And when this we rightly know,
> Thro' the World we safely go.

But is this true? Blake's words hardly seem adequate to our situation. For one thing, they don't do justice to the fact that human beings, unlike dogs and chimpanzees, can envision future disasters in excruciating detail. In the middle of the night, anxiety arises with the thought: "No matter how healthy and fortunate I may be at the moment, I am going to die. And in all probability my death will be accompanied by disease, disability, and pain. Worse still, everyone that I know and love is going to share the same fate."

Blake's words that man is "made for joy" sound promising but also present problems. What counts as joy and what causes it? Who can predict with certainty whether joys will come? And even if joy does grace my own life, will my children also experience happiness? Future states of bliss seem more difficult to imagine than intensely distressing experiences. This asymmetry in our emotions may be built into our nature, as we shall see when we discuss joy. But whether or not imbalance exists, the relationship of joy to suffering remains problematic. How can we be joyful while confronting the pain and woe of this world? In the face of great evils and in the midst of so much

1

distress, human beings desperately need to have answers to the eternal questions, *Why* do we suffer, and *how* can we cope? Is it possible to find joy and happiness despite suffering?

Admittedly, most of the time people manage to put these fundamental questions out of mind. The demands of daily routine distract us. I am as skilled as anyone in my capacity for denial, but with the coming of a crisis, defenses break down. September 11 brought one such moment. Ironically, I was going into my basement study to work on this book on suffering when I was called by my son to the roof terrace of our apartment building. From there we could see plumes of smoke billowing from the World Trade Center towers twenty-five miles down the Hudson. Immediately we rushed to the TV and stayed glued with the rest of the world for its coverage of the disaster. The phones were down, so it took some time before we could make contact with my two sons working in New York City or my mother living near the Pentagon. When we were able to get through, all were safe.

However, those of us fortunate enough not to lose family members were still unable to escape pervasive sorrow. "So many thousands gone," laments the old slave spiritual, so many lives so cruelly interrupted. Over the coming weeks as we tried to absorb the details, we would read the unending obituaries and weep again in private, as well as when attending the dreadful funerals. The attack killed many young men, so the rites were filled with brave young widows, sad children, and mourning parents. Accounts of the heroism and altruism of the fallen rescue workers brought more pain. As in wartime, whole families and entire neighborhoods grieved the loss of loved ones in the prime of life.

A communal catastrophe reopens personal wounds. Suppressed questions surface. Earlier encounters with suffering and death are relived. In our immediate family we had recently confronted our own "sudden," "senseless," and "horrible" interruption of a young life — an event that served to initiate this book. Five years before 9/11, and thirty hours after the birth of our son's baby daughter, a moment of great joy, her mother died from an unsuspected blood clot that had migrated from her leg to her lungs. Despite frantic medical efforts to save her, Ann died in pain and suffocating panic at age thirty-five, just as she had finally fulfilled her dream of becoming a mother.

In one hour, as the news came from the West Coast, Ann's family and friends moved from joyously celebrating the birth of a new baby girl to stunned sorrow, and in an instant we stumbled into a future forever changed. My husband and I flew to Los Angeles and brought our son Peter and his newborn daughter, Perry Ann Turnbull Callahan, home to live with us in our apartment. Devastated, we still had to function, one day at a time, and as with other families who find themselves violently torn by tragedy, we received an outpouring of sympathy and support, an apartment filled with baby clothes, baby furniture, and casseroles provided by our neighbors. True, disasters give human beings an opportunity to care for one another, but all the altruism and kindness in the world cannot take away the pain or resolve the larger question of why such tragic things happen.

Because fatal complications in childbirth occur only in one out of ten thousand cases, a number of unlikely, unnoticed events must converge in order to cause death, and so the rarity of such outcomes brings the terrible realization that things could just as easily have been different. For me, Ann's sudden death triggered vivid memories of an earlier senseless loss: the crushing pain of losing our fourth baby son, Thomas, who at forty-two days young perished in a sudden infant death, on March 6, 1961, my twenty-eighth birthday. Thirty-five years later on March 6, 1996, Ann gave birth to Perry, and I felt great joy at the healing coincidence — until the telephone call came the next afternoon.

In tragedies where a series of contingencies results in disaster, survivors are tortured by obsessive thoughts of why this particular train of events took place. In the 9/11 disaster why should one firefighter remain unscathed, while his partner twelve inches behind him is killed by a body hurtling down from the North Tower? Others perished who went early to appointments in the Trade Center that morning, or — as with one young man we knew who uncharacteristically forgot his keys, went home to retrieve them, and missed his train — were saved by being late. In the case of Ann's death the nagging questions centered on whether the doctors might have performed one more test on her aching legs. Would another few minutes of exploration have led to the discovery and treatment of the blood clot? With our baby's sudden infant death my anguished questioning turned on whether an earlier check on his nap could have averted the tragedy. "If only," "if only," goes the litany of grief, but it is always after the fact. Disasters come in an instant, and they cannot be undone.

Mourners can be plagued by anxiety, shock, and what has been called "secondary trauma." If death and disaster can so suddenly and arbitrarily strike down the innocent in the midst of daily routines, then no one can feel safe. Terrifying events can happen here, there, or anywhere, at any time. As a young woman survivor thinks to herself in Ann-Marie MacDonald's novel *The Way the Crow Flies*, "It will be you the icicle falls on from twenty stories up. You waiting for the bus when a motorist has a stroke and mounts the curb. To have been available to disaster once means to be permanently without a roof."[1] Tragic events break down basic trust in the beneficence of the world. Our self-confidence crumbles. Loss and bereavement deplete the human spirit. In the worst-case scenarios people suffer from numbed depressions, apathy, and an unwillingness to risk new attachments or activities. Anniversary suicides take place. Launched into the care of my newborn granddaughter, I was at times assailed by anxiety: "What if Perry should suddenly stop breathing?" In these demoralized moments, I would forget that I had cared for three children before Thomas's sudden infant death and had borne and reared three more children afterward. I would overlook the good health and general good fortune of our six grown children and succumb to irrational fear.

Such fear arises from the fact that no matter how vigilant, no caretaker can ensure completely the safety of another, though we parents and grandparents try to reenact the folktale of Sleeping Beauty. In the familiar story a baby princess is cursed by a malevolent fairy to suffer a fatal accident with a spindle. Although another benign fairy godmother softens the curse into merely falling asleep, the king banishes all spindles from his kingdom. Years go by until one day the princess chances upon a deserted tower, finds the one spindle left in the land, and pricks her finger, falling into an enchanted coma until a prince comes to her rescue. I can still see the picture in my first storybook, and now I wonder if the king was beset by bitter regret, asking himself, "Oh, if only I had searched the castle one more time?" Was he tormented by the question of why evil fortune had fallen upon him?

Of course, Sleeping Beauty was rescued by a kiss, but outside of fairy tales, tragedies cannot be so readily reversed or explained. A belief in curses and witchcraft is long gone from Western civilization, but it is quite understandable why they had such a long run: what a relief it is to blame scapegoats for the onset of misfortune. Superstitions and rationalizations that stave off the absurdity of chance persist because they alleviate our sense of meaninglessness and vulnerability. Yet the full tide of human helplessness continually comes in. "Boundless is the bitter sea," says a Chinese proverb. "All existence is suffering," states the first noble truth of Buddhism. All existence? protests the Westerner. Even birth? Can no one escape sorrow?

I live in the midst of affluent suburban towns along the beautiful Hudson River without a slum in sight, but distress still floods our shores. In the last decade, long before September 11 brought suicidal terrorist planes into sight, our parish

had lost the O'Hara family — mother, father, and daughter —
in the crash of TWA Flight 800 bound for France; only their
twin sons survived, having remained at home to go to camp.
Another neighbor couple in our town lost their sixth-grade
daughter when the drawstring of her jacket happened to catch
on the school bus door and unobserved by the driver she
was dragged to her death. A young woman was shot by her
schizophrenic boyfriend, and there has been a racially motivated killing over a parking dispute in the lot of a nearby deli.
Around the corner from the store another murder (unsolved)
took place in a home office (perhaps related to a New Jer-
sey mob?). In the same period three armed hostage standoffs
narrowly avoided lethal outcomes.

Other violent offenses have included four unsolved rapes
on the aqueduct trail that cuts through the towns and three
cases of sexual abuse of pupils by elementary school teachers.
It also goes without saying that as in most other communities
in America, a score of automobile accidents, drug overdoses,
and suicides have ended the young lives of adolescents. Such
dramatic incidents make the headlines in the local paper, but
even they take place against the background of "routine"
sufferings — bitter divorces, domestic conflicts, devastating addictions, malignant diseases, mental illnesses, dementia, and
the never-ending stream of so-called natural deaths among the
old. A so-called natural death appears to mean that an individual's dying was less horrible than it might have been. The
death was not due to anyone's intentional act of violence, nor
was it caused by some medical error or accident that cut short
the expected life span. While death appears to be built into
the genetic program of the human organism, its inevitability
does not make it easier to bear, either on the part of the person dying or those left behind. As Pope John Paul II says in
his apostolic letter on suffering, "The evil which the human
being experiences in death has a definite and total character."[2]

Indeed, death aptly serves as the symbol and metaphor for all experiences of human impotence and distress.

Nicholas Wolterstorff, a Christian philosopher of religion, lost his twenty-five-year-old son in a climbing accident and composed a moving lament for his lost child. "It's the *never-ness* that is so painful. *Never again* to be here with us — All the rest of our lives we must live without him. Only our death can stop the pain of his death." Wolterstorff voices the perennial human protest when he writes, "Death is shalom's mortal enemy. Death is demonic. We cannot live at peace with death."[3]

Our imagination also works in bringing home to us the suffering of less personal global disasters from the world's recent history. Two world wars, countless local conflicts, famines, plagues, and at least six instances of genocide have marked our era. Americans watching televised images of the World Trade Center's disaster are reminded of the footage once seen of the ash-filled streets of Dresden and Hiroshima. The crowds of New Yorkers fleeing on foot up the streets and over the bridges mirrored the endless lines of refugees we witness in newscasts from around the world.

Suffering still abounds as millions of people on earth live amid civil wars, ethnic cleansings, famines, plagues, floods, earthquakes, and political terror. Detention camps and slums all over the world display similar scenes of squalor. While technological developments and new knowledge have alleviated much human suffering, they have also added to the cruelty and misery of the world. Job's afflictions in the classic biblical story can hardly match the scale or intensity of modern sufferings, which now include sophisticated electronic torture techniques, land mines, nuclear bombs, napalm, biological warfare, and media propaganda to incite genocides and wars. Large organized totalitarian states can use secret police and trained military troops to terrorize and impose punishments upon populations.

The larger and more efficiently organized an institution or social structure, the more potential there is for oppression, injustice, and bureaucratic indifference. Impersonal forces of what we call "social sin" can inflict suffering far beyond the capacity of any individual perpetrator. Economic and social organizations exert a power that destroys individuals and the earth's resources, such that the effects upon their victims and the environment are visible, even while the deeper causes of suffering remain hidden.

Suffering as a Mystery

When confronted with all these horrors on both a large and small scale, the instinctive human reaction is to protest as Job does.[4] How can this be? No, such evils should never exist. In his sorrow Wolterstorff cries out, "Suffering is a mystery as deep as any in our human existence."[5]

To name something a "mystery" is to signal that this concern is not like a "problem." Problems may be solved, but "mysteries" are not. In the words of a Catholic priest I met once, a sacred mystery is "infinite intelligibility," and the inclusion of "intelligibility" in this definition serves to summon us all to go down the path toward comprehension as far as possible when we come face to face with a mystery. Christians affirm that the infinite God of Truth gives humans the gift of reason in order for us to seek knowledge and wisdom. So we should never refuse to embark on what one astute contemporary theologian has called "the endlessness of making sense" of God's revelations to humankind.[6] In the case of suffering, we are particularly called to seek understanding, because distorted meanings given to suffering can result in passivity and increased suffering. How many abused women have remained in dangerous destructive relationships because of their belief that their suffering was inevitable, deserved, or ennobling? Glorifying suffering has allowed persons to ignore the plight of the poor in one more instance of what has been called "the abuse of the cross." It makes a difference whether a person holds that suffering is good for you in this world, or at least good for other people. An ironic *New Yorker* cartoon shows two well-dressed middle-aged businessmen walking down a city street, with one saying to the other, "I suffer as much as you. I just don't let it interfere with my ability to make others suffer."

In the world of social policy, making decisions to launch wars, employ torture, withhold welfare payments, or build more prisons are grounded on implicit assumptions of the value and efficacy of inflicting pain and suffering on others. At the opposite pole of judgment, efforts to fund scientific research, sue for peace, increase welfare provisions, or organize humanitarian aid programs are motivated by the perceived obligation to alleviate human suffering. In private lives, countless decisions about divorce, child rearing, vocational choices, medical interventions, and dying are shaped by individuals' views of suffering. Ideas matter; concepts, beliefs, and worldviews shape public and private behavior. I have always been impressed with the maxim of the great social scientist Kurt Lewin, who said that "there's nothing so practical as a theory." A theory, or map of ideas and facts involving cause and effect, will give meaning to the confusing flow of perceptions and events. Theories guide an individual's attention to information that is relevant for future action, as well as grounding further thought. If we want to understand and cope with human suffering, we must inquire into its meaning and pin down its slippery boundaries. We may know it when we see it, or feel it, but is there any consensus as to the definition of suffering? How does one sort out the varieties of sorrow?

Suffering Defined and Described

We can all easily agree that suffering consists of an aversive experience involving severe distress — mine, yours, theirs, or ours. To be severe, the aversive experience must cross some threshold of intensity or magnitude. Mere annoyance, frustration, or irritation hardly qualify as suffering. Being trapped in a traffic jam in a car without air conditioning on the way to buy ice cream on a boiling Sunday afternoon is annoying, but it is hardly onerous enough to count as suffering. And yet, since suffering is personal and subjective, we must recognize that the threshold of intense aversion may differ for different people. As the story of the Princess and the Pea humorously points out, confirmed by modern science,[7] individuals vary in their physical and psychological sensitivities due to innate temperament and personal histories. A child may suffer differently from an adolescent who may be distressed in a different way from a mature adult or a fragile elderly person. Other obvious factors involved will be an individual's intelligence, mental and physical health, present environment, cultural conditioning, moral character, and religious faith. Abandoned street children in a Brazilian slum will differ from affluent American children in their assessments of what counts as a hardship. An impoverished Calcutta laborer will have become inured to different deprivations than a rich European professional. Yet all who suffer characterize the experience as seriously aversive and intensely distressing.

One inclusive and broad-ranging definition of suffering holds that it is "to feel pain or distress; to sustain injury, disadvantage, or loss; or to undergo a penalty. Suffering can be physical, psychological, or spiritual, and it can take many forms."[8] This description makes the point that the perceived absence or removal of a critical good can hurt as much as the onset or continuation of an aversive experience. How many poor immigrants have suffered from being denied access to educational opportunities or excluded from the employment they needed to feed their families? The constant frustration and thwarting of perceived personal abilities is painful, a form of suffering.

Another incisive description of suffering claims that no matter what form it takes, it will always be a condition or state of mind "in which we wish violently or obsessively that our situation were otherwise."[9] We want the pain or distressing condition to be reversed, the onerous penalty to be lifted, the loss restored, or the torment to stop. In other words suffering is in some way a severely aversive condition that is *imposed* upon us, something that is beyond our capacity to control, undo, or change for the better. Thus, even an experience of uncertainty or not knowing can be distressing. Intense anxieties and fears of the unknown can produce anguish. While strong individuals often can manage to control their reactions or responses to suffering, they may still be unable to do anything about its onset, duration, or causes. A firefighter may overcome fear to run into a burning building and rescue a child, but he cannot control the bodily pain inflicted by the flames or the damage inflicted by smoke inhalation. And if he is unable to save the child's life, another kind of suffering ensues for him.

Suffering in self-conscious human beings should not be identified solely with physical sensations of pain. A distinction between pain and suffering has been pointed out by the physician Eric Cassell in his classic work on suffering. He maintains that in contrast to pain, "suffering can be defined as the state of severe distress associated with events that threaten the intactness of a person."[10] When physical pain causes suffering, it is because it is felt as a serious personal threat. It signals helplessness, hopelessness, and meaninglessness.[11] Pain is always affected by its context and meaning. In rare cases pain will not induce suffering, as for example when pain reveals that a paralyzed nerve has been restored to function, or the pain that accompanies superior athletic performance. Moreover, some cultures have used voluntarily self-inflicted pain as part of their ascetic religious rites.[12] Certain Native American rituals or some flagellant practices of Moslems and Christians are instances in which modulated experiences of self-inflicted pain are invested with positive meanings. The interpretation of the pain is not that of helplessness, hopelessness, or meaninglessness, but of personal mastery, penance, or sacrificial gift. Also pain can be experienced as sexual pleasure in certain sadomasochistic practices.

By contrast, *involuntary* pain caused by various diseases and impairments points to the vulnerability of the physical organism. Such pain signals the onset of disability, disintegration, old age, and death. Something is malfunctioning, and the end will be death. Chronic pain may be particularly distressing because it destroys the hope of a future restoration to health. When the onset of gnawing, throbbing, tearing, or burning sensations of pain cannot be alleviated or controlled, then the intactness of the self as an agent is violated. Indeed, even without physical pain, the loss of the ability to function as an independent self-maintaining normal person in the world can cause suffering. Handicaps, impairments, and imprisonment reduce the self's abilities to freely operate. Illness or unremitting fatigue or malnutrition break down both body and mind as resources are depleted. Not to be able to care for oneself or nurture those we love is a grievous loss. Intense suffering can arise when a body is too weak to protect self or others in need. Seriously ill young mothers may not be in pain, but they can suffer from their inability to care for their families. In the increasing fragility of old age, as in illness, human beings can be forced to submit to "the will of the body."[13]

Most frightening of all to modern persons is the new evidence of how much the mind also operates at the will of the body, or at the will of that key element of the body which is the brain. Brain diseases and impairments or biochemical imbalances disturb thinking and emotional capacities. Mental diseases can inflict dreadful suffering on victims. Depression, for instance, has been described as a "gray drizzle of horror," "a smothering confinement" or a "howling tempest in the brain."[14] Those who suffer psychotic episodes can undergo horrible experiences of "delusions of guilt, persecution, physical decay, and impending death; visual hallucinations and perceptual distortions; rapid fluctuations of consciousness; increasing paranoia and intense panic; and suicidal and homicidal ideation."[15] A person with advanced Alzheimer's disease may no longer be self-aware enough to suffer, but persons who recognize that they are beginning to fail (especially intellectuals who have lived by their wits) can suffer enormously along with their families.

Suffering Inflicted by Others

As inclusive definitions and descriptions of suffering attest, the human journey toward death is marked by many conditions of distress from physical impairments and natural disasters. But in the midst of good health persons can suffer wounds caused by distressing interpersonal experiences. Psychological assaults and rejection can cause so much anguish because human beings live embedded in families and groups; survival and flourishing depend on secure bonding and the support of kin and neighbors. Suffering caused by betrayals, rejection, contempt, or verbal abuse may be more painful than those inflicted by physical assault. The psychoanalyst Viktor Frankl recalled that in the concentration camp when a Nazi guard contemptuously pelted him with a pebble to make him heel like a dog, this humiliation was more distressing than a brutal beating. Sticks and stones may not break my bones, but names will always hurt me.

The closer the emotional bond between persons, the greater the vulnerability. In families emotional and verbal abuse of children can produce as much damage as sexual or physical abuse; strangers can never betray trust to the same degree as a parent, a spouse, or an adult child. "It is sharper than a serpent's tooth to have an ungrateful child," laments Shakespeare's King

Lear. These words, revealing Lear's distress over familial betrayal, demonstrate how we humans use physical images to describe psychological and emotional suffering. Betrayals "stab us in the back" or "tear us apart" or leave us "twisting in the wind." And though metaphors of bodily injury describe psychic sufferings, at the same time, the mind-body unity means that mental and emotional stress do actually produce physiological symptoms of queasiness, agitation, nausea, flushing, tearing, suffocation, or numbing paralysis. Human beings are the most emotionally and physically responsive species, because of our large brains, complex bodies, and intense social attachments. We are "the self-interpreting animals," and this uniqueness increases our vulnerability to suffering. No other animal can make a promise, or suffer when it is broken.

Self-Inflicted or Blameworthy Suffering

Another dimension of King Lear's lament demonstrates just how much human suffering is self-inflicted. Like all tragic heroes Lear possesses serious character flaws that serve to destroy him, and he is an emblem of how self-sabotage marks the human condition. Freely chosen behaviors bring suffering back upon a person. Human acts produce bouts of guilt, envy, rage, shame, regret, fear, and other torturing negative emotions. So much of the world's suffering can be categorized as "blameworthy" or "merited suffering," in contrast to "innocent" suffering that comes from without in contingent events or the actions of others. The emotional suffering that we inflict upon ourselves can hurt as much as other wounds. Moral guilt from the activity of conscience was aptly known in Middle English as "agenbite of inwit," or for the poet George Herbert as "a tooth or nail to scratch." Guilt, remorse, and shame are inescapable torments because they arise from self-consciousness and so accompany us as long as we are awake, sometimes even intruding in our dreams.

While evildoers wreak destruction on those around them, they also injure themselves in subtle and not so subtle ways. A cursory run through the seven deadly sins reveals that such sins are "lethal," not only in the damage that they inflict upon others but in the harm they bring to the sinner. The proud become isolated, and the greedy, envious, and lustful remain perpetually unsatisfied. Those who rage and hate others are hated in turn and enjoy no solace. The slothful are stunted. To habitually choose evil actions can produce deadening inner lives and constant suspicion that others will seek revenge. Monsters such as Stalin or Hitler or Saddam continually feared being assassinated by their amoral accomplices or being betrayed by their many enemies. Quite often, evildoers receive their just deserts in this life. As the old maxims have it, "What goes around, comes around," and "the mills of the gods grind slowly but they grind exceedingly fine." Suffering arising from what has been called "the law of retribution" also can be helped along by informal group sanctions such as gossip, ill repute, contempt, and shunning. Human beings through long evolutionary social selection are prepared to detect cheating and unfairness and take corrective action. People will go to great lengths to punish offenders.

Torture as the Ultimate Suffering

The depths of the nightmare of history's evil may be in the suffering caused by torture, for deliberate torture plumbs the depths of suffering. A human being is tortured when subjected to intense physical pain coupled with mental and emotional torment by the use of coercive power. Women, children, slaves, outcasts, and defeated enemies have been victims of torture throughout human history, and prehistoric evidence exists of ritual torture. Indeed, even Scripture contains examples of coercive torture, as in the case of the Maccabees who resisted worshiping pagan idols. The medieval Inquisition and the

Renaissance state used torture on enemies and on religious dis-
senters. In recent centuries, rogue states and guerrilla groups
have resorted to torture, and totalitarian regimes have insti-
tuted systematic institutions of torture and loosed mass terror
upon entire populations. The S.S. and Nazi Holocaust atrocities are infamous, but the effects of tortures inflicted within
the Soviet Gulag may be more horrendous and longer lasting.[16]
Hardest to bear for Americans is the mounting evidence that
our own agents and soldiers have employed systematic torture.
Torturers are not depraved exceptions or mentally ill persons.
Otherwise "normal" persons can be trained to their tasks and
inflict policies of torture without protest.[17] In recent decades
Nazi and Communist regimes that regularly committed atrocities have been joined by a long list of other states, including
South Africa, China, Greece, Algeria, Egypt, Argentina, Chile,
Cambodia, and others. Today the practice of torture is spread-
ing and actually admitted to by 150 governments, according
to Amnesty International surveys.

In torture, the threat to the intactness of the self is a cal-
culated strategy. Degradation rituals, such as stripping, rape,
caging, and deprivation of food, water, sleep, and sanitary fa-
cilities are inflicted. The humiliating treatment is intended to
reduce a person to an object or a captured animal. Uncertainty,
isolation, arbitrary rules, and constant insults can induce severe
reactions of anxiety, helplessness, hopelessness, and humiliation, which are further manipulated by captors. The goal is to
dominate and break down a victim's intactness. One aim of
torture is to take away the victim's voice[18] so that the victim
speaks what the torturer wills. A young missionary nun ab-
ducted and tortured in a Guatemala prison by cigarette burns,
blows, gang rape, and sexual abuse is taunted by her rapist,
"Your God is dead."[19] Victims are told that they are alone,
abandoned, and have been betrayed by others they may have
relied upon. A belief in goodness and justice or any hope for

rescue must be crushed. "No one will ever know about this"; or "you will never get out of here alive."

Another goal of torturers is an effort to force victims to cooperate in the betrayal or torture of others. To be coerced into complicity with harming others induces feelings of guilt and shame. The S.S. and KGB would extract names of persons from those tortured who would then be arrested. In the Guatemala cell, the young nun's hands were held fast to a machete that her torturer wielded to cut and maim a woman held with her in the prison cell. Thus, survivors suffer from having been forced to cooperate with their torturers.

The final triumph of the evil of torture occurs if and when survivors cannot recover. Those who escape testify to their lingering sense of isolation, anxiety, shame, and depression. After such a cruel betrayal by fellow humans it is difficult to ever trust anyone again or avoid feelings of fear; the effects of torture can last for years. Some victims never recover, and thus torture has been called "soul murder" or "spirit murder." The after-effects of traumatic suffering may distort cognitive and emotional responses. Paradoxically, prolonged and extreme suffering can have the effect of numbing all feelings.

Numbness and Affliction

If suffering is defined as intense and severe experiences of aversive feelings of distress that threaten the integrity of the self, what then do we make of victims who are too benumbed and beaten down to subjectively respond to their condition? In a defensive move to avoid experiencing any more pain human consciousness can shut down. A condition of shock can curtail mental and emotional processing of information, and present perceptions or persistent memories of torment can be dissociated, distanced, or separated from awareness. Sometimes veterans returning from battle show muted emotional responses that can take a toll on their families.[20]

Other persons, deprived, impaired, or abused from birth, may never have had a chance to develop normal emotional expectations or responses in the first place. Severely neglected or mistreated children may not acquire enough language to articulate their feelings to themselves or to others. People can become so habituated to persistent suffering that it is no longer felt acutely. When the Catholic theologian Edward Schillebeeckx speaks of suffering as a "contrast experience"[21] he is thinking of suffering as distressing because it contradicts the deeply felt human expectations for love, beauty, joy, and goodness. But what if humans have been so abused and deprived, perhaps from birth, that they cannot experience the unremitting and chronic awfulness of their situation? Those who suffer most may not protest or violently wish that things were different for themselves or others because they no longer can wish for anything. Simone Weil describes this condition of numbed despair as "affliction."[22] Dorothy Soelle, another noted writer on suffering, describes a kind of ultimate suffering in which sufferers are reduced to internal deadness, when "feelings for others die."[23]

In his novel *The Plague* Albert Camus brilliantly describes the deadening apathy overtaking a city undergoing an unremitting fatal epidemic, and Camus's narrator, Dr. Rieux, observes that "the plague had gradually killed off in all of us the faculty not of love only but even of friendship."[24] People who could no longer imagine normal life revealed "the most disheartening thing: that the habit of despair is worse than despair itself."[25] Habitual despair deadens all responses, even acute pangs of sorrow.

Truly "afflicted" victims without feeling are too hopeless to struggle. Victims may even conclude that they deserve their fate. Many abused women become convinced of their own unworthiness to receive better treatment and so do not act on their own behalf. When battered long enough by an unending stream of suffering, who has the energy to protest? And to whom? Indeed, one of the inspiring features of the story of Job in the Old Testament is the fact that Job never stops complaining to God and lamenting the injustice of his sufferings. Job's comforters could never persuade Job that he deserved his suffering, nor could his wife prevail in her counsel to curse God and die. While lament and protest may appear to intensify distress, they mark the ability to retain self-consciousness, and this distinguishes humans from other animals in pain. Likewise, empathy for the suffering of others counters numbness. Empathy for the suffering of others becomes a crucial and often overlooked dimension in explorations of suffering.

Empathy and Suffering

Human empathy is the capacity to instantly, intuitively, and concretely feel what another is feeling. In infancy when one baby cries, others will wail. Children try to comfort other children in pain. Throughout life we are moved to cry, rejoice, panic, and become angry when others do. When intellectual understanding informs and accompanies empathy, humans can take the other's point of view and sympathize. Empathy and sympathy coexist in compassion when we feel another's pain and benevolently desire to relieve that person's suffering; empathy and sympathy together work to reduce the amount of suffering in the world.

But at the same time the empathy that we feel for others serves to increase and magnify suffering. Identification with a beloved person's anguish is particularly distressing. Watching strangers suffer can be dreadful, but it is even more a torment to stand by and see those we love suffer. In *The Hunt Sisters,* a novel by Elizabeth Robinson, a young woman watches her newly married sister slowly and painfully lose her battle with cancer and writes to another friend, "Watching someone you love being hurt is its own special hell. Because you are not hurt, because you are strong, you feel you ought to prevent the pain from being inflicted; her pain is blameless, while your psychic pain is laced with the guilt of knowing you didn't do anything to stop it, and the fact that you couldn't have comforts only your mind, never your heart."[26] The traditional devotion to Mary in her maternal sorrow at the foot of the cross has been an expression of this universal response. Every parent has suffered with a child's pain and torment. I will never forget my own distress in the emergency room watching my four-year-old's agony of pain and panic as he fought against the straitjacket necessary to stitch up his wounds. This quite brief episode (which seemed to go on forever) can hardly compare to what parents of chronically ill and dying children endure in countless places.

The Uniqueness of Empathic Suffering

Empathy and sympathy are intense and vivid emotional experiences that stand in contrast to numbed affliction, for the suffering of empathy is induced by caring engagement and identification with others. The feeling of pain with and for the other directs an individual's attention beyond the self. It does not narrow or diminish consciousness but expands it. Moreover, empathy and sympathy can be felt for others who are too afflicted and benumbed to feel their misery for themselves. Who has not felt distress for semi-comatose survivors of violence or those in shock after surviving a natural disaster? Concentration camp inmates, starving peasants, or neglected orphans may be mute and stare without expression, but observers can suffer with them and over their absence of feeling. Pain for another who is impaired can be felt for what isn't there, or should be there. Compassion for the demented or Alzheimer's victim responds to their evident diminishment of their condition, whether they can any longer be aware of how much they have lost. We can suffer for their loss of the ability to know and feel.

Going further, to feel compassion for the morally deformed and stunted who have lost their moral sense is also possible, though more difficult. Sorrow and pity arise, for instance, when looking at the grotesque faces of the white women and teenagers screaming and spitting at small black children integrating southern schools, making clear that empathy and compassion do not require moral approval. A love for our enemies can be brought about by empathy for their weakness, their ignorance, and their sad and deformed lives. Jesus in the parable of the prodigal son depicts a father who suffered as his unrepentant son morally debased himself. Thus, the unique qualities of empathetic suffering are important to remember when addressing the question of whether God suffers, and if so, how? The fact that empathy arises with love also brings us back to the question of how suffering can relate to joy.

Joy and Suffering

When Blake says, "man was made for joy," he celebrates the experience of humankind's gladness and rejoicing. The existence of these multitudinous experiences of joy can be as much a mystery as suffering, for how can we explain the joy we feel in love, art, truth, beauty, pleasure, goodness, or the delights of human life? Christians point to their faith in a good and benevolent Creator existing in Love, Joy, and Light for help in explaining the existence of human happiness, and yet believers confront then a problem as to how evil and suffering exist in this world made by an all-good, all-loving Creator. For unflinching atheists, evil and suffering are more easily explained: we simply exist in a meaningless universe where "the most reasonable belief is that we came from nothing, by nothing and for nothing."[27] Things are just the way they are because physical laws and the mindless evolution of matter have played these cards by chance. For such skeptics the problem is why there seems to exist intense experiences of love, joy, and beauty, which persist in surprising the wariest heart.

Christians, however, have to struggle to understand the meaning of suffering and its relation to joy. And so the life of Jesus Christ, his suffering and death on the cross, will be a crucial part of all Christian explanations and answers. Christ promises his disciples joy and also that sufferings will come, but the relationship between the two is unclear. Is there a divine plan at work?

Two

THE PLAN?

❧

W HEN FACED WITH the sudden death in childbirth of the mother of his daughter, my son Peter said to me, "I think it would be easier to bear if I knew this was God's plan and not just an awful accident." "I understand how you feel," I replied. "It might be consoling to think that this was 'meant to be,' but then we would have to say that God plans the death of young mothers, and I can't believe that." How could a God who loves each of us more than we can ever imagine cause the loss of young mothers that leave babies bereft? It asks too much of faith to imagine that a loving God plans for infants to die sudden deaths, for the young to die in terrorist attacks, for children to be abused and murdered — or for genocides, torture, Holocausts, and plagues like AIDS to afflict the world. Surely the torments and suffering of humankind could not be sent by a merciful God. Or could they?

Forty years ago, in popular Roman Catholic piety, full approval was given to such views. Every disaster was ascribed to the mysterious workings of God's plan for humankind. When my husband and I suffered the sudden death of our infant son, well-meaning friends offered words of "comfort" assuring us that God had *sent* this tragedy to us. Actually all was for the best we were told, since God never *sends* more suffering than you can bear. As one neighbor lady remarked, "Think how much better for an innocent baby to be taken to heaven now, rather than die in a teenage automobile accident!" This kind of pseudo-solace sprang from firm beliefs that God controls the arrival of suffering and death for each of us, and that every cross arrives with one's name on it. Sufferings were viewed as blessings in disguise — either as a positive test of faith, a form of necessary punishment, a purifying correction, or a general medicinal tonic for your spiritual condition. As the old Irish saying had it: "The more crosses you have here below the quicker you get to heaven." Parents who lost a second child to early death could be told that this was a sure sign of how much God loved them. The proper Christian response to suffering in this view should be welcoming submission, for true faith humbly trusts in God's providence. Suffering would ennoble and enable the ascent to holiness, as shown in the Lord's passion, not to mention the trials and travail of the greatest saints and martyrs. There was much talk of John of the Cross and the dark night of the soul; St. Teresa of Avila and St. Thérèse of Lisieux were cited for their ardent desires to suffer for Christ.

Testimonies to the value of suffering were buttressed by selected scriptural texts and other readings from tradition. Suffering was assumed to be God's just punishment for sin or granted as a privileged imitation of Christ's sacrificial death, or some combination of the two. In any case pain sent from God should be seen as in accord with God's plan. The Genesis story of the fall of Adam and Eve was understood as the explanation of the advent of all the death and suffering in the world. Humans are born guilty and deserve their punishments. Biblical stories clearly describe God's striking down of sinners, whether in Noah's sinful generation, the Egyptian firstborn, enemies of Israel, or grumbling Israelites. God's goodness was also shown through His punishments of those He loves. The Bible's description of the good father makes it clear that he chastises and disciplines the son he loves. Spare the rod, spoil the child.

This particular approach to suffering was summed up by C. S. Lewis in *The Problem of Pain,* a popular work written shortly after the Second World War and still acclaimed for its explanation of human pain and suffering. A learned Oxford don who converted to Christianity, Lewis was a supremely gifted apologist for orthodoxy and presented many difficult Christian doctrines in such clear prose that he convinced many of their truth, including myself as an eager adolescent reader. I have been intellectually shaped by his work, even though I now disagree with many of his views.

In his work on pain Lewis presents one image that has became famous. He describes God using pain and suffering as "a megaphone" to get our attention. Lewis argues that pain is necessary in God's plan because people, even good people, can become lulled by their good fortune in this world and forget to pay attention to their salvation in the next. Happiness leads to forgetfulness of God, while suffering and pain serve to turn a person's eyes and heart to Him. Pain and distress work effectively to produce the repentance that leads to conversion. Suffering is ultimately a merciful gift, because it turns many souls away from sin and indifference, and works to save them from the far more dreadful torments of eternal damnation. God deploys suffering as His instrument to perfect us. Pain now prevents eternal pain later.

Lewis quotes the Gospel texts that describe human beings as God's works of art, and in this regard he is thinking primarily of sculpture. Persons must be hammered and chiseled into the ideal persons God intends them to be, blow by painful blow. Indeed St. Vincent de Paul, in a quotation Lewis may have been familiar with, says of God's work, "He must take a hammer and knock off all that is superfluous with powerful blows, so that looking at him, you would think he was going to knock it to pieces." After the roughest portions have been removed "he takes a smaller hammer and after that a chisel..." and so on, to make the statue perfect.[1] In the same manner suffering sent by God shapes up individuals and prepares them to share God's divine life. Just as a potter shapes clay and the flames fire the pot to completion, the Father chastises his children in controlled acts of productive pain.

As an apologist for orthodox Christianity Lewis insists that an omnipotent God uses pain and suffering but is not to blame for its existence, for an all-good God cannot be the Author or Creator of anything evil. All the pain, disease, evil, death, and disorders of nature that distort God's good creation are entirely the fault of humankind, arising from the original sin of the first human beings in paradise. Human rebellion against God originated with our primeval parents in the Garden of Eden. Following St. Augustine, C. S. Lewis presents Adam and Eve as actual historical figures who lived without pain, sin, suffering, or death in a perfect uncorrupted world and who, through rebellious pride, selfishness, and misuse of freedom, turned away from God and produced not only sin, but all the world's pain, disease, disorder, and death.

Cogent as this explanation may be for humans, what about the pain of animals that evolutionary science now knows to have predated the human species? Lewis uneasily acknowledges the fact of evolution and begrudgingly grants the possible existence of animal pain before Adam. He tries to deal with this inconvenient fact by suggesting that the revolt of angelic spirits that preceded the fall of man may explain the animal pain that preceded the creation of human beings. After all Satan (who must never be seen as an independent demi-god but only as a fallen angel originally created by God as good) is shown tempting Adam and Eve to sin. For Lewis, Satan should be taken literally as the subtle father of lies who always and everywhere sows destructive evil and seeks to thwart God's will. In *The Screwtape Letters,* one of C. S. Lewis's wittiest books, Lewis warns modern Christians not to become so sophisticated that they forget that the Devil's most clever ploy is to make humans disbelieve in him. This strategy allows Satan to tempt humans more effectively and achieve their damnation.

Nevertheless, Lewis does not ignore the main point of the gospel news: that God loves the world and offers salvation and eternal joy in Jesus Christ. Still this good news depends on the bad news: the fallen state of humanity necessitates God's coming to save the race in a remedial action. After their sinful fall human beings are so ensnared in wickedness that only a divine redeemer can save them. Fallen humans created in God's image and blessed with free will must freely assent to Christ's offer of redemption. If individuals refuse the offer they incur God's just punishment. Persons damn themselves to hell by their free choices, so the sufferings of earth and those of hell do not impugn God's goodness or justice.

Yet in the end God will not be kept from His victory. He reigns eternally as an omnipotent, omniscient, and benevolent Sovereign controlling the universe for the good of all, sending Christ His Son to redeem humankind through suffering. Indeed God deploys all of human suffering to bring about His will. To illustrate, Lewis uses yet another striking analogy, comparing God to a good master who employs punishment to train his dog: what may seem cruel in the short run works for the dog's long-term benefit. A good trainer applies painful discipline to enable his dog to transcend its natural canine nature and be subsumed into the higher human world of his master. Lewis accepts the traditional assumption that a great hierarchical chain of being exists, ranging from God at the top to angels to human beings to animals. Humans can be lifted up to participate in the higher life of Christ through the discipline of suffering just as dogs can be lifted to obediently participate in human society.

Obviously a great deal of cultural water has flowed under the bridge since the 1950s. Scientific and evolutionary findings, feminist liberation movements, theological and scriptural scholarship — all have changed the contours of the religious landscape known to C. S. Lewis. Certainly when I first read his book on pain I never noticed that humans were being compared to dogs, or that God was being portrayed exclusively as male, or as a male dog trainer administering punishment. Nor did I question the praise of the heroic warrior ideals that Lewis adopted from his beloved Anglo-Saxon and Norse sagas.

At the time, the patriarchal, hierarchical, and violent assumptions underlying Lewis's theological vision of suffering and joy seemed completely normal to me. I came from a southern officer's family full of male chauvinism, respect for hierarchies extolling honor codes, and "RHIP" — rank has its privileges. Indeed, most Christians during that era would have found it practically impossible *not* to think of God as male or as anything but an omnipotent Sovereign King. While no educated adult believer would describe God as an old man with a beard or the Trinity as two men and a bird, the Lord God of Hosts was still imagined as masculine and automatically referred to using male pronouns. Traditionally God used force and as any good father or king would inflict suffering for a just purpose.

The patriarchal imagery that C. S. Lewis passed on to his readers came from a well-established tradition, both secular and theological, with literature and art conforming to this male-centered vision. Milton's great epic of *Paradise Lost* along with Dante and other classic texts shaped the Western religious imagination, and, true to form, in Milton as in Augustine's *The City of God,* there is an assumption of women's moral inferiority. It is weak Eve, not Adam, who is seduced, but Adam gallantly goes along with the woman's sin in order to remain with his consort. Eve, like all her daughters, is easily led astray and deserves to be dominated by her husband and punished with the pain of childbirth. Feminine inferiority, subordination, and women's appointed lot of suffering were part of Western patriarchal tradition.

In Chaucer's *Canterbury Tales,* feisty women like the wife of Bath may appear, but poor, oft-beaten Griselda from "Tale of the Clerk" is more representative. A victim of what we would now call "battered spouse syndrome," Griselda is used by Chaucer to teach a lesson that God "suffers us, for our good exercise, with the sharp scourges of adversity to be well beaten oft in sundry wise." In short, once again we are told, suffering is good for us.

Much earlier, St. Augustine, a convert raised as a Roman gentleman, had championed the flogging of schoolboys, slaves, and heretics. Beatings on behalf of good order and to achieve a good end were approved. Ironically, in one place in his *Confessions,* Augustine recounts how much he hated being punished in school and how counterproductive he found the rod's use in learning. However, in a later chapter he reverts to his cultural assumptions and claims that his schoolboy beatings were necessary and salutary. Augustine also does not protest wife beating. He praises his mother, Monica, for never having been beaten by his father, Patricius, while her friends were regularly subject to blows from their husbands. Augustine's point seems to be that Monica's exemplary behavior earned her exemption, not that a husband's physically disciplining a wife was wrong.

For Augustine, the severity of punishment is connected to his belief that all fallen human beings, whether male or female, adult or infant, are justly condemned to divine censure and the punishment of damnation. Unbaptized, and even baptized, babies could be consigned to Hell, along with all those who die unrepentant or have never heard the good word of Christ. Such beliefs about the narrow limits of salvation, which consigned the majority of humankind to eternal suffering, demonstrate that at the core of the classical theist tradition there was an acceptance of God's wrathful judgment and punishment. God creates and loves but also punishes and destroys. Moreover, God's omnipotence and perfection imply that God must be immutable and free from the imperfections implied in a changeable emotion such as suffering. Jesus as a human being can suffer but not God the Father. Christians had assimilated ancient philosophical ideals about what divine sovereignty would entail. God's love may be tender and merciful, but it is in no way vulnerable.

For Lewis, divine omnipotence means that God reigns as the sovereign King of Kings, a God to be worshiped as the supremely powerful agent who arranges every detail of human life according to His providential plan. Consequently, crosses and painful sufferings, like everything that happens to us, are dispensed according to God's predetermined detailed plan for salvation. Divine omnipotence and absolute control ensure that all of history unrolls according to a blueprint. The endpoint of history will be an ultimate apocalyptical event with a final accounting and judgment upon all the events that have occurred in this passing world. Mysteriously, while human beings retain free will in this drama, God foreknows what will be chosen, and is in control of whatever happens.

As one astute theologian expresses the problem with this theology, "The labyrinth is precisely the impossible attempt to figure out how human contingency, resulting from human choice, is not constrained by predestination, which is God's necessarily previous and sovereign choice."[2] Secondary causes created by God may be operating in the universe, but God still exercises control and micro-manages events. Thus, ultimately, there is no room for any concept of coincidence or a role for chance and contingency. When bad things happen to good people, as in sudden deaths and other catastrophes, the faithful must trust that a hidden meaning and positive scenario exists that is working for the divine will. Faith assures us that God's plan will someday be revealed. In the meantime believers, like patient Griselda or Job, must endure and affirm that their sufferings are blessings sent from God to lead the soul to salvation.

From this perspective the book of Job is read as providing a model of patient submission. Modern readers may be edified by the fact that Job never becomes so afflicted or benumbed that he loses his emotional capacity to mourn, and by the fact that his unremitting protest of his innocence was vindicated by God. Clearly Job's friends were shown up as false comforters, since Job was not being punished for secret sins, as his accusers insisted. Nor is there any hint in Job's story of the original sin in Eden, which justly brings punishment upon fallen humankind. But a disturbing aspect of the book is its opening, wherein God countenances testing Job's faith by allowing Satan to send a fearsome array of sufferings upon him. Job's pains and losses consist of every kind of travail from natural disasters to human hostilities — indeed, every possible affliction of the premodern age. He suffers economic ruin as his camels, oxen, donkeys, sheep, and servants are destroyed by marauding raiders. Then a sudden violent wind blows down the roof of a hall, killing his children and their families. Job himself contracts a horrible skin disease of boils. And in the midst of all these sorrows sitting on his dung heap, Job, a just and upright man, is finally subjected to the betrayal of his wife and his peers falsely accusing him of secret sins.

Job's friends are motivated by their belief in the certain operation of the law of retribution; in a just world governed by a good and all-powerful God, bad things befall those who deserve punishment, while the good are rewarded with good fortune. In reply Job steadfastly asserts his innocence and rejects his accusers. He laments and protests, but never succumbs to his wife's advice "to curse God and die." Even in the midst of ruin Job cries, "I know that my redeemer liveth."

Eventually God speaks, and Job listens and responds to God's description of His awesome grandeur as divine creator and ruler. God's mysterious and cryptic answers to Job out of the whirlwind have been variously interpreted over the centuries, as has the meaning of Job's response. Despite some ambiguity it is clear that God vindicates Job before his friends and refutes their accusations that his suffering is punishment for sin. God testifies to Himself as majestically overwhelming in mystery and power: who is Job to judge God? When Job admits, "I have uttered what I did not understand, things too wonderful for me which I did not know... therefore I despise myself and repent in dust and ashes" (Job 42:3–6), the Lord restores Job's fortunes. God gives Job twice as many goods as he had before and seven new sons and three daughters. The implication here that lost children, like stolen oxen, can be replaced is chilling, and is at least as upsetting as the notion that God had planned Job's sufferings as a test. This approach to suffering has led to a whole interpretation justifying the miseries of this world as "a vale of soul-making." God's people, like dogs, slaves, schoolboys, and women, need to be toughened up by learning to endure pain.

If pain and loss can be seen as a form of remedial divine therapy, then by analogy it was natural to assume that Christians in authority should imitate God and inflict pain and suffering for the sake of good order and communal well-being of the family, church, and state. For the glory of God and the common good, dutiful servants of God have inflicted punishment, imprisonment, exile, and death on enemies of society. The same justifications for inflicting pain permitted the use of torture and burning at the stake for witches and heretics. Until very recently, Christians defended the routine flogging of soldiers, sailors, slaves, prisoners, servants, wives, children, and schoolboys. Great saints followed in the footsteps of Augustine and cooperated in inflicting cruelty upon persons for their own soul's good and the good of the church or the state.[3] St. Thomas More hunted heretics and witches and as Henry VIII's good servant ordered floggings and burnings. A paternal administration of pain and punishment has been held to be a dutiful imitation of God's discipline. Feelings of empathy that might arise for the suffering of others in their torment have to be suppressed or rationalized away as the necessary cost of saving souls in a godly cause. Such views of suffering linger today. No one endorses burning heretics at the stake, but other inflictions of torture and suffering remain a contested issue in the present United States.

Popular Assumptions about Suffering in God's Plan

Popular Catholic piety as well as much secular spirituality still views suffering as part of God's providential plan. Certainly within Catholic devotional literature suffering can still be described as a gift from God. All the justifications presented by C. S. Lewis are endorsed along with the added belief that our sufferings can be conjoined with Christ's sufferings and offered up for the good of others. The belief that disciples can participate in Christ's work and suffering is a complex and crucial dimension of Christian thought, which will be explored in more detail in coming chapters. Here I only want to make the point that an exaggerated focus upon the intrinsic goodness and automatic benefits of suffering can exist in "folk Catholicism" and in fact go further than the Protestant stance of C. S. Lewis.

Catholic imagery and traditional devotions often feature blood-soaked crucifixes with Christ's tortured body in agony. Mel Gibson's movie *The Passion* is a recent example of one kind of traditional fixation upon blood and pain that goes beyond the descriptions found in the Gospels. Could this movie have been made by a Methodist? Would Gibson have been as eager to make this movie if Christ had been executed by lethal injection? Other grisly Catholic depictions of martyrs and their tortures and mutilations have been celebrated. Once touring a castle in Spain I found myself puzzling over a dim mural, only to discover that the odd objects next to a female figure were the chopped-off breasts of virgin martyr St. Agatha sailing through the air as she met her death by a Roman sword. On the same European trip I viewed Catherine of Siena's preserved head on display at the church of St. Dominic. At home in the United States. other Catholic iconography and devotions have featured St. Lucy offering her gouged-out eyes on a plate, St. Sebastian's arrow-pierced body, St. Lawrence burned on a grill, St. Catherine stretched on her wheel of torment, and so on. Believers may validly assert that the heroic martyrs of Christian history should never be undervalued, since martyrdom continues in new forms today, but at times a distorted message can be conveyed: dismemberment, mutilation, blood, suffering, and death are blessings and honors sent by a God who wants us to be "well beaten for our good exercise." Nothing trumps a bloody disembowelment in procuring a martyr's crown.

Current devotional collections of traditional prayers and readings still emphasize the general benefits of enduring cruel pain and suffering. Every day I pray and meditate using a booklet of readings that contains the Mass of the day, seasonal prayers, psalms, homilies, and a commemoration of the life of the saint of the day. I am extremely grateful for these selected readings, which help me pray in season with the whole church, but I sometimes demur from the homilies presented. Too many saints and spiritual writers praise and celebrate their sufferings as *sent* from God. For example, one such passage is an effusion from St. Rose Philippine Duchesne, who lived an extraordinary life of charity, first surviving the persecutions of the French Revolution and then volunteering to come as a missionary to the American frontier, where she endured more hardship. And yet I could not but wince when reading of St. Rose's desire "to live as a victim offered in a spirit of penance and love. May my whole being be the victim, all that I am and all that I have. May my own heart be the altar, my separation from the world and all earthly pleasures the sacrificial knife."

Such ardor of spirit is admirable, but her stated wishes assume two things. First, it is assumed that God can, and will, directly send pain and suffering to a victim and, second, that when the sacrificial knife falls, it is always a great blessing and a good in itself. Such ideas persisted into the twentieth century, when celebrations and descriptions of "victim souls" became popular and those who were crippled or impaired, diseased, or deformed were said to be especially blessed by God.[4] In some cases persons were encouraged to volunteer for extraordinary sufferings as a special vocation in response to God's will, carrying on ancient practices in which heroic martyrs appeared to eagerly court death and long for the sacrificial knife. In the same series of readings as that containing St. Rose's sentiments, one Dominican priest in the 1940s claimed that followers of Christ "must continue his passion, participating in both the sufferings and wounds of his divine body," a process made necessary because Christ's glory "makes it impossible for him to suffer further. However, he wishes that what his human nature can no longer undergo should be endured by his mystical body, thereby continuing his passion in us." Thus, disciples should welcome sufferings, especially those that the risen Christ is no longer able to experience. In another meditation typical of the same victim-souls piety a priest suffering from Lou Gehrig's disease affirms, "I believe that ALS is sent to me as a sign of God's love and is given to me for my own good and happiness. . . . I believe God gives me this pain and suffering."

This over-valuation of suffering also marks much "Catholic" fiction. In the novel *After Sleep* by Marc Salzman, a twentieth-century religious sister who has endured years of spiritual aridity begins to enjoy spiritual ecstasies. These experiences give her great joy as well as inspiring her to write fine poems, which garner praise from literary critics. But all too soon the nun is diagnosed with a brain tumor, which has been the source of both her artistic creativity and her ecstasies during worship. Her enthusiastic flights have disrupted the peace of her convent and disturbed the sisters' liturgical celebrations. And the sister, as a sacrificial heroine, volunteers to undergo surgery that will end both her disruptive ecstasies and her inspired poetry. Like the Little Mermaid who had to give up her beautiful singing voice in order to marry her prince and, now mute, gained feet to walk on land with the condition that every step would be excruciatingly painful, the heroic sister suffers from her muteness but sees her losses as God's will. She recalls what her first mentor, Sister Priscilla, had told her when her beloved grandfather had died: "God knows what he's doing even when we don't." Comfort can be found in the knowledge that "everything He did had a positive meaning and coherence." There are no coincidences and there is no question but that "God plans everything down to the smallest detail," including, presumably, the growth of brain tumors.

Though sensitively written by a non-Catholic, to glowing reviews, the novel's theological assumptions were never questioned or commented upon. Does God send gifts and then require that they be sacrificed with great suffering? As *After Sleep* shows, such a view of God inflicting pain for our own good according to His providential plan is pervasive even outside the church in the spirituality and attitudes of contemporary America.

Cultural Views of God-Sent Suffering and Death

One learns a lot from listening to the way people talk about God in everyday life, and I've found comments offered at funerals or after tragedies to be revealing. God is said to "take people" at "their appointed time"; God in His mercy spares certain people at one moment, while at other times hurries up a person's difficult dying. The implicit assumption is that an omnipotent God plans everything down "to the smallest detail" so that a person's death is fated to take place at a predetermined moment. Thus, it seems a blend of religious and secular fatalism is much in evidence. "When your number's up, it's up," as the saying goes. Human destiny follows a blueprint or script that inexorably determines that death will meet you in Samarra at the appointed time no matter what you do. If, and when, death is narrowly escaped, people confidently say "that bullet didn't have my name on it." Increasingly too in America, Eastern religious ideas of recurring cycles of rebirth enter popular discussion with talk of "my karma," or references to a past life's influence on this one. People are deemed to be "old souls," and destinies are thought to be predetermined.

Even in a popular self-help group such as Alcoholics Anonymous that stresses individual responsibility for changing one's abusive drinking behavior, a belief in a detailed plan and destined deployment of suffering can be found. One central affirmation of AA is that you must turn your life over to your Higher Power, as you understand Him, and that the higher power can be trusted to direct the details of your life. In AA meetings people often repeat the saying, "There are no coincidences; every thing happens for a reason." Both good and bad events are thought to be directly sent by God for our benefit. Intense personal experiences of suffering from alcohol abuse are described as "low bottoms" that are providentially sent in order to awaken and demonstrate the need for change, echoing C. S. Lewis's notion that pain acts as a megaphone to get our attention and induce conversion. The suffering sent from the Higher Power leads to good. "I became sick and tired or being sick and tired." AA heals in remarkable ways, and I think the movement can be defended as a work of a Holy Spirit — also given to anonymity. But the reality of its healing power and the intellectual explanation of its operation may not be in perfect accord with one another.

Similarly, other popular therapeutic and spiritual movements confidently describe God's beneficial deployment of suffering. "God sent this cancer to teach me to appreciate my family." Other accounts of edifying lessons to be learned from illness and loss are also proffered. Unfortunately in some "spiritual" interpretations of illness and alternative health care, an individual's disease is seen as a consequence of faulty attitudes and behaviors. Here the idea of a "predestined plan" blends with the tendency to "blame the victims for their plight." As one woman cancer patient of forty-three with two young children put it: "A cancer patient learns to see them coming, the ones who want to ask you (or tell you) just how you managed to give yourself this illness, and why you have failed so far to cure it. It is your toxic anger. It is what you eat, or fail to eat. It is your neglect of your third chakra, or your stubborn refusal to take coffee enemas. They would never be so foolish."[5] The need to explain and thereby blame the victim serves to protect the self from the fearful fact that random events can occur. Or if lightning does strike it can be interpreted as actually a timely warning from a merciful God to help avoid worse evils. The car accident, the cancer, the heart attack, or the death of a loved one can be seen as a signal from God to shape up.

Catastrophic Collective Punishments from God?

As with individuals, so with collectives. Large catastrophes and disasters have been seen as messages and punishments sent by God. A view that divine judgment is visited upon the world through natural disasters is founded on the presumption that the law of retribution also works on a large scale. Myths from many different peoples teach such lessons, but for Westerners it is a tradition amply recorded in Jewish Scriptures. Repeatedly, Israel is described as sinning and incurring the punishment of God through flood, fire, plague, poisonous serpents, sudden death, or military conquest by neighboring empires. If, on the other hand, the Israelites are obedient and faithful to God's law and covenant, they are rewarded with victory in battle, wealth, and possession of a land flowing with milk and honey. Good and bad fortune were viewed as directly dependent upon God's exercise of power in the world. Augustine meditating upon these Scriptures would apply the same explanation and moral analysis to all peoples in all ages, but in particular to judgments on the Roman Empire. A group must adhere to righteousness in order to flourish as members of the City of God or be punished for their wickedness in the City of Man. God is proclaimed as directly punishing a people's transgressions. Such views entered into Western history and have influenced later judgments of natural disasters into the present day.

In a famous instance, the 1755 earthquake that destroyed Lisbon was a cataclysm that brought forth defenses of God's providential punishments, as well as the beginning of modern Enlightenment doubts about such views.[6] The question began to be debated as to whether God was intervening in natural events to teach moral lessons, or, alternatively, was an earthquake just an earthquake? On the threshold of the European age of skepticism, many thinkers were beginning to view natural events as morally neutral, to be kept separate from the effects of punishments for blameworthy evil actions. Orthodox believers who held the line would agree with the learned Jesuit preacher's judgment, "It is scandalous to pretend the earthquake was just a natural event, for if that be true, there is no need to repent and to try to avert the wrath of God, and not even the Devil himself could invent a false idea more likely to lead us all to irreparable ruin."[7] The only question for traditionalists was, why Lisbon? Was it more sinful and deserving of punishment than other cities or was it to serve as a particularly telling lesson? Thus one modern commentator on the earlier theological debate says, "Many divines viewed the event as proof of God's mercy. The earthquake's survivors were given a chance to repent before the general apocalypse visited everyone"[8] — in other words an earlier version of Lewis's megaphone theory, in which the infliction of suffering could awaken repentance, increase virtue, and work for future salvation.

Enlightenment thinkers who rebelled against traditional providential explanations of the Lisbon earthquake were supported in their unbelief by Voltaire's biting satire of Candide, who as he roams from disaster to disaster, continually and inanely asserts that "this is the best of all possible worlds," no matter how awful the evils he encounters. For many others the Enlightenment's optimistic belief in nature's ordered goodness was shattered by the Lisbon earthquake because of the scale of the devastation and suffering. Religious believers found it more difficult to affirm that God rules everything in nature as well as in human affairs. Thus, a separation between biological/physical nature and human nature began to be made, but oddly enough, such distinctions between natural evils and man-made moral evils have lately come under question once again. Some modern thinkers considering our modern, interconnected, technological world have concluded that the devastation wrought by terrorist anthrax attacks, nuclear arms, global plagues, radiation pollution, biological warfare, or ecological disasters can "threaten to blur distinctions between natural and moral evils."[9] Malicious intent may no longer be required in assessments of the evil of a tragedy or disaster. Infected in the AIDS epidemic or subject to a genetic disease? Caught in an earthquake, starved in a famine, or thrown into the grinding maw of the Russian Gulag? The scale of human suffering resulting from different kinds of disasters serves to equalize and blend together categories.

The challenge to one's faith in God's good creation and omnipotence are similar. The philosopher Susan Nieman, whose work on evil I have been using here, views the history of modern philosophy as the effort of humans to find meaning in a universe full of every kind of evil and suffering. She warns that "debates about which blend of moral and natural evil is worse will lead us nowhere. I write in the fear and knowledge that either could destroy us all."[10]

I was struck by these words because of a recent experience of such an impasse. One afternoon I found myself in an inner-city AIDS ward conversing with the priest who serves as the hospital chaplain. He had been trained as a biologist before going to the seminary and now ministered to the ill and dying in that particular vale of tears. Our talk took place during the period when the daily news was full of the rapes, murders, and depraved atrocities occurring in the ethnic cleansings of Bosnia. As we spoke, we began to confess our distress as believers in a good God confronting the evil and suffering of this world. I said that a scourge like AIDS shook my faith in the ordered goodness of God's creation, but my ordained confrere, the ex-biologist, demurred. "No, no," he said, "You should remember that the AIDS virus is just following its natural purposes of replication and survival in its hosts." He was much more sickened and troubled in spirit by the existence of gratuitous acts of human depravity. How could human beings be created in the image of God and act toward one another with such cruelty?

I had to admit that suffering in warfare, violence, and genocides was unspeakable. The innocent are always vulnerable. Old people starve. Women are raped, and it is not unknown for pregnant women to have their wombs ripped open and their fetuses destroyed. Infants and children are dashed to death against walls before their mother's eyes. Even so, such atrocities are not caused by God but are the acts of human beings choosing to abuse their freedom. More disturbing for some believers are those cases in which an arbitrary convergence of natural events causes and increases sufferings. Chance events can magnify minor human infractions into tragedies. A person smokes in bed and "accidentally" sets fire to the house, killing four children. The AIDS epidemic may be the chance result of native African hunters becoming infected from the monkeys they trapped and slaughtered, but it is made worse by poverty and sexual license.

Upon reflection, and after reading about the Lisbon earth-quake debate, I saw that actually my priest friend and I were engaged in a futile debate. Categorizing causes of suffering does not solve the deeper problem of evil, since the very exis-tence of "horrendous evils of life-ruining magnitude" produces the problematic human questions.[11] Considering the difficul-ties of these questions it is perhaps understandable that the strictest strains of Christianity projected the causes of all evil on to humankind. God's infliction of suffering was justified as a just and well-deserved punishment in order to satisfy the affront to God of human infidelity and sin.

In our own American Calvinist tradition handed down from the Puritans, God's sovereignty was interpreted to mean that God would justly condemn many to hell while graciously predestining some persons to salvation. Eighteenth-century theologian Jonathan Edwards preached such doctrines and taught that God inflicted natural evils upon humans as punish-ment. As an intellectual and student of the current new science and philosophy, Edwards saw such discoveries as part of na-ture's workings, believing that God indeed worked through natural means, controlling and ordering every detail.[12] Living on the American frontier in a British colony did not keep Edwards from being concerned about the world's struggle against sin (the Roman Catholic Church, the faithless whore of Babylon, high on his list of opponents). Edwards routinely proclaimed to his parishioners that disasters from fire, plague, lightning strike, earthquake, hurricane, or Indian attacks were sent by God to discipline His people. A merciful God sent chas-tisements to wake persons up to the importance of attending to the salvation of their eternal souls.

And yet, as a lover of beauty, Edwards saw God's creation as filled with divine gifts such as reason, beauty, love, joy, and family ties. He experienced mystic raptures in prayer and con-templation of God's goodness and love, all the while seeing divine punishment as integral to gospel truth. In his view, no human suffering, even that of infants and children, should be seen as unjust because of the inherited and damning guilt of humanity's original sin. Beloved children might look innocent, but without Christ's salvation they were but "vipers" fit to be justly damned, a notion that led Edwards to tell his flock that those who lost children in a local epidemic should understand it as a warning from God,[13] a chastisement for loving their children immoderately, and thereby putting worldly values before heavenly concerns.

Perhaps the suffering of children should stand as a test case in this regard for either the acceptance or rejection of a belief in God's providential control over the world. Two great fictional statements of disbelief turn on the wrenching horror of innocent children dying in torment. One is the story told by Ivan in *The Brothers Karamazov,* by Dostoevsky, of serf children being hunted and torn apart by their feudal master's dogs in punishment for some small infraction. Who could believe in God's goodness in a world with such innocent suffering? The other story is a child's horrendous death in *The Plague* by Camus, in which the child who cannot be saved only suffers more pain from efforts to save his life. After the child's death Father Paneloux, the priest, gives a sermon in which he admits the child's dreadful suffering, but goes on to say that as believers "we must believe everything or deny everything. And who among you I ask, would dare to deny everything? ... Today God had vouchsafed to His creatures an ordeal such that they must acquire and practice the greatest of all virtues; that of the All or Nothing."[14]

Jonathan Edwards always chose the All. His theology asserted that God sent sufferings into individual lives that collectively were moving toward a final apocalyptic judgment where dreadful punishments would be inflicted upon the eternally damned in hell. Edwards is famous for his sermons graphically describing the terrors and tortures of the final judgment and the sufferings of hell. Perhaps the most disturbing features of these sermons is Edwards's vision of God and the saved in heaven rejoicing over the suffering and pain of the damned in hell. (Alas, this joyful acceptance of God's just infliction of torment was also taught by St. Thomas.) As Edwards paints the picture, "The saints in glory will...understand how terrible the sufferings of the damned are; yet...will not be sorry for them...when they shall see how miserable others of their fellow-creatures are... when they shall see the smoke of their torment...and hear their dolorous shrieks and cries, and consider that they in the mean time are in the most blissful state, and shall surely be in it to all eternity; how they will rejoice!"[15]

In America's recent experience of 9/11, we heard some fundamentalist preachers draw lessons on divine punishment that echoed Edwards. Pat Robertson and Jerry Falwell attributed the attack on the Twin Towers to American decadence in the form of abortion, homosexuality, promiscuity, divorce, and so on, which caused God to withdraw his protective shield over the country. Again the idea is that God sends catastrophes, or allows them to happen, in order to punish infidelity and inspire repentance. While Robertson and Falwell tried later to back away from their comments, their belief in God's direct providential rule over events in history still flourishes, even among some theologians.

In a recent reading of a respected theological journal, I came across an article explaining ecological disasters. In "Divine Ecology and the Apocalypse," theologian David C. Toole argues that large natural disasters are not really natural but sent by God. Like Jonathan Edwards, Toole maintains that natural disasters directly carry out God's just judgments and that God's omnipotence and direct control of historical and natural events upon earth include sending retribution for sin. Destructive events in history are part of God's plan. God "will take action to rid the earth of wickedness.... God is in control of everything, even the weather."[16] Toole goes on to argue for his claims and warns his readers to beware of the many skeptical "liberal" Christians who are guilty of avoiding their moral duty to teach the "truth," i.e., that divine punishment for sin is directly visited upon us.

But why, ask protesters against this Sodom and Gomorrah approach, must so many innocent victims, especially the poor, suffer in God's acts of divine retribution? Typically, after a recent earthquake in El Salvador, a survivor is reported to have asked, "What have we done that God should send us such destruction?" Toole, along with others of his persuasion, admits that in any ecological calamity the poor will always suffer more than others. However, goes the argument, these unfortunate realities must be accepted by faithful Christians as part of the evil effects of the sinfulness of a fallen world. Unmerited suffering is the inevitable and unavoidable price to be paid in the overall operation of God's justice. In this steely "all or nothing" approach to human suffering, it would be very easy to go even further, as some actually do, and claim that AIDS is a direct punishment visited upon the sinful. If you believe that God directly controls the movement of tectonic plates and the weather, why not microbes?

Unsolved Contradictions

Needless to say, contradictions abound in the theological assertion that God directly sends individual or collective suffering to humankind. How can it be that God creates a good universe out of overwhelming love, yet wounds and destroys it in acts of wrath? Does a merciful, patient God love, forgive, and heal, yet torment and punish? The prophets proclaim that the Lord "plans for your welfare, not for woe! plans to give you a future full of hope" (Jer. 29:11). They claim that God wills comfort, peace, human happiness, and joy for all creation, so can heavenly joy come only to a select few who will rejoice in the eternal suffering of others? Is this the good news revealed to us in Christianity? No, not if God is that One of whom no greater perfection can be imagined and who is revealed in Jesus Christ. With the help of God's infinite wisdom, further reflection inspires believers to seek a fuller Christian story of suffering and joy.

– *Three* –

GOD AND CREATION

SOMETHING IS WRONG with the idea that God directly sends suffering to discipline, punish, or perfect people as part of His plan. Can countless dead children, victims of natural disasters, survivors of torture, contribute to God's artistic project of perfecting creation? C. S. Lewis in his acute grief after his wife died a lingering painful death from cancer said that he now understood why people call God the "Cosmic Sadist" who "vivisects," and yet Lewis in this work *still* affirms that God is like a surgeon who hurts in order to heal. As he cries out to God, "Already, month by month and week by week you broke her body on the wheel whilst she still wore it."[1] God is like the good surgeon who "the kinder and more conscientious he is the more inexorably he will go on cutting."[2] Lewis believes in a God who tortures us for our own good. He finds this conviction logically necessary because of his belief that God is absolutely omnipotently in direct control of every detail in the world, including the deployment of pain and suffering. As he says, "If God's goodness is inconsistent with hurting us, then either God is not good or there is no God: for in the only life we know He hurts us beyond our worst fears and beyond all we can imagine."[3] These words echo those of believers who think that it is an all or nothing choice when it comes to God's power.

Christians like myself who reject the view that God sends brain tumors, cancer, earthquakes, AIDS, or sudden infant deaths do so because they believe that God is not as Lewis and this tradition imagine. Instead, we believe that God is purely positive and does not harm or hurt. If God sends no suffering to creatures, then God's love, God's power, and God's relationship to creation must be understood and reinterpreted. Today new theological visions are being reclaimed and developed within mainstream Catholic Christianity. The post–Vatican II explosion of new scholarship and theological reflection, along with revolutions in science, have opened new possibilities for understanding. New voices, such as those of women and Third World thinkers, also add new perspectives. Fortunately theologians are no longer threatened by secular knowledge arising in either science or the humanities, faithful biblical scholars use new textual research, archeological findings, and sophisticated methods of interpretation to move the church beyond simplistic or narrow literal readings of Scripture. As the church constantly responds to the counsel of the Holy Spirit, Christian understandings of God and the Gospels can deepen and be weighted appropriately. Within this ever evolving awareness and array of resources Christians can wrestle anew with the troubling question of how a God-for-us, all-loving, all-healing, all-liberating, and all-merciful, is related to the reality of human suffering.

But first it is worthwhile to explore whether non-Christian perspectives offer any helpful solutions to the problem of evil and pain. Are there nothing but claims of nihilism and meaninglessness out there in the cultural marketplace beyond the church? One set of alternatives that comes up from time to time explains human suffering by asserting that God is dead or gone.

God Is Dead and Gone?

In many circles, it is assumed that "God is dead," or that God never actually existed in the first place except as an illusion, so that only self-deceptive superstitious folk persist in thinking the universe and human lives have any ultimate meaning or final purpose. To ask why there is something rather than nothing is a meaningless question, a waste of time. This stance considers the problem of evil and the existence of suffering as an irrelevant question since misery is just part of human existence. Granted, unbelievers may be given pause by the universe's ordered rationality and their subjective experiences of beauty, joy, and love, but these puzzling phenomena can likewise be dismissed as signifying nothing. Life is nasty, brutish, and short, and the only meaning to be found will be what human beings manage to construct for themselves. Dedicated scientists and intellectuals continue to investigate the universe and human life in order to discover how things work, but in any "respectable" search for scientific truths, religious questions about what "it means" are taboo. The cosmos and all that exists are seen as shaped by random materialistic evolutionary processes, and while the human brain in the course of its development has admittedly produced some surprising by-products, any claim of a "Creator" behind this phenomena is wishful thinking at best and potentially dangerous.

Dogmatic assertions that God is dead do not, however, convince the masses of ordinary people living in a world prone to faith, and we see everywhere new spiritual movements emerge whenever traditional monotheistic orthodoxies lose influence. Often the belief in a personal God who intervenes in history gives way to affirmations of hidden "spiritual" forces, both positive and negative, that operate in the world. Fluid religious syntheses provide meaning and comfort, as people adopt practices aimed at spiritual growth. Today in developed Western countries decidedly non-Christian spiritualities proliferate, blends of Eastern faiths such as Buddhism and Hinduism, including elements culled from Sufi, Native American, or pagan nature worship. But even with such pluralistic practices, questions of evil and suffering do not disappear. The challenge

remains. Some pantheistic approaches affirm that since everything is divine, the ultimate spiritual reality can be manifested
in Shadow as well as Light. Evil and suffering are but another
element of the divine unity. Or, alternately, suffering is but another illusion that arises from the unenlightened person's need
to cling to a "self" and insist on differentiating some aspects
of reality as "evil." When there is an acceptance of the impersonal laws of karma, then present sufferings can be explained
as being caused by evil deeds committed during past lives.

One intriguing post-Christian perspective of the God-is-
gone variety is the notion that God exists but happens to
be on leave, or otherwise engaged. Indeed, earlier Deists of
the Enlightenment period envisioned God as a great cosmic
watchmaker who created the world as a perfect operating
mechanism, and then left it alone to run by itself; in an intriguing modern version of the absent God, God leaves creation to
its own devices for more mysterious reasons. An ineffable transcendent divinity, like the mysterious dynamic whirlwind deity
of Job, turns away from creation and human concerns — but
who can know why? Maybe out of divine boredom or attraction to some more compelling project elsewhere. Why, after
all, should humans imagine that God should care about them
or their petty troubles? How anthropocentric of human beings
to worry so obsessively over this world's woe.

This lofty approach shares a traditional Christian vision of
a transcendent, ineffable God who dwells in unapproachable
Light but decidedly denies the central Christian belief that the
transcendent God is also God-for-us ardently desiring communion with humankind. A postmodern view of this divine
detachment is captured by a character in Nobel prize winner
J. M. Coetzee's novel *Elizabeth Costello,* which presents the life
and thoughts of a celebrated woman writer of our day. At one
point Elizabeth is being interviewed and is asked whether she
believes in God. She thinks to herself that "this is a question
she prefers to keep a wary distance from. Why, even assuming

that God exists — whatever *exists* means — should His massive, monarchical slumber be disturbed from below by a clamour of *believes* and *don't believes,* like a plebiscite? So in response, she says, 'I have nothing to say.'"[4]

By contrast, Christians over the ages have had plenty to say. Bolstered by Scripture and tradition, the faithful vigorously deny that God as pure act and loving creativity could ever exist in a "massive, monarchical slumber." Nor can the God in whom we move and live and have our being turn away from intimate, passionate concern with each and every human being created in the divine image. Every hair of our head is counted, each thought and every desire of the heart is known, for God cares for us more than we can think or imagine. To see God as absent, or as an impersonal cosmic spiritual force, may help resolve the problem of evil, but it does not satisfy Christians. Those who believe in Christ affirm the most anthropocentric religious story ever told. Through Christ God enters history as fully human and bonds eternally and irreversibly with humankind. Thus, Christian approaches to suffering and joy must be congruent with this gospel proclamation of a God who becomes fully visible in Jesus Christ.

In contrast to the image of a divine watchmaker, God's incarnation means that God continues to create and act always and everywhere through the Holy Spirit as well as in, with, and through the minds and hearts of humankind, making creation, incarnation, redemption, resurrection, and a renewed creation one unified, ongoing event. When God's Word takes flesh in Mary's womb in one moment of historical time and is born as an infant, God operates within creation. Jesus grows up in Nazareth gradually increasing in grace and wisdom. As a young adult Jesus seeks baptism from John, receives a manifestation of the Spirit, and enters into his ministry. Fully human, Jesus prays for discernment as he enacts his passion and death, and when Christ rises from the dead, a new reality begins — Christ has come, Christ is risen, and Christ will come again — fore-shadowing a final future day of fulfillment when God will be all in all. In this new creation groaning into birth, the church as the body of Christ grows and evolves through time and increases in understanding of God's good news on its pilgrim journey of work and love. The church is an ever learning church responding to the Holy Spirit's gifts of good counsel and wisdom.

Consequently the more we come to know of creation, the deeper our understanding and appreciation of the good news. No longer reading the Genesis story of creation as a literal account that takes place in seven days, we now see this story as a symbolic poetic account of God's wondrous work of creation. Through our knowledge of the cosmos, the ordered complexities of matter, and the amazing evolution of life, we Christians feel an increased sense of awe and gratitude for God's gift of the good creation that produced us. Always, scriptural texts must be interpreted within Christ's church community with Christ as guiding template and the inspiring counsel of the Holy Spirit. Christ is the Word and exists as both the message and the medium of God's good news. For all these reasons, today we seek a deeper understanding of suffering and joy by turning to Christ in order to explore three interrelated and relevant realities: God's love, God's power, and God's relationship to creation.

God's Love

What does it mean to say that God is love and that God loves the world? Because one's understanding of love shapes beliefs about God's loving agency and use of power, over the centuries Christians have reckoned with various dimensions of love, and the human understanding that emotion, intellect, and will are all essential to love. If love, either human or divine, is seen as a unilateral action emotionally separated from its object or existing over against it, one who loves could be intent on an outcome that involves inflicting pain and suffering upon the beloved for its own good. The monarch, the master, the trainer, the inquisitor, the surgeon, the vet all are fitting images for a "loving" God who exercises supreme control over a separate subject for his own divine purposes.

In this one-way version of love, short on empathy and union, divine punishment and pain can be rationalized as necessary retribution or reparation for God's offended honor or sinners' unpaid debts. God is viewed as so grievously offended by the disobedience of human beings that only suffering can undo the offense, to the extent that even saints might take joy in the torments of sinners in hell. What such a misunderstanding of "love" has denied to God, however, is an essential characteristic of true love, that is, an empathic identification with the beloved, whereby the lover is united with the beloved in a dynamic mutual relationship. In distorted notions of God's love, this empathy and mutuality is missing.

Love always includes empathy and mutual union, along with a desire to alleviate another's suffering felt as one's own. Thus, empathy is the foundation of justice and morality, since it moves one to take the role of the other and consider her well-being from her point of view.

Today the faithful can approach those scriptural passages that are traditionally quoted to support a vision of God's love as punitive in a different, less literal way. Instead, texts referring to God directly sending suffering to sinners might be understood as evidence of an incomplete understanding of the nature of true love. Because ancient people had little concept of natural causation of events, they found it easy to attribute everything that happened to supernatural causes, and so we find scriptural "texts of terror" describing deadly events or immoral actions, such as genocide or misogynous treatment of women, as commanded by God as punishment. While these texts reflect the ancient writers' fully human (and flawed) views, they can also emphasize the importance of justice, righteousness, and fidelity in God's kingdom, where sin has no place and moral conversion is necessary. Nevertheless, even if punitive passages and images make the point that wickedness and immorality are incongruent with God's justice and beneficence, taken literally, these images and metaphors of God inflicting pain and suffering are in the end incongruent with the more dominant and essential core of the whole gospel message, namely, love. As God's saving love and merciful redemption of creation is proclaimed over and over, in text after text, we come to see how this message must be taken as a whole, with the person of Christ as God's Loving Word made visible governing our understanding of Scripture.

The good news that Christ brings to the world is one of love and mercy. Christ comes to save and to heal, not condemn. Yes, of course, sin, oppression, and wickedness are contrary to God's will and must give way before the power of divine love and justice, but justice, says Jesus Christ, is no more than love's absolute minimum and a true love of neighbor must go much further, must be demonstrated in forgiveness and active works of mercy to end the others' suffering. In this way Christ will overcome the world's sin by love and truth. In light of such teaching on love, therefore, today the church teaches that hell is not literally a place but rather is the absence of God, an image of emptiness that results when love is absent and rejected. Hence, sinners experience the sufferings of hell here and now. Jesus uses many vivid and powerful Jewish images that speak to the heart's distress: the wailing and gnashing of teeth in outer darkness, the lonely isolation of being cast out from the joyful marriage feast. But a positive vision of God's love and life of joy is conveyed in equally vivid images; Christ comes to liberate us with God's mercy, lovingkindness, and healing presence. A kingdom of justice and a life of blessedness are God's gifts on offer, and the call to life is for everyone. Even those who come late are rewarded. Christ's promise has been given: "I shall open a door before you that no one shall close."

Thus, Jesus fulfills the earlier promises God made to rescue the Hebrew people, who throughout their history experience a loving God who continually opened a door to life and joy. God led Abraham to a new land and gave him a son, and when his descendants were suffering, the Lord rescued them through Moses. God is moved by the anguished cries of his suffering people to come to their rescue. God's bond and covenant with the chosen people are sealed with loving care. Food, water, and safe passage are given. Even the terror and awe of meetings with Yahweh are balanced by encounters of tender concern. Yahweh acts as a tender mother to the people and is likened to an eagle that supports its fledglings with its own wings, or to the shepherd who carries the lambs and pregnant ewes of the flock to pasture. As a faithful forgiving husband to his bride, Yahweh is the giver of new life, riches, happiness, and abundant blessings. As we shall see in chapters devoted to the emotion of joy, countless scriptural passages manifest poetic genius in exulting praise for the goodness and kindness of God; God's love inspires joy, praise, thanksgiving, and celebrations of music and dance. Such Jewish testimonies to God's tender mercy and care far outweigh descriptions of God as Tyrant inflicting pain and punishments. Rather, the Jewish revelation is one of a God who is all good and merciful: "A bruised reed I will not crush or a flickering wick extinguish." These prophetic words of comfort and acceptance came to be applied in the Gospels to Jesus and aptly describe his life and teaching.

For Christians Jesus fully reveals God's love and brings God's promises of rescue and transformation to fruition. In Jesus we see God's desire to save, heal, and rescue humankind from sin, suffering, misery, and death. Jesus is the good shepherd incarnate who brings the flock up from the dead, consoles all broken hearts, and offers sinners God's merciful love. In going about his nonviolent ministry of truth and lovingkindness, healing, and teaching Christ constantly rejects retribution and destructive terror. No fire is called down upon disbelievers or sinners. Rather, enemies and those who persecute the good are to be loved. Jesus himself forgives his murderers and in so doing demonstrates God's infinite loving mercy, a love and goodness that will overcome sin and death in a resurrection that gives birth to a new creation and validates all of his testimony to God's infinite love. Jesus reveals God to be a loving father, the source of all life and goodness who can transform his people and his creation into God's kingdom.

The many loving paternal and maternal images of God in Scripture help us to understand God's love. As Jesus taught, even a human father does not give a stone to his child who asks for bread. Though some scriptural texts reflect the ancient world's view that a father's duty entails physically disciplining his son, as in "spare the rod and spoil the child," more powerful for us Christians is rather the loving and magnanimous father in the parable of the prodigal son, who forgives his children's transgressions, both the dissipations of the younger son, and the envious resentment of the elder. This loving father forgives and rushes out to meet his returning son, even before the prodigal says he is sorry, and then patiently tries to persuade his elder son to come and celebrate. Would this loving father have chosen to teach his prodigal son a lesson by inflicting more abuse upon him as he lay starving among the pigs? Disciplining, testing, soul making, and delivering just punishments are not part of the father's program.

Like the father in this parable Jesus offers a "maternal" image for himself, describing himself as a mother hen desiring to shelter her chicks under her wings. Does a mother forget her child, whom she has fashioned in the womb? Does not God treat humankind as a mother does her nursing infant? The prophet Isaiah expresses the divine care, "As a mother comforts her child, so will I comfort you; in Jerusalem you shall find your comfort... as nurslings, you shall be carried in her arms, and fondled in her lap" (Isa. 66:10–14). In passages in Hosea God proclaims, "yet it was I who taught Ephraim to walk, who took them in my arms. I drew them with human cords, with bands of love; I fostered them like one who raises an infant to his cheeks."

When the forgiving nature of God's love is fully understood, then we Christians can embrace such maternal images for a God who holds us close as nursing infants learning to walk in the light. The church's long devotion to Mary as the Mother of God who tenderly carries and nurtures her babe has been important because images of God's maternal love speak the truth. A loving mother-child relationship reflects God-human love, complete with a mutual gaze and mutual delight. God Our Mother does not afflict her nursing infants with punishing wrath and painful suffering. Today we hold even the most benighted human parents, teachers, or caretakers to high standards of protective nurture, or else prosecute them for child abuse. Loving parents do not take up the hammer, the surgical scalpel, the rod, or the chisel to shape their children into artistic perfection.

Beyond images of Father or Mother newer understandings of God as Trinity also give a fundamental insight into God's love. When love exists, there is a mutual relationship seeking further union, since all loving arises from the interpersonal loving and communion of God as Trinity; Father, Son, and Holy Spirit; Three in One. Giving a real and not just notional assent to the theological doctrine of the Trinity has practical and positive consequences for Christian thought and practice. The Holy Spirit comes into vivid focus as the way God creatively works *within* the world and within hearts. Reality is known as essentially relational, and conversation, dialogue, and communion mark the reality of God's creation. The one God who is a Loving Trinity of Persons exists as a dynamic divine interpersonal relationship of giving and receiving. Why is there something rather than nothing? Why is there a universe and why are we here? Because the dynamic mutual self-giving love within the relationships of the Trinity overflows in abundant creativity.

The divine love as three in one reveals that dynamic diversity can exist within unity, and this truth helps to explain the infinite richness, variety, and pluralism of the universe. Our God of Love engenders lives that can participate in the divine life of love and joy without losing their own identity. When God is known as Loving Trinity, existing as freely and mutually communing persons, then loving interpersonal communion and participation in relationship is *the* ultimate truth.

For ordinary Christian disciples the practical consequences of the realization that the God they worship is a dynamic loving Divine Union of Persons will be to increase their appreciation of the developing and transforming actions of God's love. As theologian James Allison says, "By the Holy Spirit we are being taken to the inside of God's life, so that our very 'I' might become part of the 'I' of God who has risked sharing that with us.[5] Humans become adopted children of God and brothers and sisters of Christ, God's son, who are invited to grow up into adulthood in God's family. The traditional theological terms of "divinization," and "theosis" refer to the transformation of humans into God's family through participation in God's life. It is ever and always a daring thought. As the early church fathers proclaimed, God becomes human so humans can become God.

Moreover, when the nature of God's transforming love is fully understood, God is recognized as calling humans to participate in God's own work, as created co-creators of the new creation. Because divine love is creative and co-creative in its mutuality, humans are drawn into the birthing process. Our creative activity, as well as our worship and receiving of peace and joy, are essential in the abundant dynamic life of God's family. Older static images of an immutable God implied that a passive eternal rest would mark the life of heaven, but creative activity always accompanies the loving life of a God justly celebrated as "the Divine Liveliness." A God of mutual love and creativity becomes seen now as also a God of Play, of Beauty, of Joy, and of Surprise. Such a God magnetically attracts and enkindles human hearts. Delight in God's presence and fruitfulness holds out a divine invitation: come and drink from the living wellsprings of water; come take part in God's glorious marriage feast and come as friends to work in bringing in God's kingdom where suffering will be no more. Love engenders life and joy. God does not harm or hurt or rule by pain and terror.

Of course, awe is always a part of any encounter with God. The infinite, transcendent, ineffable light inspires wonder and is too much for us, but such "holy fear" can be engendered by the truth of God's love for us. This good news is probably the hardest thing for Christians to truly, really, actually believe and accept. Yes God loves creatures beyond all reason. The Holy Spirit loves, heals, liberates, redeems, inspires, consoles, enlivens, and transforms creation. God's infinite light and infinite love exist without negative shadow or wrath. As theologians of today can affirm, "If God is really God, he is pure positiveness."[6] Or, in another formulation "She Who Is" is pure benevolence. This is a mystery that is hard to grasp for finite human beings, emerging out of a disordered conflicted world filled with domination, violence, and sinful cruelty. The good news seems too good to be true; the great mystery lies in the wonder that our God desires friendship with us and loves the troubled world so unconditionally. Meditating upon the nature of God's love produces new insights into the nature of God's power.

Power

When God is revealed as Love, existing as a trinity of giving and receiving, then we come to see that God's power is not exercised as a unilateral act of force over and against subjects. The relational nature of love makes clear that courtship, not conquest, is God's way, for slavish, fearful obedience of one to another has no place in any truly loving relationship, whether in family, friendship, or religious community. Love seeks a voluntary mutual union, and this mutuality of relationship necessitates as much freedom and equality as it is possible to have. A slave or a dog may adore his owner, but friends and lovers reject such disparities of power. Mothers seek to enable their infants to take part in an ongoing family and so encourage growing up by renouncing control, coercion, and micro-management of their children's lives. Spontaneity requires freedom, creativity needs mental spaciousness, and moral maturity rests on autonomy and freely willed acts. No good parent wants her child to be nothing more than a puppet, obedient robot, or talking doll. Control, especially control through violent superior force, destroys the mutual consent and freedom inhering in a loving relationship. In love and friendship, influence is exercised instead through persuasion, truth telling, demonstration, and magnetic attraction. And so with God's love.

Just as friends and lovers are humble and seek equality and freedom in their love, so too the Christian God of loving benevolence does not act like the gods in the pagan religious narratives of Greece and Rome. They operate within dominating hierarchies that manipulate and exploit those with lesser power. The Greeks accepted the fact that Zeus, who himself narrowly escaped being eaten by his father, would abuse his powers to trick, deceive, coerce, or rape females at will. On Mt. Olympus was the site of competition, conflict, deception, favoritism, and struggles. How different the model of divine perfection shown forth in the Trinitarian God of love and unity.

Mutual self-giving in humble equality dispenses with competition or dominance or hierarchy. When theologians speak of "the humility of God" they echo Jesus' words describing himself as meek and humble of heart. The meek are blessed and will inherit the earth. Humility brings joy through an openness that can receive wisdom and goodness. Consequently, in free and equal unions there is no destruction or diminishment of another's identity, or of their agency and potential. No loss of individuality comes from the loving union, but instead, growth, expansion, and flourishing. Lovers, friends, and families desire not submission and uniformity but for the other to increase to the fullest possible extent. The more one is united in loving friendship with God, the more one gains the capacity to become unique and actively free.

Unlike slaves, prisoners, or fearful subjects in thrall to the rulers and gods of the ancient world, the friends and family of God will grow up into the liberty of God's family as co-heirs. In the economy of divine triune loving, individuals increase their freedom by the giving that is also receiving; to give is to receive, to receive is to give and gain joy. God's power, like the power of Beauty or shining Light, attracts us, draws us magnetically toward God Self while transforming us. When Moses talked with God his face became radiant. God, the ancient beauty and radiant light of truth and goodness, entices us onward into love with the divine creativity that makes all things new. The power of love and work enjoyed by liberated creatures is made possible through keeping company with God. The loving relationship is both the goal and the means to the goal.

Secular Notes on Power

It may come as some surprise that certain secular analyses of power in modern social science actually give support to the theological truths of power we have been exploring. In such analyses, "power" is defined as influence or as long-term effectiveness in gaining an object or goal. This influence is opposed to "force" or "violence," which is acknowledged as capable of establishing temporary control, but which has the drawback of being effective only while a superior force is present. Effective and lasting "power" is achieved when a goal or objective is voluntarily adopted and internalized by an agent who then pursues it independently. In other words, persuasion leading to consent produces an internalized agreement that will be effective continuously, whether or not force is present. Thus, true power comes from achieving the free assent, consent, and conviction of another. Political regimes that win the hearts and minds of their people will function best; their laws will be obeyed because they are in accord with the inner consent of the governed.

When an agent has internalized and identified a goal, an agent's independent initiative and resources will be engaged. Every successful empire or colonial system must depend upon agents who will carry out its commands and laws. An effective army or police force depends upon group loyalty and cohesion. Internally adopted goals have staying power because they are owned by the actors. Colleagues and friends will take initiative for a common project, whereas slaves and forced conscripts await orders or defect at the first opportunity. Though self-interest, ambition, and greed may motivate cooperation with a conquering power, love, respect, and inner assent to truths inspire greater and more reliable cooperation.

Similar conditions of consent have been described as constituting a form of "enabling power." "Maintenance leadership" or enabling power has been defined as the ability to sustain group cohesiveness and to inspire its members to act together. Holding groups together is necessary for all cooperative action, whether in a family, school, work group, or cultural celebration. Whereas one kind of power lies in directing or enacting a task or a plan, another kind of influence lies in tending to the emotional needs, care, and well-being of the participants in an ongoing relationship. To inspire morale, kindle good feeling, and ensure cooperation among persons is a form of real "power." Another aspect of "enabling power" is encouraging the growth of others. To inspire and help other people to fulfill their potential is a form of social or nurturing power. While a basic form of enabling power is that of the good mother nurturing the family, others such as teachers, physicians, nurses, psychotherapists, coaches, group therapists, and other spiritual leaders exercise a lasting influence, because like good parents, they effectively nurture growth.

The desired goal of all these practices and forms of enabling power is to give power away. Parents rejoice when a child grows up to be an adult who can love and work. All other educators, caretakers, and healers take joy and satisfaction in the growth and fulfillment of those they have cared for.

God's Love and Power in the Creation

God's power can be understood as a form of "enabling power" bringing creation to fulfillment. Many scriptural verses refer to the desire of God to give hearts of flesh to human beings to replace hearts of stone. God seeks a special covenant with created persons with their voluntary consent to grow in God's ways. Jesus refuses to lord over others as pagan rulers do. Instead he wishes to create friends who will know what he knows and work as he works. To flourish and become a true friend, a person must be given autonomy and freedom to grow up. In all these ways, God gives power away so that creation may flourish and God's family be enabled to live and love. God's power is a generative power that allows human beings to imitate God's own love and creativity. Only with free inner identifications with God can human persons be enabled to create, to rejoice, to play, and to cooperate in God's work and joyful celebrations.

New scientific understandings of cosmic evolution are compatible with an understanding of a creator God who continually works and makes all things new. The important notion here is that in both loving personal relationships and in evolutionary processes, freedom and openness are necessary. Chance and contingency must coexist with law and ordered principles for novelty and change to take place. Similarly, as elements of freedom, time and space are also necessary. Friends and lovers require time and freedom to grow together, to give and receive delight, to surprise each other, and to give mutual support in creative work.

Human infants require time, space, and the nurturing relationships of their parents interacting with the gift of autonomy and freedom. Human persons learn and mature through choices and action. If God out of gracious love wishes to create separate others, who can become unique friends, lovers, adopted children, fellow artists, and co-workers, then God will give the humans independence and freedom to act autonomously over time. As many religious thinkers, inspired by new scientific and theological ideas, have noted, creation seems to be continually self-organizing and moving toward complexity as it plays itself out. God appears to will "created co-creators" of every kind.

Some Christian philosophers in the past and present have expressed such ideas by viewing God as the primary cause who creates secondary causes that then operate in the world. This approach helps solve the problem of the independence of creation but leaves the question of how God as primary cause is related to secondary created causes. Some thinkers affirm an evolutionary approach in which the universe has been created with enough freedom, openness, and contingency to produce an incredible variety of novel forms of life. God creates through order and through chance, in a dynamic interaction that produces an evolving process.[7] In this view, the openness of probabilities, contingencies, interacting with the constraining constancy of mathematical and physical laws, together produce ever more complex and conscious forms of life. Human beings on earth live by the light of a second-generation star and are themselves made of stardust from past explosions of the cosmos. Human life and thought have evolved as the results of many huge cosmic events along with billions of years of small chance events and occurrences interacting with the laws of physics. Nonbelievers see the evolving process of chance and lawfulness as having no purpose or meaning, without any original creator or final goal, but believers see God's creative purposes in processes that are actively, subtly, and wondrously working.

This notion of freedom and openness has been breaking open the certainties of an older worldview characterized by a mechanically programmed determinism. The reductive naturalism, so dear to atheists, is hard pressed to integrate these new scientific discoveries. Clearly, the universe is no giant ticking watch set to run predictably. The recent discoveries of quantum physics and speculations about the existence of other dimensions and parallel universes serve to introduce theories of unpredictability in the universe. No one now understands the nature of different kinds of matter, or what is the nature of time. But it can be affirmed that all known systems interact with each other and are somehow mutually entangled in a dynamic evolving process. If only "the theory of everything" could be discovered! In the meantime scientific theories and findings can support new theological affirmations of a continual dynamic creation. As John Polkinghorne, one of the most astute scientific theologians, says, "An evolutionary world is theologically to be understood as a creation allowed by its Creator "to make itself." The play of life is not the performance of a predetermined script, but a self improvisatory performance by the actors themselves."[8]

Theologians influenced by evolutionary thought affirm that the evolving creation is incomplete and groans in its birthing toward fulfillment. For an evolutionary theologian such as John Haught the universe is moving, or being drawn, toward its ultimate fulfillment in God. God is Our Future. The evolutionary processes that began with the Big Bang are continuing with a dynamic role for human creativity. Haught also speaks of "the humility of God" in giving creative power away to creatures and allowing them their autonomy. Since humility is a characteristic of enabling power and all relationships of love, it makes sense that God's love has long been expressed as *kenosis,* or self-emptying gift. Traditionally, a theology of kenosis has been based upon those scriptural affirmations that Christ as God's Son and Word humbly chose to give up divine power in order to fully bond with humankind in the incarnation. Christ chooses to become like a slave, even undergoing death, out of love for humankind. This humility of God produces the communion of love and love's rejection of coercive power.

Therefore, as we will see when turning to Christ's saving life and death in the next chapter, his offer of God's salvation to humankind is one that requires free assent. No fire is called down from heaven, nor are persons stunned into assent by violent displays of might. Signs must be read and received; healing miracles are demonstrations of God's love and an invitation to a new life of justice and truth. Christ's call to discipleship is a courtship in which heart speaks to heart, light to light, spirit to truth.

The philosopher Søren Kierkegaard tells a parable to make the point of God's tactful and humble efforts not to overpower human beings with grandeur. In his story a great king who loves a poor maiden disguises himself as a beggar in order that her love for him will be freely given and not influenced by his riches and power. But even this story does not go far enough or deep enough into God's ways. God's incarnation is not a temporary disguise. If so it would recap the old heresy claiming that Christ is only God in a Jesus suit, not fully and forever human. The king is not just adopting a strategy of pseudo-equality with the ulterior purpose of returning to the palace with a bride. No, the king must be born into the maiden's tribe, take up residence, and become part of her family forever.

Feminists, refusing patriarchal assumptions of God as a powerful male, might devise even better stories to describe self-limiting strategies of divine courtship and persuasive, pervasive influence. For instance, every good mother who bears and nurtures an infant must care and entice the child into its new life. The courtship and partnership is one of giving and receiving, as while constantly engaging and adapting the stimulation that can be received in each stage of development. Nurslings need milk, physical protection, and tender love communicated by mutual gaze, touch, soothing sounds, and stimulating play such as peekaboo. The nurturing dance of attention sets the stage for what has been called the child's love affair with the world. The partnering of care and emotional attunement changes as the child grows, with ever greater freedom and autonomy given over to the developing self. Today, mothers are warned against overcontrol, intrusive suffocating supervision that stunts development. To become a separate self a person must be given the freedom to feel her own emotions, think her own thoughts, exercise her own agency, and enter into self-initiated social relationships. A good mother provides a supportive "holding environment" and subtly provides the conditions and influence that will nurture the growth of her child's free independence. Does not God provide the holding environment, the great sustaining of creation in which humans can grow up? The loving care of parents provides one image for God's dealings with humankind, as Scripture and tradition attest. Surely, the great seated Madonna figures found in medieval shrines, supporting the Christ child on their laps, provide a potent symbol of God's maternal sustaining creation and nurture of the world. Good parents care, lure, persuade, and tactically help their offspring into their own adult lives of love, work, and creation. Family bonds, however, continue forever.

Other imaginative analogies have been offered to describe God's continuing creativity in cooperation with creatures. One metaphor used is that of God as a jazz musician improvising and elaborating musical themes with creatures within creation.[9] In the openness of the creative process different outcomes are possible. God has also been seen as weaving complex living tapestries in cooperation with the free responses of humankind. Instead of adhering to a rigid blueprint, or predestined detailed plan, God's continuous co-creation with humans can be envisioned as evolving in a multitude of ways, with variations and novelty of responses. Given God's infinite creativity and resources for artistry, it makes sense to imagine that many different plans and acts may be possible.

Another metaphor employs the analogy of authorship, imagining God as the Author and Producer of a divine drama. In my version the drama starts off with a bang in which God builds the sets, prepares the music, and assembles a company of actors to join in the creative enterprise. An outline of the plot is provided, certain key parts are assigned, but as in improv theater the actors express themselves and contribute to the plot. This freedom and active communal collaboration has been chosen by the Author in order to develop a company of mature co-creative artists. Improvisations that are actual performances reflect the adventurous and indulgent Author's risk taking, again displaying the "Divine Liveliness." Together players and Author shape the action of the scenes. The Author is all good and purely positive, so no negative or harmful turn of the plot ever arises from this author and producer, but the construction of an unfinished, unscripted production can leave room for disorder, disasters, and chaotic upheavals as byproducts of the contingent and joint process. Members of the company can misuse their freedom to insert destructive turns to the script. How can the Author, who has given the actors and performers their freedom, creatively influence or rescue the performance? At a crucial point in the drama the Author joins the cast as a member of the company. Now the ensuing acts can be more directly influenced by the original goodness of the Author.

But even in this playful theatrical metaphor, crucial questions arise: Will the plot go downhill and disintegrate into tragic disaster? What happens to the players when they have had their turn upon the stage? How long will the drama run? Is a grand finale and happy ending already determined? Such queries replay many theological debates concerning the limits of human freedom within creation. If God has truly given away power to co-creators, how complete is God's self-limitation? Some theologians would claim that God's self-giving in the incarnation has been absolute, even to the point of submitting to time's process. In this view God's omniscience about the future has also been renounced. The final victory of God in the end times may be undetermined. But in my mind, proposing such a degree of irresolution in the process of creation hardly does justice to the creative powers of the loving God revealed in Scripture. Most orthodox Christians will affirm in faith, as I do, that yes, God is our future; this confidence asserts that in the long run creation's collaborative drama will have a joyful finale — with every tear wiped away. The resurrection of Jesus is our assurance that the drama of creation is a divine comedy, not a Greek tragedy. Christians trust in the power of God's divine creativity and steadfastness so that in the *end* "Paradise is God's finished work."[10]

On the way to a finale, however, the continuous and free collaborative process of co-creations may include surprises. New discoveries on the part of humans will certainly take place, but an even more daring thought is that the ongoing freedom of the universe could produce developments that have not yet been created and would be unknown even to God. This question will be another issue that turns on the nature of time and how our time and God's time relate. But in our present ignorance we can affirm that God is all Good and all-loving, and that God acts in creation in a purely positive way. God is God for us; suffering and evil arise from resistance to God and the incomplete birth process.

Does God Suffer with Us?

The question arises, does God suffer with us? I believe that the only logical answer, in light of the above, is yes. Those who have denied that God ever suffers have done so to affirm a view of God's perfections; divine omnipotence they thought could not coexist with the vulnerability and diminishment of suffering.[11] If God is a Spirit that is eternal, immutable, self-sufficient, all-powerful, and controlling, then how could God be affected or in any way moved? Philosophical ideas about an unmoved prime mover were applied to God's nature, which could never change, much less be disturbed or diminished by suffering. Since emotions are dynamic and changeable responses, then God would never be subject to the transitory movements of passion. Love was considered a form of abstract willed benevolence.

Granted, such concepts of an unemotional God do not sound like the Yahweh who is revealed in the Jewish Scriptures, the God who self-identifies as "I am Who I Am," and personally converses, promises, instructs, reproaches, regrets, and forgives. Yahweh is revealed as uniquely transcendent and beyond all imagining, but at the same time moved by passionate and personal feelings and thoughts. The God of the Jews is intimately and emotionally involved in the details of His chosen people's lives.

Perhaps a treatise devoted to God's emotions could put to rest the temptation to let intellectual philosophical abstractions dominate religious thinking. Philosophically, God was thought to be beyond suffering because the all-powerful God who is the source of all being, or the Prime Mover who exists beyond time, could never be affected or changed by anything external.

While Christians could always understand that Jesus Christ as a fully human being suffered as humans do while on earth, some Christians wondered about how and how much Christ suffered. Did Christ's divine nature really allow suffering? Or perhaps the human suffering was only a temporary episode that like other human characteristics was over and done with once Jesus Christ was raised to the right hand of the Father. We will discuss Christ's suffering and God's suffering in the crucifixion in the next chapters, but in general God too can be seen to suffer if we more fully understand God, love, and the different kinds of suffering that exist.

As we have noted, there has been a Christian theological recovery of insights into God's dynamic Trinity as an eternal interpersonal relationship of love. God is faithful and yes, immutably, eternally steadfast in love, but also exists as a relationship characterized by dynamic movement and responses. Our whole sense of divine perfection has changed to include liveliness, creativity, and novelty. One image is that God is a fountain of creativity. So why should the intense emotions and affects scripturally depicted in God (and in Christ) be absent from the divine communal life of love?

If we accept that all love arises from the Trinity's interpersonal giving and receiving, God's love for us includes God's being affected by us. As the eminent contemporary theologian David Tracy puts it, "God alone affects all (by providing the relevant possibilities) and is affected by all (by changing as our actual decisions and actions occur and affect God)."[12] God is perfect in being the infinitely responsive One in infinite relationship with all. Thus God does suffer with us in empathetic response, but the empathy with those who suffer is different from other kinds of suffering that God has come to rescue us from. The human suffering that accompanies physical pain, disease, and death arises from possessing a finite vulnerable body as a member of homo sapiens. Christians assert that Jesus Christ as a fully embodied human being suffered in these ways in his earthly life. But God the Creator existing as transcendent infinite Spirit does not suffer disease, physical pain, or death, nor does a perfect God of Love suffer from negative human emotions that arise from sin and error, such as guilt, shame, contempt, rage, or disgust. If one element of suffering arises from a threat to the self's integrity, then God does not suffer from this vulnerability as humans do, nor does the human suffering that arises from social structures of oppression directly threaten God's integrity. Yet one kind of suffering experienced by human beings does affect God: the suffering that arises from loving empathy.[13] Perhaps no suffering is as acute as that of a loving parent suffering with of a beloved child, and a self-conscious person made in the image of God, capable of loving empathy, suffers with another's pain or distress. The distress we feel through loving empathic identification is not caused by direct personal limitation, loss, or diminishment; in fact, empathy stretches and expands our hearts. So too with God: it is the suffering engendered through expanded empathy that characterizes our divine Lover, Parent, Friend, and Creator.

Both Jewish Scriptures and Gospel narratives reveal God's suffering with those in distress, and such a view of God's genuine empathy gives the lie to other characterizations of God as pitiless or punitive. Because empathy does not require moral approval, one can feel empathy for those who sin, or for the sufferings of our enemies as well as for the good and innocent. God does not refuse love to lost sheep or to rebellious evildoers any more than an ill infant. When we creatures impose suffering upon ourselves or fall into depravity and hurt others, Scriptures tells us that God's empathy for us does not fail. Christ's love of his enemies reveals the character of divine empathy for us all.

Does such divine empathy reduce the joy, light, and love of God? Those who deny that God can suffer make their strongest argument here, saying that nothing can destroy God's joy in

God's interpersonal life of the Trinity. However, God's joy is not curtailed or stunted by empathic suffering: infinite empathy does not preclude infinite joy. Indeed, many theologians, such as David Tracy, have affirmed that God's nature is complex, di-polar, simultaneously possessing both transcendent and immanent poles,[14] and priest-physicist John Polkinghorne likewise speaks in his works of God's di-polar nature. Such views help us to imagine how God can suffer with us while simultaneously rejoicing in the love of the Trinity. This ineffable God infinitely is beyond us and intimately within us.

When we experience God as immanent and alive in our hearts, we also affirm that in the incarnation God has become human and has bonded with humankind forever. Yet at the other transcendent pole we worship God as the *mysterium tremendum,* the ineffable Holy of Holies, ground of all activity, dwelling in unapproachable Light. The traditional form of mysticism, termed "apophatic," understands God as beyond all imagining and comprehension and urges us to give up all inadequate images of God. Hence the commandment to make no graven images. In the apophatic path, believers approach a transcendent God through a "negative" way, embracing the mysterious emptiness and unknowing that leads to God. At the other pole, termed "cataphatic," the mystical path approaches God through meditating upon God's revelation in all of creation and specifically in the person and life of Jesus. Here the believer finds God in all things and seeks union with God through others.

Like many another Christian I've puzzled over how God is both ineffable and beyond all imagination and thought, while at the same time intimately Self-disclosing, a Spirit of Love within us and within all creation. The answer is that God is both.

Perhaps humans can gain some insight into the nature of God as di-polar since we, too, experience double consciousness in a limited way. One feature of our self-awareness is the way we can experience different dimensions of our self at the same time or over time, a dynamic coming and going, rising and fading of different emotions, thoughts and states of alertness in what William James called the "stream of consciousness." I can become absorbed in abstract reasoning and soar above the present moment, or I can remember the past and imagine the future. I can feel extreme states of immersion in pain or pleasurable ecstasy, with moments of the loss of self-consciousness, along with the onset and fading of other emotions. If a timeless free "I" is one pole of my being, then an embodied, socially constructed, ongoing emotional "Me" who lives with others in historical time is another pole of my personal reality.

Thus, God's infinite di-polar nature implies that while God suffers in empathy with me, this is not God's only experience. Yes, God knows me and mine and can suffer with me in my suffering and pain, but God feels more than "just" that. God is not confined to being "a fellow sufferer" with creation. The divine Trinity can simultaneously exist in perfect joy and happiness while God the Holy Spirit can continue to exert influence for active healing and comfort in empathizing love. The active loving and rejoicing of God working within creation cannot be turned off or destroyed or be engulfed by empathetic suffering with us. I can believe that God is with me and with others intimately and completely responsive to our pain, as well as at the same time transcendently present to all the joys and beauties of Godself and reality. Christians can affirm that God can be affected and moved and can empathetically suffer with us without being limited or diminished. Divine transcendence and di-polar existence mean that More always exists with creative power, plenitude, and fruitfulness. God's loving relationships within the Trinity always produce joy, and so do loving creative relationships with the world and creatures. God can abide in joy and empathetic suffering at the same time.

Similarly, we think humans in our own complex di-polar consciousness can also have certain experiences of joy in the midst of suffering. A father who has survived the tremors of an earthquake hears his child's cry from under the rubble. The father agonizes and responds with empathetic suffering for his child's distress, and yet in the midst of this pain he feels surges of joy in knowing that his beloved child is alive and that he will be able to rescue him. If joy can coexist with the suffering that accompanies love with us humans, how much more is this the case for God. And for Christians, it is the person of Jesus Christ to whom we turn to understand God most fully. Jesus Christ is God's answer to the suffering of the world. We cannot truly understand the role of suffering and joy without confronting what the life and death of Jesus mean — for us, for creation, and in the life of God.

– Four –

JESUS SAVES

S EVERAL YEARS AGO I was at a sophisticated dinner party
on the Upper West Side of Manhattan when one of the
guests announced to the room that he considered the Christian doctrine of a God who had sacrificed his son a deplorable
regression to pagan practices of child immolation. By contrast
a superior religion such as Judaism had moved beyond child
sacrifice, ever since Abraham's plan to offer up Isaac had been
rejected.

"But what can you mean?" I replied, rising to the task of
politely defending the faith over cocktails. "I am afraid that
you misunderstand Christianity. Your view that the Christian
God is an abusive Father committing filicide gets the Gospel
story wrong. First of all, Christians believe that Jesus Christ
is God, so Jesus, as divine, *freely* gives himself up to death
in order to show his love for the world. Second, you must
remember that the horrible death by crucifixion that Jesus suffered was not inflicted upon him by God, but by the Romans
and those elites who served their regime. And by the way, you
might be interested to know that there are different theological interpretations in Catholic thought on just *how* Christ saves
humankind." At this point, the hostess and guests around us
began to look faintly distressed, so we all changed the subject and began to talk about the latest Broadway play. And a
good thing too, since at the time I knew only enough theology
to realize that different theories of Christ's saving death had
been proposed in the long history of the church, but I was

none too clear about whether there were views still currently held that endorsed the notion of redemption accomplished by blood sacrifice.

After I began this work on suffering and joy, I did encounter such theologies in both academic and popular religious culture. For example, in the film *The Apostle,* Robert Duvall plays a charismatic southern preacher who before being hauled off to jail for manslaughter gives his last sermon in a small country church. In the mounting enthusiasm of the swaying congregation, Duvall leaps down into the aisle to hold up the hand of a toddler in his mother's arms and shouts out: "Could you as a Daddy nail your own baby son's hand to the cross? No? Well, God could. And He did. In order to save you and me from our sins. Come, come to Jesus."

Such a description of God intentionally crucifying His son could be dismissed as an unschooled or garbled version of the Christian gospel, but similar assertions are found among even learned thinkers. In C. S. Lewis's meditation on grief, he agonizes over his wife's tortured death from cancer and reflects that it would have been useless to look for relief from God. And why? Because, Lewis says, when we look at the way God treated Jesus we see that, "He crucified him."[1] Lewis expects that no end of suffering in this world will be forthcoming when God directly inflicts a horrible death upon His own son in accord with His divine plan. And other even grislier Christian versions of Daddy God nailing his son to the cross exist. Such beliefs hold that God increases the sufferings of Jesus by first forsaking him and then laying on more and more painful tortures. Why? Only in this way could God's offended honor and divine justice be fully satisfied. Some early theologians in the era of a literal belief in demons added the twist that Jesus served as bait to outwit Satan's evil purposes.[2] Satan thought he had triumphed by obtaining Jesus' death, only to find that through the resurrection God was victorious. Jesus snatches Satan's victims away.

Unfortunately in such theological versions of how Jesus saves the world — "soteriologies" to use the technical term — Christians not only have to exalt suffering but are asked to envision a God so offended by wrongdoing that He plans to exact retribution. God's offended honor requires God to inflict pain and suffering upon Christ as a substitute for fallen humanity, for Jesus is the only one innocent enough to serve as an acceptable sacrifice to ward off God's wrath. These harsh views of a God demanding the punishment and sacrifice of his innocent son give ammunition to Christianity's enemies who have claimed that the Christian God is a "Tyrant-Abuser" a "Cosmic Sadist," or "Sadomasochist." For instance, an unbelieving character in James Wood's novel *The Book against God* rails against his minister father's defense of God's use of pain: "The most charitable image of this particular God I can produce is that of a father who breaks his son's leg just so that he can watch his son learn how to appeal to his dad for help in mending it."[3] Even when God is thought to be volunteering his own suffering in His divine-human Son, Jesus as fully human is still intentionally tortured. What's gone wrong in this particular soteriology?

First and foremost, a story that views Christ's passion as a punitive blood sacrifice is grounded on untenable assumptions about God. God is seen here as vengeful and possessing an honor that is easily offended, not humble, not patient, not infinitely forgiving, in other words, a God *un*like the God consistently portrayed in Jewish and Christian Scripture. Only pain and blood sacrifice will do.[4] Moreover, if God is indeed a divine bookkeeper who tallies sinful debts and payments due, then the implication is that God suffers from a scarcity of spiritual resources so that a balance of payments must be restored, and Christ becomes man in order to right the ledger. That God suffers from a lack of any kind is a manifest contradiction.

Nevertheless, such distorted theological views of God and Christ's role in salvation have led to much grievous harm, a glorification of suffering, and a justification for oppression. Suffering is not only necessary but a good thing. If it's good for God, it's got to be good for us. Back to C. S. Lewis and those who affirm that God directly sends suffering, pain, and natural disasters to punish, discipline, warn, or test persons. A warped sense of God's love, or indeed of all loving, is presented. The imposition of pain can become fused, identified, or confounded with love, so that enduring pain or, even worse, inflicting pain is thought to be an act of love.

In this particular narrative, Christians can conclude that their primary religious duty is to imitate Christ by submitting to suffering, passively enduring and acquiescing in the divine plan. This passivity and glorification of victims can be seen as an "abuse of the cross," because the call to live, love, and work with God to transform the world and end suffering becomes secondary or totally obscured. When the cross and passion of Christ are misinterpreted, the healing and teaching of Christ's ministry becomes separated from his death, and even the resurrection is obscured and slighted. Here it is easy to forget that historically Jesus was executed by the reigning authorities in Roman Judea because of his revolutionary preaching of God's kingdom with its call to end suffering and oppression of the poor. God in Christ's reversal of history with its overthrow of the world's powers is sidelined. Paying for past debts shifts attention to the past rather than focusing upon God's new future. God making of all things new is ignored. Good Friday overshadows Easter Sunday. There is little good news in this harsh view of God and God's plan for the death and suffering of Jesus.

Thankfully, other views of God and other soteriologies of Christ's saving action are alive and flourishing, and always have been part of the tradition. It is enlightening to explore ways that Christians in the past and in the present propose understandings of Christ's saving actions that more fully reflect God's love and mercy — the God that Jesus makes visible.

Glad Tidings of Salvation in and through Jesus Christ

The wonder of the life, death, and resurrection of Jesus Christ has inspired continuing efforts to comprehend God's relationship to humanity. How can a believer begin to understand the abundant riches and plenitude of the Christ event? Some theological reflections have focused upon how Jesus fulfills the past revelations and promises of God to the Jews,[5] as the ultimate prophet, teacher, and priest who fulfills God's covenant with Israel. Jesus as prophet proclaims the revolutionary coming of God's kingdom of justice to earth. It is a saving realization to know that God's victory and God's kingdom are prior to and more powerful than the evil forces afflicting the world. Human liberation from the yoke of oppression and enslavement has arrived with Christ's advent, resurrection, and victory over sin and death. Jesus not only fulfills the prophetic tradition of Israel but also embodies the wisdom tradition of the Hebrew Scriptures. God's wisdom and God's Holy Spirit shine forth in Jesus, who as the Word and Light of God illuminates the ignorant and darkened world and brings God's truth and light to those who sit in darkness. In Jesus Christ the past promises of God in the covenant with the Hebrew people are now made good. Jesus as the eternal high priest through his priestly offering of himself achieves the reconciliation of God and humankind. A new and eternal covenant and unity between God and humankind now exist in and through the life, death, and resurrection of Jesus. The author of Hebrews who writes to Jewish Christians uses this traditional imagery of priesthood and Jewish worship in the temple in Jerusalem to show how Jesus fulfills the role of priest.

Today, other threads of the tradition come together in a contemporary Christian theology that focuses upon God as interpersonal Trinity with special attention to the work of God the Holy Spirit. This Trinitarian approach, never better expressed than in Catherine Mowry LaCugna's *God for Us,*[6] counteracts a soteriology of blood sacrifice by providing an understanding of God as dynamic and interpersonal, God as Three in One, God as ever loving, ever giving, and ever receiving. The overflow of divine loving and creating results in the gift of our creation and its fulfillment through the work of God's Son and Word becoming human in the incarnation of Jesus.[7] Through the power of God the Holy Spirit, Jesus as incarnate Son comes from God and returns to God with a saved people and renewed creation. God becomes human so that humans can become God and participate in God's life. God the Holy Spirit sustains creation and draws all life into God's life of love and joy. Jesus, who is both fully human and fully divine as the Son and Word of God, comes in love to save the world. This nonviolent coming of God begins with a loving woman freely assenting to the birth of a beloved baby and ends with a risen savior who creates an eternal new family of God. Indeed, familial images of birth and dynamic development convey the good news well; a maternal loving God has created the world, and creation is moving toward its fruition in and with God. Jesus brings the whole of humankind into God's divine liveliness and joy. As adopted children and co-heirs with Jesus Christ human beings are "created co-creators" and will take part in God's ongoing work of creation and birth.

In this view of overflowing, trinitarian abundance, Jesus saves by giving the power of God's Holy Spirit to his beloved people, engendering the church as the body of Christ. Thus a new birth is offered through the rite of baptism into the risen Christ's eternal life, and the power of God's Spirit and love, not the satisfaction of debt through blood-vengeance, makes it possible for each of us to overcome sin and death. Everyone and everything is being reborn in God's love and life, with and through Christ's life and resurrection. Jesus as divine and human is, therefore, the firstborn of many brothers and sisters who can live anew with him and share in the joyful company of God. This news of rescue from death and birth into God's family can seem too good to be true. As an astute modern theologian, Romanus Cessario, writing of the revelation of God's transforming gift of love, points out, "Only one of the divine Persons authoritatively could make such an extraordinary declaration."[8] The declaration announced by the "incarnate Son" is that the Blessed Trinity exists as both the final cause of all human activity and the true perfection of the human person. God is going to perfect human beings so that in the risen life we shall be like Christ. This astounding promise is demonstrated through Jesus' historical life, death, and resurrection. The empty tomb and the post-Crucifixion appearances of a risen, embodied Jesus confirm the disciples' faith in Jesus' promises, with the result that they, now we too, believe in his saving power as Lord.

Without Jesus' resurrection with its experiential evidence of God's saving power over sin and death, there is no good news. Christianity would not exist.[9] At best Jesus would be mourned for a time by a few people as another exemplary man who was crushed and tragically killed by the forces of injustice and evil. Our views of the meaning of human suffering and joy would be very different. But the resurrection and the coming of the Holy Spirit engender faith in the gift of living with Christ in God's new eternal life of joy. In this theology of salvation, God becomes human out of love and desire to give birth to joy, truth, and life in a transformed human family. Our God is a God who is *for* us, not against us, not over us, a God *with* us. As the poet John Donne eloquently sums it up in his Holy Sonnet XV: "Twas much that man was made like God before, But that God should be made like man, much more."[10]

This understanding of God's dynamic Trinitarian love also implies that God always and everywhere seeks union with an evolving creation, desiring to bond with human beings by becoming one with humankind. The incarnation is not solely a remedial rescue operation, but is rather a divine act intrinsic to God's overflowing and generative self-giving love. God is proactive and creative. Consequently, the story of Adam and Eve's disobedience with the resulting coming of death to a fallen, flawed world is interpreted differently and less literally than in earlier eras. The story is not seen as referring to some past event, but rather as a narrative dramatizing the ever-present limitations of flawed, incomplete, immature, evolving human beings in a disordered world. One can acknowledge that humans are in absolute need of a transformed life with God without claiming that once upon a time we were different. With greater knowledge of the evolution of the cosmos and the history of life, the myth of a lost paradise is seen rather as symbolic, depicting a crucial development in human evolution, i.e., the advent of reason, self-consciousness, and language in primates. This emergence of self-consciousness and its consequent awareness of death undoubtedly produced new fears and intensified human competition to survive. With self-consciousness and knowledge, free and intentional actions could be undertaken with the aim of harming others in a calculating fashion hitherto unseen in animal species still governed by fixed programs of development. Sin, and social sin, enters the world with increased self-knowledge, for with such awareness, humans can intentionally seek self-advantage and use intelligence to support aggression.

With Christ's coming a new story is told, one that promises a rescue from death, aggression, and all the suffering that exists in the world. Creation will be completed and fulfilled in God; a paradise in which there is no sin, suffering, and death lies not in the past but in God's future. In a new garden with an empty tomb human beings will find liberation and new life. Jesus Christ, the new Adam, accomplishes a great leap forward for humankind, leading creation into new freedom and fulfillment. In a sense the advent of Christ is like God's gift of a new great mutation that makes a new form of Godly human life possible. And like all newly emerged forms of life in evolution the new

capacity is a gift of birth, not a willed achievement. Those atheists who rail against the idea of being saved through Christ's
actions on their behalf should remember that no humans ever
earned their own status as homo sapiens. All of their capacities
of creative intelligence and autonomous human freedom come
to individuals not through effort but as a gift from their birth
into the human family. And no human can survive or mature
without dependence on the nurture and care of others. In the
same way the new life in Christ is a gift and must be received in
faith. Humans can open themselves to the new life but cannot
achieve it through individual willing.

Jesus made possible a new birth and beginning in a communal life of loving mercy. The past can be left behind because
God makes all things new. By forgiving the sins that close us
off from God's life and healing what has been broken, Jesus invites us to forgive others and open ourselves up to them and to
God. Defects, wounds, bitterness, and hate no longer shape relationships, and every act of forgiveness is a new birth, a new
start, an act of "yes," instead of "no." The "yes" that Jesus
utters to God and his "yes" to his human brothers and sisters
makes our own human affirmation of self, others, and God
possible. Christ's yes opens the door to God's life, a door that
can never be closed.

But what of those who have resisted and rejected God and
goodness? Or worse still, what of those who have consciously
chosen evil or cruelly harmed others? As God's love and truth
made visible, Jesus Christ has the power to withstand evil and
overcome resistance. He can heal human hearts, engender repentance, give birth to the desire for God and fulfill that desire.
When the heart is touched, the mind and will can move toward God. Jesus gives testimony to the good news that God
loves the world and is seeking to be known and loved. In this
way, Christ draws humankind to himself and to God. Our
own inner consciousness of divine love is aroused through the
magnetic attraction of Jesus Christ. Persons who encounter

and receive Jesus experience a conversion of life, for Christ enkindles the desire for God. The fire of the Spirit burns away those obstacles inhibiting new beginnings. The great physician heals the suffering; there is a balm in Gilead that heals the wounded heart.

Giving birth is one vivid and compelling metaphor that describes Christ's saving work. United with God, Jesus begets a new family of God. Christ on the cross, therefore, can be envisioned as in the final stages of labor in a cosmic childbirth, resurrected life being born in a renewed creation. A contemporary feminist theologian, Mary Grey, sees the passion as the crowning moment of Jesus' laboring to bring forth God's transforming life,[11] and this re-visioning of the cross as a process of birth is entirely consonant with the core gospel message that human beings are brought forth into a new life through steadfast love in action. As fully God and fully human Jesus is the new Adam bringing into new life all the rest of his human family. Because we share Christ's human nature in one species, we can share his divinely transformed humanity. If Jesus were only God and not fully human, then full sharing in his life could not take place. If Jesus were only human and not God he would be a great and good man but he would not be able to make us like him through the gift of the Holy Spirit's transforming power. Since Jesus Christ gives birth to our new life, he becomes our mother, as well as our brother, the firstborn of a new family. A new heart of flesh is born within us, and we take part in a new and universal company of kin.

Jesus himself uses images of childbirth and being born again in the Spirit to describe his work and to reassure the disciples that their present sufferings will be followed by joy in their new life; he refers to the coming catastrophes before the end of time as birth pangs before the coming of God's kingdom. Paul too uses the metaphor of childbirth, speaking of the whole creation groaning in travail as it awaits redemption and fulfillment. At other times Paul refers to himself as giving birth and nurturing his new communities, first with milk and then with solid food.

Christian spirituality through the ages adopted these images of Christ as a mother laboring to bring forth our new life. Many mystics, both male and female, have used maternal and generative symbols to voice their gratitude for Christ's nurturing care and encouragement on their journey. One vision of Christ's maternal love is perhaps most engagingly expressed by the great medieval mystic Julian of Norwich, who describes God as our mother and Christ as a tender, mothering one who gives birth to us through his passion and nourishes us with the Eucharist. Devotion to Mary as the Mother of God has also helped to strengthen an image of God's love as maternal.

God, our divine Lover, our tender Mother, our nurturing Father, gives birth by way of a gradual process that requires patience, through a pregnancy and labor that are both prolonged and arduous. In this great birthing story of God, the original maternal act of creation described in Genesis is brought to completion by Christ's giving birth to a new resurrected form of life. The creation story and the story of Christ's saving labor are one and the same story. Before the crowning moment of fulfillment, childbirth can include both suffering and joy, often simultaneously. But it must be remembered that in the Gospel joy and the victory of love are stronger than death. As the letters to the Hebrews expresses it, Jesus endured the cross for the joy that awaited him. In the risen life, joy, love, and happiness last forever while suffering fades away.

Birth into the new Christian family is enacted in the church's ritual of baptism by water and the Spirit, as the death of an old, limited self opens up into the birth of a new self, able to live and love as Christ does. Through baptism, we receive the mind of Christ within us. In uniting ourselves with Christ, we seek to live as he lives, completely open and obedient to God, or as Hans Urs von Balthasar defines obedience best, we live in "readiness for everything."[12] This readiness to do whatever it takes to live in God's love and truth is the source of Jesus' saving power, and through this readiness and union with God, Jesus becomes our peace. Jesus binds humankind to God because he is one with God; faithful to his mission to the bitter end, he does not turn back. This absolute openness and union of Jesus with God's divine life makes it impossible for death to have a hold over Jesus, and his loving union or at-one-ment with God is made manifest in the resurrection.

Christ is our peace, the one who bridges the distance between limited, flawed, sinful humans and the infinite, perfect, transcendent God. Finite, immature, conflicted, benighted, rebelliously flailing human beings can now be healed, perfected, and born into new life. Scripture expresses the good news in a multitude of images in addition to the generative maternal and familial ones. Jesus is the way, the truth, and the life, the one who is able to lead the rest of his brothers and sisters into the risen life. Jesus is the good shepherd bringing his sheep up from the dead, he is the gate to eternal life, the bread of life, the true vine, the living water, the bridegroom, the physician, the light of the world, the friend, the cornerstone of the new temple, the anchor, the rock, the morning star, the Alpha and Omega — the savior of the world.

Christ's Fully Human Life

Through living as a fully human being Jesus saves humankind. The presence of the divine Spirit in Jesus as God's Son and Word does not suppress or overwhelm his humanity. Rather the Spirit releases the deepest fulfilled humanity of Christ. So too, disciples living in Christ are human beings who receive the power of the Holy Spirit to live in a new fulfilled way. Christians can be given the capacity to love God with all their heart and mind and their neighbor as themselves. Living in love and truth they can carry out God's works of mercy and healing. The Holy Spirit transforms human beings so that they can work to end suffering and bring God's justice and mercy to birth in the kingdom. Learning from Jesus his disciples seek to follow him, become like him, and go and do likewise.

We Christians living in today's more psychologically aware era desire to understand how Jesus came to be fulfilled as a person who is like us in all but sin. Beginning life as a specific individual formed by his time, place, family, culture, and religious tradition, Jesus was born of a woman, lived through infancy and youth, and came to adulthood in a conquered Palestinian province of the Roman Empire. As Jesus grew in wisdom and grace he lived and worked as a Jew in Nazareth, a "hidden life" that prepared him for his public ministry. Spiritualities emphasizing the hidden life of Jesus call attention to the fact that the majority of the time in God's earthly life was spent in a humble existence of work. Jesus prayed to discern God's will. With complete readiness to answer and obey the Spirit he moved toward his public ministry after a time of spiritual preparation in the desert. Baptized by John and confirmed in the Spirit Jesus began then to preach prophetically, to teach with authority, and to heal and comfort the ill and suffering with compassion. The power of his personal charisma, the witness of his deeds, and his example of a fully lived whole and holy life brought Jesus disciples and local renown.

But soon the disturbing revolutionary teaching of God's truth, with its demand for justice, repentance, and conversion, stirred up opposition to Jesus from those who did not wish to change or to give up their power and privilege. Jesus encountered, rejection, persecution, hostility, arrest, torture, and execution. Since Jesus lived in readiness for everything that his work and love of God would bring, he freely gave over his body, blood, mind, heart, and life for God and his people. His wholehearted love and willingness were never diminished or deformed by violent hatred for his enemies; his openness to and union with God gave Jesus his authority, his merciful love, and his joy.

Giving all to God, Jesus received all back in perfect integrity. Jesus taught with authority because he lived with the inner authority of an integrated undivided self totally open to God in love and truth. His humanity and God's Spirit gave Jesus power to live and love others in a new way. In Jesus, we see all the diverse human capacities, multiple powers, and different levels of human consciousness integrated into a free, harmonious, and ordered whole, or holiness. The Gospels record a rich range of word and deed, dialogue and teaching stories of Jesus, each of which displays his nuanced responsiveness to people along with his intense love and empathy. This fully human personality is like us, yet different. The intensity of his love and desire, the confidence, the wit, the magnetic assurance astound observers. His focus, his union of will and heart, give Jesus spiritual power and a liberating freedom, unmarred and unmarked by even the slightest separation of himself from God. He is the holy one without sin, an undivided self, without inner conflict or fragmentation. In Jesus, we see no inhibiting anxiety, rage, shame, guilt, or disgust. As a fully human being he is not omniscient but, through constant prayer that sustains him, he is wise and ready for everything. He can suffer, but not from apathy, paralysis, or sin; when Jesus does display anger or impatience with others, it is always in reaction to others' failure to love or to the sinful hypocrisy of religious elites and the greed of the rich. Even in his most scathing denunciations, Jesus does not threaten vengeance. Rather, he seems sad and sorrowful that such hardness of heart exists in God's children. When Jesus himself suffers from the evil and sinful actions of others, he does not retaliate but instead asks for the forgiveness of his torturers and expresses sorrow over the fate of those who reject him. Jesus suffers intensely in his life and in his dying without faltering in love and faithfulness.

Jesus the Man of Joy

For all his suffering Jesus also is a man of joy; his is a liberated and joyful heart. The deeper humanity that is released and developed in Jesus includes a deeper capacity for joy, happiness, and celebration. An abundance of love and infinite wellsprings of living water and healing powers flow from Jesus. In him God reveals what He has in mind for human beings created in His image and adopted into His family life. Christ's disciples can rejoice and exult; they too can become whole and say, "I am who I am"; they too know that they are the beloved children of God. Rescued from death, sin, and futility, disciples rejoice with Jesus the man of joy.

Jesus rejoices as he brings good tidings to the world, a world longing for the day of salvation and rescue from suffering and woe. He tells his disciples that they should be glad because they are witnessing what so many people in the past have longed to see. Now is the long-awaited day of the Lord. The Kingdom comes. Jesus rejoices in fulfilling God's promises and the past witness of the prophets of Israel.

Two dramatic moments of glory and radiant joy are recounted in the Gospels that mark Christ's possession of God's Spirit. On the day that John baptizes Jesus a voice from heaven announces that he is God's beloved Son. Later when praying on the mountaintop with his disciples Jesus is radiantly transfigured and enjoys an intimacy with God and the greatest of prophets. Here is a peak experience of ecstasy that overwhelms his companions. But Jesus comes down from the mountain to complete God's work amid growing difficulties. Still, in the midst of all of his days and during all of his teaching and healing, Jesus rejoices and gives thanks to God for God's loving intimate presence and bestowal of good things, for now the yoke of oppression is lifted. Healing and restoring the ill to health allows Jesus to give them back to their relatives and friends. Those who are healed leap for joy. Jesus professes that he is sent to do God's work and that it is his meat and drink; for this he was born. He eagerly enkindles the fire that will set the world ablaze as it will sweep all sin and evil away. To rescue the poor and oppressed gives joy to the liberator; to comfort the brokenhearted and heal produces in Jesus and in all who are touched by him a shared happiness.

Celebration and feasting are constant themes in the teaching of Jesus, with images of a king's banquet, wedding feasts, and the joy of eating and drinking in unity constantly recurring. The joyful father kills the fatted calf and prepares a feast for the return of his prodigal son. Rings, fine garments, and music add to the festiveness of the celebrations. In John's Gospel Jesus begins his public ministry at a marriage feast, and at the request of Mary his mother he adds to the merriment by providing fine wine. The joy of a marriage celebration of love and joyful unity becomes a central image in his preaching. He is the bridegroom and those who are with him will rejoice, eat, drink, and be happy.

Jesus in his turn takes delight in the company of his friends. His circle of followers includes both men and women: Mary and Martha, Lazarus, and Mary Magdalene are part of his company of disciples. Jesus celebrates and shares meals with those he meets. He tartly dismisses the criticism of those who claim he is a drunkard and those who are offended that he eats with everyone, going beyond the purity taboos and reigning customs of the time. Such inclusive table fellowship represented a significant revolutionary act meant to convey the crucial message that God's mercy and love include all.

In these images and stories of celebration, we perceive how Jesus as a devout Jew has inherited the rich tradition of Hebrew worship. Joy and praise, psalms and prophecies of Scripture ring and resound with countless soaring expressions of delight. Dancing, singing, music, and merrymaking celebrate God's glory and the wonders of creation. Psalmists sing that "the precepts of the Lord give joy to the heart"(Ps. 19), as do the beauties of the creation. God delights in humankind and wishes them to be happy in having their desires fulfilled.

Jesus promises blessedness to his disciples in the Beatitudes, a series of teachings describing happiness, which can be recognized as a kind of self-portrait of Jesus' own joyousness. Being meek, merciful, and pure of heart will make seekers of God able to receive knowledge and mercy from God as well as their inheritance of the earth. Peacemaking brings joy to the peacemaker since it shows him or her to be a child of God. Even persecution for God's sake brings happiness, because the disciple is accomplishing God's saving work in the world. Jesus constantly tells his followers that giving, serving, and loving will bring blessings and joy: in giving one receives. The Beatitudes disclose the good news of love; they describe the inner relationship of God as Trinity, the ground of all human experiences of joy.

In the Gospel accounts when Jesus proclaims his teachings on joy and happiness, those who hear believe because his own joy witnesses to the truth of what he says. The crowds follow Jesus because of his magnetic presence; he teaches and heals with the authority of true happiness. Jesus lives what he preaches and manifests what he promises. Jesus radiates joy, and "the crowds listen to him with delight." The people go "looking for him" and "try to prevent him from leaving them." Even to get near him and touch him will bring relief from suffering. Jesus' joy in God constantly infuses the images he uses in his teaching to describe God's favor. The kingdom of God can be likened to the joy of finding a pearl of great price, or to the joy of finding a treasure hidden in a field, or to the possession of a wellspring of living water. In many different ways and times Christ assures his disciples that "I give you joy that no man can take from you."

Most appropriately, Jesus uses the image of the joy of childbirth to describe the new life in God. Babies and children are especially blessed and appreciated by Jesus, and he teaches that the openness and delight of a child in life is like that of those who inhabit God's kingdom. Similarly, God's lovingkindness is likened to that of parents who give to their children. The delight of the forgiving, generous father of the prodigal son is perhaps the most vivid image of parental love. And the sulkiness of the envious elder brother who cannot rejoice in the feasting is an example of how sin and lack of love can keep us from rejoicing in the beauty and goodness of God's love.

Often in Jesus' parables, joy springs from surprise at an unsuspected reversal. What was lost is found. The woman who finds her lost coin is delighted. The shepherd feels intense joy when he finds his lost sheep. Virgins who do not despair and keep watch are ready when the bridegroom suddenly comes to join in the marriage feast. The beggar Lazarus, who lay at the gate with dogs licking his sores, reclines upon Abraham's bosom. The last will be first, for God does not judge as the world judges, but sees into the heart. God loves all without partiality and cares for each person, to the point of numbering each hair on our heads. Those who repent and turn again are received with special joy. Workers who come late are given the same reward as those who work all day. All are invited to take part in the great eternal banquet prepared by God even if they are stragglers. After death a future life will exist where the risen Jesus will await. Jesus promises to prepare a place for those who follow him. The disciples and crowds who hear Jesus respond to the wonder of the good news; through the force of his joyful confidence they come to believe and overcome their doubts and sadness. Yes, their thirst for happiness and liberation is going to be fulfilled, their broken hearts consoled. With Jesus they can live in joyful hope; in his presence their hearts burn within them.

Perhaps the greatest reversal is the joy of the resurrection; the disciples see that death is not the end. The stunning news of the resurrection is a great turning point in human history.

While many Jews of Jesus' time believed in a general resurrection at the end of time, the individual resurrection of Jesus was unexpected and surpassed all his disciples' expectations. To know that the scourge of death, oppression, and suffering have been overcome produces ecstatic joy and gratitude. In God's love the ancient promises to Israel will come true; when God is all in all every tear will be wiped away and there will be no more death or suffering. Christ's resurrection is the first fruits of a coming victory of God's compassion and glory. Joyful relief, happy expectation, and glad gratitude to God inspire the disciples. Their experience would prepare them to receive the fire of the Holy Spirit at Pentecost and begin their journey as the church proclaiming God's good news. Throughout the church the joy of Christ's presence is celebrated in the ritual feast of the Eucharist. The feast is a reenactment of Christ's triumph over death and a participation in the joy and glory of God.

But what of the suffering that is still present in human life? How does the suffering of Jesus relate to his triumph of joy and love; how are suffering and joy related in the Christian life? The answer affects disciples seeking to live with Jesus. How, then, is Jesus the man of joy also the man of sorrows?

– Five –

JESUS THE MAN
OF SORROWS

JESUS SAVES, Jesus suffers, Jesus brings us God's joy in this life and the next. What do we need to understand about the suffering and joy of Jesus in order to be united to Christ and live as his disciples? The creed states that for our sake Jesus suffered, died, and was buried. But the interpretation of Jesus' suffering has been much contested, and, as always, different views will have practical results in Christian lives. How essential, for instance, is it for us to suffer? Was the suffering of Jesus necessary for his saving work, and what kinds of suffering are we talking about? The claim has been made that Jesus not only brings us with him into a risen new life in God's family, but that he does so through his sufferings. As the saving Lord he understands all of our present travail because he suffered as we do. Jesus is like us in all but sin so he can encourage and sustain us in every sorrow. Consolation comes to us through the man of sorrows. When we look at the crucifix we take heart from the reminder of the enormity of God's love for us.

Does Jesus still suffer with us even though he is risen and lives in glory with God? If so, a puzzle emerges: how can a glorified human body united to God suffer? This question returns Christians to the complicated question discussed earlier, of whether God suffers.[1] A no less difficult issue is whether, or how, we share in the suffering of Jesus. Again the problematic relationship of suffering and joy in the Christian life emerges as both a theoretical and practical challenge.

Jesus and Human Suffering

Jesus living as a devout Jew was familiar with the suffering and joy in the Hebrew scriptural accounts of God's covenant with His people. In the founding narrative Yahweh responds to the cries of His suffering people enslaved in Egypt and acts to rescue them. Moses leads his people to freedom, and they pass safely through the Red Sea, praising and rejoicing in God. In the songs, celebrations, and Scriptures of Jewish worship, magnificent expressions of joy and gratitude are offered to God for His favor and care. But at the same time there are commemorations of the sufferings entailed in the long struggle to get to the promised land of milk and honey, and the later travails of Israel's history as a people are remembered in many scriptural accounts of backsliding, violent rebellions, warfare, defeat, exile, and subjugations to oppressive regimes. The psalms and traditional lamentations of Jewish Scripture recognize the pervasive presence of evil, loss, and suffering in a harsh and cruel world, suffused with longing for the final victory over suffering that will accompany the coming of God's Messiah. He will bring justice and joy to the world.

Heir to the Hebrew tradition of lamentation, Jesus also lives in a time when his people are groaning under the oppression and exploitation of its rulers. Subjected to the imperial regime of Rome the poor suffered from unjust taxes and laws that served the rich and powerful landlords allied with the occupying powers. Many uprisings took place against the Roman regime and were cruelly suppressed. Rome's superior military force backed up their local puppet rulers who had been installed in the region. In the decades before Jesus' public ministry, several false Messiahs had appeared and been executed. Jesus himself refers to the sufferings of those Galileans who had been condemned to death for their rebellion. The suffering and woes of his people were clear to Jesus, whose teachings reveal a knowledge of traditional Hebrew prophetic protests and hopes for the reign of God's coming kingdom.

In the teachings and parables of Jesus he demonstrates intimate familiarity with the many different kinds of human suffering and losses. He has obviously lived among his people and been someone upon whom nothing is lost. Many blameworthy self-inflicted sufferings that people bring upon themselves are described by Jesus. In the famous parable of the prodigal son, the young man has acted as an ungrateful wastrel, indulged in promiscuous living, and finally finds himself suffering destitution and hunger among the pigs. He has brought his misery upon himself, and when he comes to his senses he acknowledges that his sufferings are his own fault and resolves to go and beg his father's forgiveness. In other stories with less happy endings, greedy men who foolishly spend their lives getting and storing up riches for themselves suffer fear when they face death and their souls are required of them. Rich and worldly men who turn away from God are said to be like people who build their houses upon sand instead of rock. Foolish virgins are shut out of the wedding feast because of their carelessness, lack of preparation, and inability to keep watch. They are fast asleep when the bridegroom comes. The rich man who for years ignored the needs of the beggar Lazarus lying at his gate covered with sores ends up in the flames of hellfire, while Lazarus lies in the bosom of Abraham. Did Jesus mean for these physical sufferings of fire after death to be taken literally as just punishments for ignoring God's commands to give alms to those in need? Perhaps, but if these fires are meant to be symbolic they are appropriate representations of the kind of excruciating sufferings that can arise from guilt, shame, and regret. So too the images of wailing and gnashing of teeth in outer darkness are vivid descriptions of the self-inflicted suffering of isolation that comes from rejecting God.

By contrast Jesus also tells us of unjust suffering inflicted upon the innocent. The poor are forced into debt. Wayfarers are compelled into military service by Roman soldiers. He describes physical attacks and beatings — for example, the man assaulted while traveling on the Jericho road or messengers arriving from the owner of the vineyard who are attacked and murdered. A bullying servant unjustly and cruelly throttles an underservant with less power. Children are harmed. Women are stoned. Closest to home, the prophet John the Baptist is imprisoned and murdered by "that fox" Herod, joining a long line of God's messengers who are rejected and killed. Sinners, who are threatened by a prophet's courageous witness to God's demand for righteousness and repentance, execute the just ones.

In addition to physical injuries and sufferings inflicted upon the defenseless, Jesus describes the contemptuous scorn and wounding insults inflicted upon the vulnerable and the outcasts. Under the law not only could an adulterous woman be stoned, but a prostitute or woman of the town could be shunned as unclean. Jesus recognizes the suffering such humiliating treatment produces, and he even goes so far as to say that a person may be in danger of hellfire from calling another "a fool." To be treated with contempt and labeled as unclean is to suffer a form of personal assault. In stratified caste societies the dominant and powerful elites strive to inculcate shame and a sense of inferiority in those below them. To be called unclean, untouchable, or polluting is to be despised and abandoned. The morally unclean, along with the leper, are ostracized as threats to purity. Jesus indignantly criticizes the scribes and Pharisees who misuse their religious status to impose burdens and strictures on the people, without ever offering to help them. Such hypocrites impose suffering on many in the name of religion, and some, he notes, even neglect their aged parents.

In all these cases, when Jesus encounters the sufferings around him, he acts to relieve them. He accepts the outcast, touches the unclean, and eats with all. He has deep pity for the sick and impaired, healing the blind, the deaf, the dumb, the demented, the diseased, and the paralyzed. The dying and the dead are resuscitated. Jesus seems especially responsive to the anguish of parents whose children are demented, ill, or dying. These conditions and impairments are not blamed upon the sins of the victims, or on the victims' parents or on sins committed in a past life. God does not punish people through suffering but instead, in Jesus, heals all. When demons and demonic possession as such are the cause of an illness, then Jesus demonstrates God's loving power by exorcising the demons. Jesus acknowledges that victims of unforeseen events are not at fault. When towers fall upon innocent bystanders, Jesus makes the point that they have not been punished because they have sinned more than others. Death for human beings is horrible and is not willed by God. Jesus makes this judgment most dramatically when he raises the dead and restores them to families and friends. The suffering of those who mourn the loss of their friends is felt by Jesus; Lazarus dies, Jesus weeps. As the good physician who heals body, mind, and spirit, and comes to bring God's kingdom of justice, Jesus understands the depth of human suffering.

The Suffering of Jesus

Alive to human suffering, Jesus himself suffers. The question has been asked whether Jesus in his life and death suffered as much or more than other human beings. Older people enduring years of intense chronic pain have been heard to mutter that they envy the fact that Jesus only suffered on the cross for three hours. It also can be wondered whether or not in the torture chambers, hospitals, battlefields, prisons, and concentration camps of history, other victims might have experienced equal or greater amounts of pain and suffering than Jesus for longer periods of time. Severe suffering arises from the individual's impotence in the face of threats to the integrity of the self, which may occur with or without physical pain. Moreover, because of the innate human capacity for empathy, acute suffering can be felt with the suffering of others — especially beloved others whom one cannot protect or help. In the Gospel narratives Jesus suffers in all of the above ways, both directly and indirectly for others.

In his public ministry Jesus meets rejection, hostilities, calumnies, harassments, accusations of insanity, misunderstandings, and death threats. On the way to his execution Jesus suffers the abandonment of friends, their betrayals, mockery from the crowds, and the degrading tortures of a criminal's death. After being arrested and imprisoned Jesus endures physical abuse and deprivations. And the more we know of the Roman practice of crucifixion, the more we understand its gruesome cruelty. In addition to the pain of being flogged and pierced by nails, the victim suffers the agony of gradual suffocation as he weakens and can no longer pull his nailed body upright in order to breathe. Modern torturers presently engaged in interrogating and abusing helpless prisoners with near drownings can note, "There is something more terrifying than pain, and that is the inability to breathe."[2] As with Jesus, tortures by asphyxiation are increased when they are "combined with stress positions, sensory and sleep deprivation, and direct 'physical coercion,' or beatings." Stripping of clothing and taunting are also ancient and modern torture techniques. In Roman crucifixions the agony of the dying process could be extended for days. For Jesus, death came more rapidly because of his body's depletion from prior abuse and assault.

Adding to the sufferings of Jesus' execution is the moral indignity of being punished while innocent. Jesus knows he is innocent and has done all things well. Like so many past and future victims, Jesus is despised and killed for who he is, not for doing wrong, and so he shares the fate of all innocent victims massacred in genocides, pogroms, holocausts, atomic attacks, carpet bombings, terrorist attacks, and guerrilla actions. In fact, Jesus as the man without sin is especially hated for who he is: his goodness, his charismatic holiness, and his dedication to God's loving truth are felt as an affront. Goodness and holiness provoke hostile responses, because they induce inner self-judgments of guilt by comparison. As the Book of Wisdom expresses it, the just one is "obnoxious" in his difference and holiness; "to us he is the censure of our thoughts; merely to see him is a hardship for us, because his life is not like that of others" (2:14–15). As great literature has also shown, for instance, in Melville's *Billy Budd* or Browning's *My Last Duchess,* perception of another's goodness brings to consciousness one's own failings and sins; the resulting defensive anxiety and envy motivate the destruction of the innocent.

Jesus suffers, but does not let rejection and hostility deter him in his work. His steadfast uniting of his life, love, and will with God's loving will, despite suffering, is the essence of Christ's saving action. His complete self-giving love and openness to God produce courageous fidelity. Faith and love overcome the temptations toward flight. Nothing can separate Jesus from his Father, and his love triumphs over human weakness and the powers of evil. Although Jesus suffers, he does not turn back. His passionate love and dedication, his union with God, ensure that the suffering and dreadful death of Jesus give birth to a new risen life for all humankind. Jesus is sinless, faithful, and true — wholly at one with God, wholly at one in his human nature, and wholly at one with his brothers and sisters loving them no matter how sinful they are. Without Christ's integrated, focused life of holiness and love of God and neighbor, his pain and torturous death cannot be understood, nor would they possess saving force. Human suffering and death in themselves have no positive value. The suffering and death of Jesus bear fruit because of who he is and because they carry through to the bitter end his faithful love and union with God. But ironically, his love and unity with God may increase Jesus' suffering.

If suffering is partly a contrast experience, then Jesus' joyful intimacy as a beloved son with his Father would intensify his agony. Suffering and dying are in complete contrast to Jesus' own joyful and loving experience of God's life. Jesus, who rejoices in knowing himself as the anointed son of God, endures the degradation and humiliation of a criminal's death. One can argue that Jesus suffered more deeply and more intensely than any other human being because he possesses a greater empathy and love than any other. If empathy or identification with others produces suffering and compassion for others' travail and woe, then Jesus' divine capacity for loving his people means he will suffer their pain in a uniquely intense way. His own agony can be increased by his compassionate sorrow for his mother, his friends and disciples, and all the others in his human family. Hanging on the cross he can neither protect nor comfort others. On the way to his death Jesus laments his inability to draw his people to him as a mother hen gathers her chicks under her wings. He pities the daughters of Jerusalem and those who have failed to recognize him as God's word bringing their day of salvation.

And as a prophet, Jesus foresees how in the future the world and its inhabitants will suffer for rejecting God's goodness and truth. In his love for humankind Jesus can prospectively feel sorrow for all the woe that humans will endure: from fear, apathy, sinful betrayals, cruelty, injustice, natural disasters, diseases, wars, and death. In empathy and love Jesus suffers not only his own pain and distress, but all the world's past, present, and future travail. Moreover, as we have seen, empathy can be felt for the ignorant and deformed evildoers who in their moral wickedness reject the light and remain in darkness. In this sense Jesus bears the burdens and sins of humankind. He is innocent but through loving empathy can suffer for the lethal and sinful lapses of his people. His bearing of the sins of the world is not a passive punishment laid on Jesus by God, but rather it is a voluntary act of love and empathy for the human family. A mother mourns and suffers vicariously in and with her children's destructive sins, and so Jesus suffers for us. Mothers freely bear pain for the sake of their children and long to hold them in their arms. Jesus suffers from others and for the sake of others, but in his love and empathy does not desire to take revenge. As the new Adam he transcends the innately human built-in drives to exact revenge or punish wrongdoers. The evolved human predisposition to injure those who injure you and yours is strongly imprinted in the species and violently reinforced. But Jesus reveals that in God's mercy, vengeance is transcended by love; no more sacred violence and killing of victims on behalf of a vengeful God, no more eye for an eye or tit for tat, no more blood sacrifices and blood feuds. Jesus as God's son forgives those who bring about his death and prays for his enemies. Jesus suffers from his persecutors but also with and for them — hardened and brutalized sinners who are to be loved and pitied as God's creations that have become deformed. Yet disappointed sorrow over the world's rejection of his prophetic mission adds to the suffering of Jesus.

But can we say that Jesus was disappointed? Those who doubt this would claim it to be impossible since they judge Jesus' divine nature to confer upon him God's omniscience. The claim has been made that from the beginning of his life Jesus was completely aware of his destiny to suffer and be crucified according to the divine plan. Such claims in effect reject the affirmation that Jesus Christ was truly human as well as truly God. As an embodied, fully human being Jesus lived in historical time and was subject to human limitations, vulnerabilities, and ills, including sufferings and death. Earlier efforts to emphasize the divine nature of Jesus as God's Son even led to denials that Jesus ever actually suffered or could be limited in human knowledge or in any capacity.[3] But as a real man born of a real woman in a specific time and place, Jesus grew and developed from childhood to maturity, *increasing* in wisdom and grace. He lived as a devout Jew and would respond as such to his ongoing experiences and culture. Through a life of intense prayer and meditation, Jesus develops an *increasing* understanding of his inspired vocation and identity. He may not have known from the very beginning how his prophetic mission would turn out. Long before the Second Vatican Council, the great Catholic writer Romano Guardini speculated in his classic work *The Lord* that Jesus' message and good news could have been accepted. If all who heard Jesus had repented and acclaimed him as God's Word, then God's kingdom could have been ushered in on earth through a great messianic conversion. Jesus could have been acclaimed instead of crucified.

Guardini's ability to imagine an alternative outcome to the Gospel story showed his understanding that God's creation was open to human cooperation and co-creation. God's gift of real freedom to creation ensures the possibilities of different outcomes in encounters and events. Acceptance as well as refusals of God can take place. I remember that when I first read about this idea, the concept of an open evolving creation and co-creation was too puzzling for me to grasp, especially when applied to Jesus. Influenced by C. S. Lewis and his traditional narrative and interpretation of God's omnipotence, I was in thrall to belief in a predestined, detailed divine blueprint in a fully determined universe. After all, in the science taught at that period, the universe was pictured as a fully determined machine, operating by the rigid and necessary laws that govern billiard balls. But now science and theology have moved on. God's purposes and desired goals may be differentiated from divine detailed micromanaged plans involving coercive control. Many theologians remind us that God is continually creating and that within an evolving creation, God's will can be fulfilled in a creative plenitude of potential ways. "Behold, I make all things new." Could not Jesus, who was conscious of God's love and promises, have hoped for the immediate acceptance of the good news of the kingdom? Jesus might have had hope since he knew that he himself had freely obeyed God's call. Certainly the initial response to Jesus by the crowds was enthusiastic, and the final outcome of his mission may have been uncertain.

Jesus as a fully free human being, like ourselves, was not simply passively following a clearly outlined plan. In *Prayer and the New Testament* Robert Karris describes the way that Jesus prays constantly throughout his life to discern and follow God's will.[4] Always he prays thy will be done, even when at the last he asks, "If it be possible let this cup pass from me." From the beginning, as the examples of his initial temptations in the desert demonstrate, Jesus understands that there are alternatives open to him at every turning point in the great drama. Jesus might have stayed in the countryside and avoided going up to Jerusalem with its dangers. Earlier he had found no difficulty in facing down a lynch mob in his native Nazareth, and when he wished, he could slip away from the temple authorities who sought to arrest him. Jesus prays to be ready for anything that God's love and truth will require of him and makes his decisions accordingly. He always says yes to God.

Views that imply that Jesus was completely omniscient and always knew exactly how everything would turn out do not accept the full humanity of Jesus. Jesus was not God merely pretending to be human, or a being who was not subject to suffering and other human limitations. To think in this way does not fully honor Jesus for his courage, fidelity, and loving gift of self. Today theologians understand the hymn in Philippians describing God the Son's self-giving to human estate to be a complete self-emptying and irreversible union with human nature. This central truth of the incarnation means that in his full humanity Jesus can suffer physical pains and emotional sorrows and be hurt and disappointed by rejection.[5] Despite the crowds who flocked to hear and see him preach, teach, and heal the ill, it soon becomes clear that opposition to him is growing.

Any expectation for the immediate acceptance of God's messenger and the good news are dashed. Criticism and hostility to Jesus mount. His teaching and healing miracles on the Sabbath offend the religious establishment, but even some of the ordinary folk begged him to leave their neighborhood after he heals the demoniac. Why? Because of awe and fear? They report that Jesus is "too much for them." Present disciples can understand such a response to Jesus' focused dedication to God; his fullness of life and willingness to give completely judges human mediocrity and the comforting security that apathy provides. The new wine is too inebriating. It becomes clear that people are not going to repent and turn to God. Jesus, who "knew what was in everyone" (John 2:25) could read the signs of the times; he saw that he would be rejected like God's previous messengers. Once again a prophet will be without honor in his own country. In what Jesus sorrowfully describes as an "adulterous and sinful generation" (Mark 8:39) too many "loved darkness rather than light because their deeds were evil" (John 3:19). Jesus too will have to face death if he goes to Jerusalem where God's prophets meet their end. One portent of the coming persecution is evident when Herod imprisons and executes John the Baptizer because of his faithful witness to God's truth. Evil continues to exercise its lethal power in the world (often personified as Satan, the prince of the world). Christ understands that if he remains faithful, he too will face suffering and death. In an effort to prepare his disciples, Jesus "began to teach them that the Son of Man must undergo great suffering and be rejected" (Mark 8:31), a bitter and unwelcome message. Jesus comes down from the ecstatic experience of radiant transfiguration on the mountain and sets his face steadfastly toward Jerusalem. Peter, who thinks it would be a fine idea to stay safely on the mountaintop forever, voices his pained objection to courting danger and prophetic martyrdom. Why must Jesus face such a death?

Many others have wondered why Jesus had to die and endure such a tortured and public execution by crucifixion. Would it not be enough of a saving action that Jesus unite his mind, heart, and will completely with God's loving will, and thereby engender in the Spirit a new family of God? If it is truly the union of Christ's humanity with God's divinity that saves, heals, and gives birth to the new transformed creation, does the manner of dying make a difference? Perhaps Jesus could flee and hide in the countryside, living a holy life until old age and death end his years. These kinds of arguments over the necessity of Jesus' suffering and crucial death are useful in countering views of Jesus' death as a necessary kind of ritual blood sacrifice, or a Godsent filicide, predestined and required to placate an offended God. At least exploring the possibility of an alternative scenario for the end of Jesus' life makes clear that Jesus freely lays down his life for God and humankind rather than being a passive victim of fate.

But alternative narratives are inadequate because they ignore the character of Jesus as a person. Wherever Jesus lived he would still be himself. He is a prophet passionately on fire to proclaim God's loving will for the world. The good news of salvation he brings and his message for the need of repentance and revolution burn within him. Jesus desires to set the world on fire and usher in God's reign of justice and charity. This enkindling zeal and blinding light can hardly be hidden under a bushel. Jesus recognizes that God's kingdom cannot come without a converted world committed to God's righteousness and justice. A solitary holy individual in ecstatic contemplation on a mountaintop cannot bring about a new transformed and transforming community that will bring mercy, justice, and relief of suffering to the struggling multitudes on the plain. God's good news and work must overcome the embedded powers of evil and liberate everyone who suffers.

Moreover, Jesus could hardly suppress his intense love and pity for the suffering and wounded, which move him to heal the ill and comfort the brokenhearted. Wherever the Great Physician finds himself, he heals, teaches, and proclaims God's truth. Such dramatic events displaying unprecedented powers and magnetic charisma could never be kept secret. The crowds follow Jesus everywhere in hopes of being healed. Inevitably a confrontation with the established powers and authorities would take place; a crisis demanding acceptance or rejection would follow. A prophet threatens the injustice of the status quo as he or she proclaims God's word through symbolic public actions that embody God's message. Cleansing the temple was one such disturbance. The powerful who benefit from the status quo reject and hate the challenge of a prophet; when he becomes too prominent a threat then he must be removed, discredited, and destroyed. In this sense, a public execution of Jesus could be seen as a social and political necessity for the powerful oppressive regime. It was "not accidental."[6] Of course, Jesus might have been tortured, killed, or executed in some other publicly humiliating way, but he could hardly have died peacefully at home in bed after a long and peaceful life.

Suffering public execution for the sake of God's truth is a witness worthy of the Hebrew prophets who went before, such as John the Baptist, the Maccabees, and other great servants of God. Jesus was willing to lay down his life for God and his people, for both his friends and foes. In his absolute trust that God is a loving God of the living who keeps promises, he is ready to endure the full force of the world's evil in hope that God's will be done and God's reign be imitated. Jesus believes that he goes to God and will bring his disciples and the world with him into a new life. When Jesus is lifted up he will draw persons to himself. Jesus dies in his trust that God's love and truth are stronger than death and also stronger than the fear of death that enslaves humankind.

It seems a grievous misunderstanding of Jesus' suffering to think that it is added to by God's abandonment or by Jesus' conviction that he has been forsaken by God. These views would be appropriate in an approach to Jesus' death as a victim who must be tormented in order to placate God's offended honor.[7] But if Jesus freely offers himself in love and witness of the truth and constantly unites his whole self in union with God, then it would not be consistent to see him as forsaken or despairing. He is not a hapless victim broken by an unforeseen and meaningless accident of fate. Yes, Jesus suffers agonizing torture and pain, as well as the sorrow of rejection, betrayal, and abandonment from his people, but not from God's abandonment. It seems misguided to take his cry, "My God, my God, why have you forsaken me?" as evidence that *in extremis* Jesus loses his faith in God and his own mission. To interpret these words in isolation ignores the rest of the Passion as given in the different Gospel accounts. Other recorded words of Jesus on the cross show him promising paradise to the thief being crucified at his side, giving his grieving mother into the care of his disciple, praying to God to forgive his executioners, and finally commending his spirit to God. His words, "It is finished," reflect a sense of a mission accomplished, not a sense of desolate despair. Indeed, even the psalm that Jesus appears to be quoting when he cries, "My God, my God, why have you forsaken me," proceeds from its opening line to a final affirmation of trust in God. For that matter, when Jesus cries out to *my* God, he is uttering a prayerful lament to God. Hebrew prayers of lament, protest, and complaint reveal an intimacy with God and are offered by the faithful in the midst of agony and suffering. By contrast, broken, despairing persons who are afflicted by overwhelming suffering are muted, numbed, and incapable of expressing feelings for self or others.

Over the centuries Christians reading the Passion narratives in the different Gospels have observed the discrepancies and the different emphases given to the event and its suffering. The agony of Jesus is more salient in one Gospel and his confident faithfulness in his mission more present in another. One conclusion has been that since these characteristics seem different, a choice has to be made between them, or between the early Christian communities that preserved them and passed them on, but such is not the case. As noted elsewhere here, the stream of human consciousness moves and changes in multi-leveled, multifaceted, and complex recursive movements. Since brain and body have evolved with different complicated modules, systems, and circuits for positive and negative emotions, it is possible for us to feel both positive and negative emotions simultaneously or quick interacting in alternating ways. One does not cancel out the other. In human evolution, positive and negative emotional systems have evolved from different origins and to serve different functions. Different emotions and thoughts can instantly rise from different sources and then fade away; human consciousness can range through different degrees of intensity and interact in complex ways with moments of joy and woe. The psalms and other poetic expressions, especially those of lament, gain their emotional power through reflecting the richness and fluctuation of contrasting human feelings.

While no one could ever say for certain what Jesus consciously experiences while undergoing his Passion, from the accounts traditionally handed down to us it seems probable that Jesus may be suffering more than any human being ever has, *while* simultaneously possessing more love and trust in God than any other. Since Jesus recognizes that he has been wholly faithful and true in his life and love of God, he remains united to God's will and may even perhaps feel surges of joy in completing God's call, despite the agony. Many other martyrs for God have expressed intense joy and intense suffering at the same time. In Jewish traditional accounts, for instance, of the martyrdoms of the courageous Maccabees, the old father Eleazar at ninety is tortured because he will not renounce his faith or accept the exemption offered. As he groans in agony he cries out, "The Lord in his holy knowledge knows full well that, although I could have escaped death, I am not only enduring terrible pain in my body from this scourging, but also suffering it with joy in my soul because of my devotion to him" (2 Macc. 6:3–31). The Maccabees also trusted that after death they would be vindicated by the living God.

And as the whole world must attest, whether believing or not in the Christian interpretation of events, the execution of Jesus is followed by an astounding outcome. The routine killing of one more troublemaker in a provincial backwater is followed by an unexpected aftermath. A demoralized group of ordinary men and women experience encounters with a risen Jesus and turn the world upside down. The first Christians believed that they met a resurrected Christ who promised them that they would receive the Holy Spirit and God's power to carry the good news to the whole world. The disciples gathered in the upper room at Pentecost and experienced a transforming power. They began to preach and live as Christ's disciples and created the Christian church as a religious movement. They proclaimed that Jesus Christ conquered death, appeared to them in living form, and could save all humans who believe in him from death and sin. Without their empowering faith in their experiences of the resurrection and the coming of the Holy Spirit, this nondescript group of disciples would surely have scattered in the same way as the followers of past failed messiahs who were put to death. No one would have heard of the teachings of Jesus, and if by chance they did, they would remain as another instance of the story of man's longing for the good.

Faith in the resurrection event produces the joy of Easter, which is decisive for the effective faith of Christians. Christ's triumph over death and suffering has been celebrated in the church's liturgies ever since. Indeed, the medieval church would mark the good news of the resurrection with masses featuring rites of "Easter laughter" as an expression of triumphant joy. The core experience of the early Christians was joy and trust in the risen Jesus; Jesus was alive, victorious over death, present, and through his gift of the Holy Spirit granting them the power to transform themselves and the suffering world. If Christ is not risen, Christians are of all men the most to be pitied and the most deluded. And what of the risen Christ's glorious life with God: does the risen Lord still suffer?

The Risen Jesus and Suffering

Christians believe that Jesus has been raised, sits at God's right hand, and is already victorious over sin, death, and evil. But the earthly fulfillment of the victory is "not yet" accomplished, as evidenced by the present suffering condition of the world. In the interim time before the day when Jesus will come again and God will be all in all, evil, sin, and suffering remain on earth. Persecutions, disasters, diseases, deaths, and a multitude of sorrows mar the life of human beings. This being so, Christians believe that the resurrected Christ, who lives in union with his human family and his body the church, does continue to suffer with his brothers and sisters and share the travail of those on earth. When Paul is felled on the road to Damascus, the voice of Christ asks him, "Saul, Saul, why are you persecuting me?" In Christian teaching whatever is done to, or for, anyone else is done to or for Christ. Whoever abuses his brother or sister is abusing the Lord; whoever does good to another is doing good to Christ. The communion and unity of humankind is a reality that transcends time and place. Even those theologians who would deny that God the Father as infinite transcendent creator and origin of all things can suffer, will acknowledge that Christ as fully human can suffer. One of the Trinity suffers. But how can the risen Christ suffer?

As a glorified resurrected human being Jesus cannot be suffering from the kinds of ills and assaults that he endured in his earthly ministry. He cannot die or suffer physical pain, torture, hunger, thirst, illness, fatigue, or fear of death. Nor can Jesus as the sinless one have ever suffered directly from self-inflicted sufferings caused by sin, such as guilt, anguish, shame, hate, rage, envy, or despair. But there is one kind of suffering that does not spring from personal sin or human vulnerabilities to betrayal, pain, or death: empathy, compassion, and loving identification with others' sufferings and sins can produce vicarious or indirect suffering. Since the risen Jesus continues as a human being to be united with his people, he can suffer in loving empathy with all of their sufferings. Wherever the Lord went in his earthly ministry he was deeply moved by the sorrows of those he encountered. The ill and diseased, the poor, the bereaved and bereft, brought forth his pity and compassion. Jesus also was sorrowful for those who were ensnared in sin and rejected him and God's goodness. And in his risen life Jesus still suffers with us. When Jesus looks at Peter who is betraying him before the cock crows, his sadness is unspoken and also a portent of Jesus' future disappointments with his disciples. Sinful cruel behavior can no longer crucify Jesus, nor can fear, apathy, or indifference lead to Jesus' execution, but our sins can cause sorrow to the one who loves us more than we love ourselves and eternally hopes for our conversion and transformation.

In this very real sense our sins do grieve Jesus today as they once did in his earthly ministry. He bore with our sins and still bears with us. More empathic suffering can arise as the risen Christ is present in and with those victims who are innocently suffering torture, oppression, abuse, and executions from the wicked actions of others. The sexual abuse and exploitation of women and children, prisoners and the poor, cause sadness from identification with the victims and sorrow from the moral deformities of the victimizers. The risen Jesus shares every trouble and misery, every pain and sorrow with us, his beloved family.

While the risen Jesus suffers with us in empathy, it must be remembered that this kind of suffering does not diminish or constrict consciousness as other forms of pain and suffering do. Whether in heaven or on earth, loving empathy expands the heart and mind because there is an outward movement into a shared identification with the other; a sense of "we-ness" and communion is born. The intense mutual and positive relationships of this loving beneficence or compassion overcome isolation and narrow selfishness. Nor does this kind of suffering turn the sufferer away from God as the blameworthy, loveless suffering from sin does. In fact the opposite is true since love and compassion give embodied reality to the presence of God. Christ is worshiped as the Compassion of God. Moreover when the risen Christ suffers with us in empathy, that is not all that is happening. Jesus Christ risen in glory, sitting at God's right hand, is simultaneously enjoying God's plenitude, joy, and delight in the company of the saints or adopted family of God. With God glory abounds, and within the inner life of the Trinity mutual love is continuously generating joy and creativity. Christ's wounds no longer bleed, and his sufferings from empathy do not darken, obscure, shadow, or extinguish joy. He has overcome the world and brought victory over evil and suffering. Christ who is fully human and fully divine can suffer with us and at the same time participate in God's transcendent life of Light and Joy.

There is a double reassurance in this for Christian disciples. In our most extreme sufferings here and now, Christ's loving presence is with us, and after this time of trial, future joy will come. Those in pain can receive an enfolding, sustaining love and comfort in Christ, also hope and trust that the troubles of the present will give way to future joy. Hope stays alive and engenders courage. Christ shares our every moment of suffering and heals all wounds. And how do we disciples in our turn share in Christ's suffering?

Sharing in the Sufferings of Christ

Disciples are commanded to prevent, alleviate, and end the sufferings of their neighbors by efforts known as the works of
mercy. They are to take up their cross as Christ did in order
to love, serve, and help their neighbors flourish in every way.
These actions can bear good fruit. But at times the sufferings
and disasters encountered in life are completely intractable and
have nothing but negative and destructive effects. Nothing can
be done, and no possible earthly or spiritual good can come
from certain disastrous and tragic events. As Karl Rahner puts
it: "The children burned to death by napalm bombs were not
going through a process of human maturing."[8] In overwhelming horrendous sufferings that produce the numbed desolation
of affliction, no wisdom accrues, no empathy is enhanced, nor
is human solidarity strengthened. Rather, the lethal power of
evil goes unchecked, leaving no opportunity for creative outcomes. Can Christians still affirm that Christ is present in these
circumstances of extreme intractable sufferings? The answer
must be yes, because of Christ's unjust suffering and death on
the cross. When Jesus as the innocent God-man suffers torture,
he reveals that God is present in the very depths of horror. In
the midst of meaningless agony, God's Word is present, and the
Word is that love that is stronger than death. God in Christ ab-
sorbs the worst consequences of the world's sin and overcomes
through love. He suffers without hate and without seeking revenge. Jesus on the cross is giving birth to a new risen life.
The good news is that meaninglessness, evil, and cruelty do not
have the definitive word. The death making of the world's evil
is reversed in the creation of a future with God. In the interim
time of "not yet" before the last things, suffering Christians
can unite their most painful moments with Christ's suffering;
they can hope to share in his victory of life and love.

Can disciples hope to unite their intractable sufferings with
Christ and participate in Christ's work, bringing the new

creation to birth? Again the answer is yes, if whatever is done in word or work is done for the glory of Christ. The "whatever" need not refer only to fruitful works of mercy that succeed but can include failures and losses, pain and sufferings. The suffering and agonies of Jesus in his life and death give witness that our own experiences of suffering can be offered to God as gifts. Even more momentous is the belief that our gifts of sufferings can be joined with Christ's sufferings and play their part, however small, in God's birthing of the new creation. Failure, torment, and isolated distress that is meaninglessly absurd in itself, or a grotesque instance of evil, can be given meaning because they are joined with Christ's self-offering on the cross.

This truth has been expressed in the traditional Christian language of "offering up your suffering." Even though this concept has been abused by encouraging passivity and the valorization of victimization, it is too important an idea not to be recovered and reinterpreted. Clearly to alleviate, prevent, and heal suffering is as much a part of the Christian's vocation today as ever. Failure of active deeds, however, need not be the end of Christian efforts to effect good and transform the world. Because of the gifts of self-consciousness and free will, humans are able to lift heart and mind to God and offer up to God our will and loving intentions; through such self-conscious acts of free will, the Holy Spirit draws humankind and creation toward God's fulfillment. Each thought, word, or deed offered in Christ's name increases the order and active energy of love in creation. Meaningful order is formed through every intentional act. Formless chaos recedes through humanly initiated acts of love and will; God's new creation is birthed. Paul preaches this truth when he rejoices in his suffering, which will be used to fill out and complete Christ's saving work. This belief is not an example of masochism but of extreme optimism. Christ's power to save the world can be exercised and manifested through love, weakness, and suffering. This message of hope for the positive spiritual use of suffering was repeated in Pope John Paul II's reflections when he said, "A source of joy is found in the overcoming of the sense of the uselessness of suffering, a feeling that is sometimes very strongly rooted in human suffering."[9] When efforts to rescue and heal, to alleviate suffering, fail, loss and pain can be offered up as an acceptable gift, united with the offering of the crucified Jesus. In our most helpless moments of torment and loss, and especially at the moment of death, we Christians can say with Jesus, "It is finished," and "into thy hands I commend my spirit."

Yet this particularly Catholic spiritual attitude of "offering up" suffering has puzzled many observers. Several years ago I met a young television interviewer who asked me what this religious talk about "offering up suffering" meant? He knew a Catholic woman with an impaired, chronically ill child who told him that she kept going only by offering up her sufferings to God. He could see that she was living a heroic life of loving service, but he could not understand what she meant when she spoke of the spiritual solace she had found. I tried to explain to him that this traditional practice in Catholic piety is grounded on the belief that all human beings are intimately united as members of Christ's body. What happens to one happens to all. What is done by one can benefit all. Indeed, the theological teaching about our participation in Christ's suffering is supported by new ecological and scientific understandings of the unity and interdependence of life in the universe. For Christians, just as the many can be saved by the one God-man Jesus, so all humanity is able, through God's Spirit, to participate in Christ's ongoing creative work. In transforming the world, prayers and intentions count as actions, though not visible to the eye. True, the act of nursing an ill or retarded child is clearly visible, and good works benefiting the world are also clearly evident when people build a school, set up a hospital, or enact laws for human welfare. But a Christian faith in God affirms that there are invisible spiritual realities and that private personal activities of directed consciousness can be beneficial to others as well as to oneself. Persons can love and pray for one another and affect the good of the world. Such works of love can operate at a distance, as well as in face-to-face relationships.

As modern thinkers now express it, all life, consciousness, and matter are interdependent and "entangled." In this unified reality persons affect and influence one another. Paul teaches that "the life and death of each of us has its influence on others" (Rom. 14:7) and instructs disciples "to pray all the time, asking for what you need, praying in the Spirit on every possible occasion. Never get tired of staying awake to pray for all the saints and pray for me" (Eph. 6:18). This belief in the power of prayer and intentional self-offerings in a larger spiritual communion is expressed over and over in many different ways by Christians. As the exemplary religious scholar Baron von Hügel writes to his niece, "I wonder whether you realize a great, deep fact. That all souls — all human souls — are deeply interconnected? That, I mean, we cannot only pray for each other, but suffer for each other."[10] Christians believe that in Christ they can benefit others not only through direct service but also through lovingly offering up their sufferings for them as Christ has done for us.

Offering or lifting up something to God consists of actively attending, focusing, intending, and willing it; one directs loving energy and personal consciousness and will toward a desired goal acceptable to God. Human intelligence gives persons the freedom and awareness to direct attention toward an infinite number of things that are perceptually present or past, or imaginatively projected future events. Selective attention can be fixed and focused on images and thoughts emerging within the constantly moving stream of consciousness, and images and thoughts can be purposively induced, called up, or kept in mind. Making plans and making decisions require the same purposeful acts of focusing and fixing attention. The conscious act of offering up something, such as intractable, useless, meaningless suffering, to God is a personal act of directed will infused with the emotional investment of love. Focusing personal attention and feeling is not easy, as anyone who has tried to meditate can attest. Praying for the living and the dead has been called a "work" of mercy, because it takes effort. Sustaining an attentive focus does not come naturally to the ever-scanning human mind. In offering up gifts to God for the sake of others we voluntarily direct loving feelings and thoughts toward the achieving of another's good. Just as I can help others alleviate suffering by giving of my concrete resources of time, money, food, land, possessions, and labor, so I can add to or intensify the collective conscious energies of love and meaningful order in the universe. Older ideas of "the treasury of grace" can be newly understood.

The Christian belief in the communion of saints rests on the affirmation that there exists a continuing interdependent unity of love and shared interpersonal concern between visible and invisible reality. Bonds of love exist between the living and the dead, and between Christ and his human family. Christians faced with intractable sufferings can draw courage and comfort from their faith that they are never isolated, never alone in their suffering, nor must their experience remain meaningless. Attending to Christ crucified and risen into new life, disciples are nourished by hope. They feel Christ's indwelling love and understanding, and know themselves also to be surrounded by a cloud of witnesses, a loving, encouraging company of friends and family, saints known and unknown. Their suffering and that of others is not without recognition. "Say not the suffering naught avalileth," as the Victorian poet avers in a sentimental line that also happens to be true. Christ's saving act has been completed, but until the final day the work of healing continues with its joys and sorrows. The disciple's mission is to be another Christ and carry out Christ's liberating and healing works.

However helpless persons are, or physically constrained, intentional acts of prayer can provide meaningful action and bear good fruits. Passive suffering can become active through self-conscious, free acts of attention and love that create meaning. This power of human freedom has been affirmed in our time by the psychologist Viktor Frankl in his classic book *Man's Search for Meaning*. As a young Jewish psychiatrist Frankl was imprisoned by the Nazis in the Second World War. Amid the cruel torments of the concentration camp he came to believe that humans remained free in one respect: while completely coerced by brute force they could still take up an attitude to what was happening to them. Prisoners could not prevent themselves or others from being cruelly beaten, starved, or killed, but they could in their consciousness and conscience morally condemn the evils. As a secular thinker Frankl does not refer to God but simply says that humans can act worthily and give meaning to their sufferings before the unseen witness of humanity. But on reflection one problem remains.

What do Christians make of the many situations of suffering that thoroughly destroy, maim, numb, or distort the operation of consciousness in an individual human agent? Physical and mental illness, drugs, torture, or other conditions of traumatic shock and impairment can distort, skew, twist, or numb a human being's sense of self, or conscious exercise of free will. Frankl's claims that we are free to take up an attitude to whatever happens may not always be true. Victims of torture, traumatic accidents, drug abuse, physical and mental diseases, dementia, and genetic impairments can be too maimed or impaired in mind, heart, and will to function with normal conscious capacities. Taking up an attitude or having the capacity to offer up suffering would be impossible. Many individuals have had lives that from birth are stunted, injured, deformed, or twisted by tragic circumstance. Ill infants or the severely retarded and demented may never be able to develop any capacity for self-conscious agency. Their diminished awareness may diminish their ability to feel pain and suffering, but it might also be argued that without a sense of the future pain is intensified. (This aspect of the problem of pain and suffering is a problem in regard to the suffering of other animals besides ourselves.) Of course, at the other end of the intelligence spectrum there are highly functioning persons who can clearly take up an attitude to their suffering and that of others, but their chosen attitude is one of indifference, or worse still, to take pleasure in causing the suffering of others.

Facing the reality of so much obstinate indifference and numbed affliction, it becomes clear that most of the world's suffering will not be directly offered up by those who suffer. Humans would rightly despair if they did not have the faith that the human race exists as one body or one interdependent human family. If one human Savior is born, lives, suffers, dies, and rises for the sake of all, then even sinners, the afflicted, and the impaired can be carried by others. Just as Jesus seeks the lost sheep and saves them, so members of the body must carry each other home. What cannot be done by some must be done by others who can, and Christ holds all things together. Christians take hope in their belief that this world is not the end of the human story. Faith in Christ's resurrection and victory over evil and death give the assurance that the sorrows and failures of this world can be transformed in the risen life to come. Cultivating an apocalyptic imagination is important for Christian faith.

God's merciful love does not give up on God's creatures. The God who continually makes all things new can engender creative future healing. God's power can lay a saving hand on the past and overcome futility. As theologian Elizabeth Johnson writes: "God is ABBA, on the side of the one rejected, able to give a future to someone who has none. Henceforth, we can trust God to have the last word on our behalf, as indeed

God had the first, and that word is *life*."[11] In the life to come we can expect more chance for recovery, restoration, growth, and healing of wounds. As we will discuss in the chapter on transformation, Christians have long affirmed the doctrine of purgatory, which claims that in the fullness of God's time, more opportunities to learn and grow exist after death. The traditional Christian belief that on Holy Saturday Jesus goes to offer salvation to the dead, also known as the triumphant harrowing of hell, provides another hopeful image of rescue beyond our brief and limited space-time.[12] In God's fullness of time, the creativity of love can find ways to mend, heal, and bring to flower the unfulfilled, stunted, distorted, silenced lives suffered in this world. Jesus has told us that with God all things are possible. Christians can constantly offer up their work, their prayers, their joys, and their intractable sufferings in hope that they further the salvation of those who never could, or never would, do so for themselves.

Joy and Suffering Together

Living in, with, and through Christ makes it possible to become transformed and to transform the world. Love produces healing, joy, and gladness as fruits of the Christian life — even while recognizing the full horror of intractable sufferings. Jesus suffers with us and we suffer with him as we participate in his saving work. At the same time Jesus rejoices, and we receive the gift of joy. Gladly celebrating the resurrection gives proof of the presence of the Holy Spirit. Joy, empathy, and love for those who suffer inspire ceaseless labor to end suffering. The double commands of Christ are given clearly: "take up your cross," and "rejoice without ceasing." But exactly how do we follow these commands in practice?

– Six –

SUFFERING
IN PRACTICE

❧

HOW DO DISCIPLES of Jesus follow in his path of suffering and joy? The double command to "take up your
cross" and "rejoice always" can produce puzzling questions. Is
there some proper balance to be struck? How do we avoid
signing on to a skewed cult of sacred pain, or on the other
hand avoid flight from works of mercy that may bring suffering? Earlier simpleminded views that glorified suffering victims
are not adequate. A modern theologian writing about suffering wisely warns against the "traditional piety that sanctions
suffering as imitation of the Holy One. Because God suffers
and God is good, we are also good if we suffer."[1] This line of
thought easily slides into assumptions that suffering should be
eagerly sought and embraced as a blessing since it automatically makes you good. And if suffering is good for you, then it
should also be inflicted upon others for their benefit. If victims
have a head start on holiness, then disciples should seek to become victims. In this reading, to take up your cross means to
go and seek pain and suffering — the more self-annihilation,
the better.

Should the crucified Jesus be worshiped and glorified as a
passive victim with his suffering on the cross held up as a model
for imitation? Certain believers have talked "of desiring to be
nailed to the cross with Christ."[2] But the theologian Sebastian
Moore writes that such aspirations contribute to a Christian
cult of suffering. He explains that the death of Jesus "is not

123

for imitation," because "the agony in which his earthly life ends . . . is not chosen by him as a way of life." It *is* voluntary, and it is embraced as necessary to end suffering and death forever, "but it is not like choices that we admire and try to imitate in our heroes." To think otherwise would turn Jesus' example into masochism. Yes, Christ suffers as a bloodied, tortured, executed victim of a cruel regime, but as the Gospel account makes clear, Jesus voluntarily gives up his life *for the sake of* God's saving love. He suffers in order to overcome evil's power, suffering, and death. The cross is proof for us of Christ's victorious and steadfast love; Jesus the God-man is bringing to birth the new joyful life of God.

Distortions of perspective on Christ's suffering and joy have produced spiritual practices that valorize suffering and pain. Devout persons have embraced actions that have harmed themselves and others in misguided zeal. Unfortunately over the course of Christian history, emotional fervor and a near lust for suffering have motivated suspect acts of bodily and psychological self-abuse. During World War II Simone Weil, an impressive and noble spiritual pilgrim, ruined her health by virtually starving herself to death. As a French Jew she escaped the Nazis and reached safety in England. Once there, she refused to eat more than her starving compatriots who were left behind. She desired to fast as an act of solidarity. She could not, however, give any of her renounced portions of food to relieve any actual person's hunger. She also remained undeterred by the pain of her family and friends watching her waste away. Her premature death ended her work in the war effort as well as her luminous writing career. In a real sense, Simone Weil elevated suffering to be her primary religious value.

Other zealous religious believers have basked in the role of victim, even holding up the idea of the election of special "victim souls" designated by God to receive the blessings of affliction. Idealizations of victims and their suffering lingered on into the twentieth century as legacies of past pieties.

The Problem of Glorifying Suffering

Nontheological analyses of the overvaluation of suffering echo theological critiques. Modern feminist thought has pointed to the ways that an idealization of suffering has harmed women, encouraging them to remain victims in society and family life. Popular books describe women who "love too much," who stay in abusive relationships with men, embracing a mystique of "sweet sorrow" with self-destructive consequences. Feminists point out quite rightly that suffering per se should never automatically be equated with virtue or used as a proof of true love, since the emotional and physical abuse of women has been rationalized as a necessary ideal. Ever since patient Griselda, many Christian women have been encouraged to think of themselves as the good and self-sacrificing sex.[3]

Of course there also exist masculine versions of the cult of suffering, for men too are told that suffering is good for them — "no pain, no gain" — and should be borne in silence. To display silent stoicism and indifference to pain has been thought to be the sign of manliness.

In certain families and subcultures a covert message is given early to both male and female children. "You are good and worthy only when you suffer or fail." This conditioning may not be explicit or conscious, but it can implicitly guide basic underlying attitudes and behavior. Pain and suffering validate self-worth. Pain is good for you; happiness and joy are always suspect. If it feels good it must be wrong, and if it hurts it must be morally good. Individuals may internalize the message that they must suffer in order to be loved.[4] Parents pass on what they have learned, but it also serves parental power when children are docile and subject to threats of guilt, shame, and loss. The uses and abuses of suffering as a strategy for controlling others in families and other institutions have been analyzed in the clinical literature and in social scientific analyses of dysfunctional groups. In extreme cases of pathology self-mutilation appears. Troubled adolescents may actually cut themselves in self-inflicted acts that have been seen as a cry for help and an effort to offset numbness, alienation, and depression. To feel "something," even something physically painful, proves that one is alive. Deeper anxieties over self-worth can be avoided by embracing wounds and self-destructive strategies. Self-starvation through fasting and vomiting is another way of implicitly exerting control through suffering. Such acts can become suicidal. Oddly enough, self-inflicted pain, starvation, and vomiting can become as addictive as alcohol or drugs. Distressed persons can cling to their suffering and resist any movement toward health and happiness as a threat. Misery is familiar and safe. There may be a common human existential attraction to suffering. In the last century Dostoevsky seems to have understood this perverse dynamic when he commented, "Man is sometimes extraordinarily, passionately, in love with suffering."[5] A tortured spirit himself, Dostoevsky knew the attraction of unhappiness, the dramatic pride that could be reinforced by clinging to suffering, which produces arousal in isolation. Active self-giving to others may bring happiness, but such love requires humility and moral effort. "I will not serve," cries Lucifer in Milton's *Paradise Lost,* proudly choosing damnation, a "heroic" and "romantic" stance. The drama of bearing pain appears more exalted than accepting mundane contentment.

Yet many who have suffered through the large traumas of recent history vigorously reject romanticizing suffering, and warn against the idealization of victims. For instance, Norman Marcus, a Romanian Jewish literary critic who in his life endured both Fascist persecutions and Communist oppression, observes that "suffering does not make us better people or heroes." As a child during World War II, Marcus had been deported to a concentration camp, survived the ordeal, and returned home to grow up under the misery imposed by a totalitarian Communist regime. Thus, he speaks from experience when he says, "Suffering, like all things human, corrupts, and suffering peddled publicly corrupts absolutely."[6] Individuals or groups damage themselves when clinging to their status as victims, when they allow their suffering to become the justification of a sense of entitlement fueled by resentments.

Worse still is the abuse of suffering that occurs when pain is co-opted for use in personal or political agendas. In the nineteenth-century campaign for suffrage, middle-class white women identified themselves as "co-sufferers" with Negroes living in the brutal system of chattel slavery, while remaining virtually blind to the differences imposed by the privilege of their race and class. Such obliviousness "obscured the role of white women themselves in maintaining the institutions of white supremacy."[7] A more contemporary example of such co-optation in twenty-first-century America is when pictures of suffering children or wasted, anorexic, or heroin-abusing models are used in clothing advertisements to capture the attention of consumers and boost sales. Hints of sexual abuse and sadism infect media images of a world mired in violence, and slide into an unsavory voyeurism of pain as TV and newspapers disseminate graphic pictures of victims of war, famine, and disaster. The titillation of observing suffering fosters moral corruption when it focuses upon personal feelings and avoids taking any action to alleviate the suffering. It is easy to mistake the arousal of sentimental emotions for moral sensibility. It is no virtue to shiver and shudder, and then turn quickly to the next stimulating image of horror.

Another past instance of glorifying feminine suffering was the resistance to ending the pain of women in childbirth. The travail of childbirth was considered to be religiously warranted by the Genesis story of God's punishment for Eve's sin. In different eras and locales, the invention of anesthesia and the innovation of newer psychoneurological Pavlovian conditioning techniques for pain relief were resisted. The opposition to employing modern breathing and relaxation conditioning for childbirth existed until the 1950s and 1960s. I know because as an early advocate of the new conditioned birthing techniques aimed at achieving a drug-free, painless birth, I encountered antagonism. One obstetrician actually asked me in an irritated tone, "But, Sidney, what do you have against pain?" I was so disconcerted by the question that I could only manage to mumble something about it "hurting." Later I could see that much of the resistance I struggled with as a pregnant woman revealed implicit but lingering assumptions that women were fated to suffer. Queen Victoria may have demanded to receive anesthesia for the pain of childbirth, but other women should not challenge their ordained destiny.

Ironically, few physicians, or anyone else at the time, had ever heard of the papal teaching of Pius XII justifying the use of anesthesia and natural childbirth conditioning techniques to relieve suffering. His address explains that the biblical verses in which Eve's future punishment will include suffering pain in childbirth should not be interpreted as prescriptive, but simply as descriptive of the vicissitudes and travails of living. For their part, Christians should be active in providing pain relief for laboring women in accord with God's merciful will. Furthermore, the pope averred, the fact that new, painless Pavlovian-conditioning birth techniques were developed in "Godless" communist Russia should not be a deterrent to their use by Catholics. Christian disciples are called to use every good medical discovery in their mission to prevent, alleviate, heal, and end suffering. These efforts to meet and minister to suffering are works of mercy, a central commandment required for membership in the Christian church.

The Works of Mercy

All of the traditional listings of the corporal and spiritual works of mercy consist of the relief of human suffering in its physical, psychological, and spiritual forms: feeding the hungry, comforting the sorrowful, clothing the naked, instructing the ignorant, sheltering the homeless, admonishing the sinner, forgiving all injuries, and praying for the living and the dead. Such acts of loving service are not carried out easily by the weak and sinful. To love as Christ loves requires conversion and a transformation of persons. Disciples must take on a new human nature and live with the mind of Christ. To perform works of mercy all the natural virtues and strengths, such as courage, temperance, justice, and prudence, must be cultivated and developed, and the God-given virtues of faith, hope, and charity must be received. The gifts of the Holy Spirit will empower persons and make it possible for disciples to grow in Christian love of neighbor. The Spirit's gifts of counsel and knowledge also help Christians discern when and how to best act to relieve suffering.

Preventing suffering is thus an important task in bringing God's reign of justice to earth. The first small Christian house churches acted to minister to the needs of their own and to the needs of surrounding neighbors. Since Christ did not return immediately, these works became more important in the not-yet interim time. Indeed, Christianity spread through the ancient urban world partly because of its practices of charitable service to those in need. Christians did not flee from the cities during the plague; rather they stayed to nurse the ill and dying, thereby often gaining converts. Over the centuries as the church grew in size and influence, it began to develop specialized institutions and religious communities to carry out good works, nursing, teaching, and helping the poor. And it is still the case that wherever Christianity has a presence in a society, Christians will work for justice and peace in the larger social and political realm. Today there is a new understanding of the way social systems and institutions function, giving rise to a body of teachings called the Social Gospel, articulated to sustain Christians in their age-old task of alleviating human suffering. Christians desire to create societies "where it is easy to be good," as Dorothy Day described her vocation in the Catholic Worker movement. Recent papal teaching expresses this call as the Christian effort to bring about a "civilization of love," where justice is love's absolute minimum. But the fact of the matter is that when Christians seek to carry out the works of mercy, they will meet resistance as Christ did. Christ suffered in order to end suffering forever, and his followers may have to take up their cross in imitation of him.

Taking Up the Cross

Of course, the command to imitate Christ does not literally mean to seek torture and criminal execution, or to choose to be victimized and suffer as a goal in itself. Since creation is good and in the process of being transformed, the amount of external suffering to be encountered by disciples will differ, as their particular circumstances vary. The phrase "taking up" the cross implies rather that, as with Jesus, there is a voluntary act of self-giving. The cross of Jesus is a labor of love endured for the sake of others, not self-inflicted mutilation or suicide. The pain and suffering that results are imposed by the evil and sin of outside forces of resistance.

Sorrowfully, it appears that calls for justice and equality in unjust societies will arouse rejection and hostility. People with power, entrenched in oppressive systems or institutions exploiting the poor and vulnerable for their own profit, rarely accept admonition calls for correction without instituting reprisals. Prophets who challenged King Herod and the Roman emperor, or Hitler and Stalin, were quickly silenced and forcefully removed. "Taking up one's cross" means recognizing that the Christian works of mercy and justice can result in the same suffering as that inflicted upon Jesus: ostracism, hostility, slander, detention, arrest, torture, trial, imprisonment, and execution.

By the time the Gospels were being written, early Christians had begun to suffer persecution for their faith, as evidenced in the accounts of the lives of Stephen, Paul, and Peter. Yet at the same time remarkable and widespread conversions to Christianity occurred and rapidly spread the faith throughout the ancient urban world. Often missionaries were initially successful, but subsequently or in nearby locations they could meet bitter hostility. This mixed pattern of acceptance and rejection of Christianity has existed ever since. In the twenty-first century conversions around the globe swell the number of Christian believers, while bitter hostility, persecutions, and martyrdoms continue to arise. Even an activity such as teaching poor Central American children to read and write has been enough to get missionary sisters murdered. In every age the revolutionary message of God's demand for equality, justice, truth, and charity has incited enmity. Christians seeking to love their neighbor and end their sufferings may encounter suffering.

The important distinction to be made here is that the suffering of disciples should be like that of Jesus, not sought as a way of life or a good in itself. Rather the cross is an evil imposed by those who reject God's Word. Christians do not desire to experience pain, disease, persecution, imprisonment, torture, and assassination, but they may be called to endure them if they cannot be avoided in good conscience. As they carry out God's work, Christians seek peace with others, as did the earliest Christian communities. To court unnecessary danger and harm can be criticized as tempting God. Suicide, direct or indirect, is always forbidden, and a line must always be drawn between altruistic acts of sacrifice for others or of a witness to the truth and self-destruction. Disciples may decide to risk suffering in order to continue their work, but they do not seek out painful outcomes.

Disciples have been taught by Jesus himself to pray, "Deliver us from evil." When meeting rejection, disciples on a mission are advised by the Lord to shake the dust of that place from their feet and move on. In a disaster and time of destruction those who flee to the hills are called blessed. Jesus himself walks away from the Nazareth lynch mob threatening to throw him over a cliff and later eludes being stoned and apprehended by the temple authorities. In his final necessary confrontation and arrest he seeks to save his disciples. Christians always pray for deliverance from every evil. When arrested, Paul appeals his case to Rome in order to obtain his rights as a Roman citizen. When imprisoned, Peter is miraculously led to freedom through the prayers of the church.

Throughout Christian history many rescues, escapes, and healings have been attributed to prayer. As we will see in a subsequent chapter on prayer, different kinds of saving events are seen as evidence of God's willed intervention to bring about the health and happiness of God's people. Pleas for deliverance have been offered in the confident belief that God desires only good things for all creatures.

Does Christian hope include the conviction stated by St. Paul that all things, even suffering, can work together for good for those who love God? Yes, Christians can affirm that in the long run, suffering offered to God and joined with Christ's love can participate in the great co-creative work of God. But in the short run, on our present earthly pilgrimage is it also the case that suffering sometimes leads to wisdom?

Suffering as Creative?

From the days of the ancient Greeks it has been asserted that suffering leads to wisdom. Most famously, Aeschylus proclaims that "Wisdom comes alone through suffering." Other thinkers have confidently declared that individuals undergoing great trials benefit from them. Nietzsche's boast has been often repeated: "That which does not kill me makes me stronger." Persons who survive misery are thought to grow hardy and stronger. In this view, pain is the great teacher. Twelve-Step programs speak of "hitting bottom," the moment when intense suffering gives rise to the movement to seek help, and those in recovery express gratitude for the fact that they were so broken that they gave up resistance and could begin to heal.

Should we really claim that it is the pain alone that induces such healing? I would argue no, because the changes really come from the person's new and different *response* to the pain and suffering, that is, from the positive surge of hope that change is possible. The sinful prodigal son suffering among the pigs is moved to action by remembering his Father's love and goodness. The first step toward relief of suffering is motivated by a *new expectation* of what may now be waiting.

The only salutary aspect intrinsic to suffering is that, in pain, an individual encounters a reality beyond his control to stop it. The other necessary realization that comes with suffering is that I am sharing a common human experience. I know that other persons suffer as I do because of the innate human ability of normal individuals to read emotional signals and share other persons' feelings. Yet a person can still respond in different ways to suffering: either negatively and aggressively, or positively and lovingly. Individuals in pain can curse their condition and struggle to reassert their self-centered and autonomous will. They can reject any identification with others who are suffering. "Victims" must be differentiated from myself because they threaten my uniqueness and superior status. I am not like those others. It is possible to suppress feelings of empathy and refuse to share in common humanity. Proud distancing and separation from other sufferers can be choices. Or safety and dominance can be sought by striking out and harming others who are more vulnerable. Victims can choose to victimize others. Overoptimistic and romantic observers have too easily believed that suffering will automatically increase empathy and virtue. George Sand, the great nineteenth-century woman novelist, said in her autobiography that she thought that suffering comes to us in order to let us learn how terrible it is to be hurt, and thereby resolve never to inflict suffering upon others. She forgets the potential of humans to suppress empathy, turn away, and inflict suffering to prove their superior strength. The equalizing and humbling effect of empathetic suffering can be nullified in order to reject identifying with victims. Sometimes suffering can corrupt and by itself does not lead to wisdom. Creative and positive effects of the experience of suffering will occur only if persons are able and willing to respond to positive promptings of hope and charity.

A chilling expression of the isolating despair that suffering can produce is found in Randall Jarrell's poem *90 North*. The poet decides that for him all his life's painful journey has been meaningless. It is only in a childish "Cloud-Cuckoo-Land" that it can be imagined that there is a world "where people work and suffer for the end that crowns the pain." It is icy cold and dark, for "I see at last that all the knowledge I wrung from the darkness — that the darkness flung me — is worthless as ignorance: nothing comes from nothing. The darkness from the darkness. Pain comes from the darkness and we call it wisdom. It is pain."

But other contrasting testimony also exists. Suffering and the response it calls forth in some has led to meaning and wisdom. A movement from despair toward God as one's Higher Power begins a spiritual journey. The wisdom that is won from suffering may be "unwanted wisdom," as described in theologian Paul Crowley's reflections on his experiences of the intense sufferings of the AIDS pandemic.[8] With an acceptance of a spiritual reality beyond the self, our connections and relationships with others increase. Our innate response of empathy to others who suffer is not suppressed. When we share another's pain, our sensitivity and attentiveness to the condition of others expands, and with such attention comes more understanding and more insight. Empathy motivates acts of loving caretaking, and the mind and heart expand. A person who cares for others is no longer isolated in cold and meaningless darkness.

When our proud self-sufficiency is given up, suffering can create bonds with others. "Only connect," says E. M. Forster in *Howard's End,* and mutual suffering may help to forge the links. The modern therapeutic concept of the "wounded healer" rests on the assumption that suffering increases empathy and healing wisdom. If the wounds are no longer bleeding and recovery is well along, then persons who have been afflicted in the past can counsel those who suffer. The successes of Twelve-Step and other self-help support groups give evidence that those who have found the road to recovery can help others. Once rescued from the mire of paralyzing despair and led to solid ground, survivors can help others find the way. Persons recovered from addiction, or breast cancer, or sexual abuse, or the murders or suicides of family members can share their experiences and give testimony to human resilience. Without false illusions or romantic idealization of pain, many who have suffered testify that the experience brought them wisdom. Some feminists also, who vigorously reject damaging idealizations of women's suffering, can give convincing witness. Kristine M. Rankka expresses this understanding in her fine book *Women and the Value of Suffering.* "In my view, here, both God's grace and one's faith, working together, can meet tragedy on its own terms — in the realm of the unexpected, paradoxical, mysterious, and incomprehensible."[9]

For Christians the hope of responding well to suffering is founded upon the belief that Christ suffers, dies, rises, and appears with his wounds healed. God ultimately overcomes the destructive power of sin and evil and is always working toward the good in every life at every moment. The Spirit seeks to draw forth any potential good during and after any suffering that comes. God as love creatively comforts, inspires, heals, and seeks to mend what is broken. God never sends suffering, but when it comes God wills and enables human resilience and recovery.

Two other deeply entrenched human responses to suffering can be overcome by attending to Christ's suffering and death on the cross. One is stigmatizing victims, and another is retaliating against enemies.

Healing the Stigma of Victims

Indirect healing properties arise from Christianity's faith that this man Jesus, suffering in agony and dying as a tortured victim, is divine. This is God's Son being cruelly abused and executed as a criminal. This death of this divine-human victim will change the way all suffering victims are viewed. This event begins the uprooting of human predispositions to loathe, despise, and avoid victims. Aeschylus was correct when he said that "it is the nature of mortals to kick a fallen man." Yes, it is the case that altruistic responses to suffering are also innate, but there is no denying the strong human tendency to mistreat and stigmatize victims. Fear of being hurt or suffering a similar fate urges individuals to join in an attack or flee from the threatening. The horror of injury, mutilation, disease, and dying also results in religious taboos concerning pollution from blood, bodily fluids, and corpses. The wicked may instigate brutality to victims, but ordinary persons can shrink from them. This means that those who survive great suffering can suffer further from the stigma of having been a victim. They can be blamed as deserving their pain and treated as outcasts.

But once God in Christ has been beaten, tortured, humiliated, and killed, it signals a divine judgment on behalf of victims. Suffering does not invalidate the moral worth and dignity of a human being. Jesus Christ has shared a similar fate. The millions of victims who are tormented, mistreated, or killed by powerful oppressors can be recognized as other beloved children made in the image of God. No evil treatment or brutality can take away their dignity and worth. Victims can not be degraded or polluted by what has been inflicted upon them. The primitive response that suffering evil will stain its object forever is overthrown by the cross. Jesus has been there and is with everyone who suffers. After torture and a terrible death Christ has risen to new life and brings all human experiences with him into the birthing struggle of the new creation. The suffering of each victim is joined to that of Jesus and is never forgotten by God. The scriptural phrase "by his stripes we are healed" has deep meaning for those whose wounds are despised. God in Christ has plunged into the depths of horror and rises to vindicate all victims.

But healing for victims may be difficult and prolonged. When victims are assaulted cruelly in body and mind by pain and suffering they can begin to have their sense of worth and dignity depleted. Bitter psychological wounds of heart and mind are inflicted by hostility, abuse, and abandonment. Loss of self-efficacy and a sense of helplessness add to misery and demoralization. Malicious mistreatment by other humans is more injurious than the physical suffering that arises from natural disasters or from processes of disease and old age. Many victims in their own irrational thinking begin to internalize the evil and hostility that beset them. The old beliefs in the law of retribution that bad things happen to bad people revive. The disdain, contempt, and hostility thrust upon victims tend to seep into the psyche and fester. Abused and helpless persons can suffer from depression, stigma, and shame, even though they had no part in causing the evil events overtaking them. Rape victims, sexually abused children, adolescents abused by priests, genocide victims of ethnic hatred, or those who have been imprisoned and tortured can feel polluted by their forced contact with wickedness. Post-traumatic syndromes can be real and prolonged, and are no respecter of persons. Jesus understands these evils, and he warns his disciples that those who kill the spirit are more dangerous than those who kill the body.

The innocent God-man's degrading and humiliating death forever removes the stigma of victims because no one can defend the side of powerful abusers against God. The process of sacrificing victims is no longer justified as a ritual that brings order to a group. There is no more justified silence and shame for the vulnerable coerced by oppressors. God is with the powerless, not with their oppressors. The Christian savior turns the world upside down, forever. God in Christ has not been dishonored by being cruelly abused, and neither are any other victims. The Lord is with them. As the African American spiritual cries, "Nobody knows the trouble I've seen, nobody knows but Jesus." Black chattel slaves in the midst of their suffering and powerlessness against oppression could recognize Jesus as one of them. "Were you there when they crucified my Lord?" Wherever a human being is powerless and suffers, or is unable to prevent their families' pain, Jesus is there.

While all victims are not cognizant of the meaning of Christ's suffering for them, Christian disciples are. They know that they must never give in to the temptation to flee or ignore victims. The flawed self may be tempted to join in the struggle for selfish survival, but victims cannot be abandoned or treated as polluting. Those dying with plagues such as AIDS must be cared for as one would care for Christ. Love casts out the fears of the diseased, the impaired, and the needy because love and trust in God calm the anxiety over self-preservation. Humans shrink from victims because of primitive fears that suffering is contagious. "If I get too close, I will be infected, engulfed, or drawn down into their fate."

Popular devotions — such as the way of the cross, honoring the crucifix, meditations upon the sorrows of Mary, and the sorrowful mysteries of the rosary — work against stigmatizing suffering. These practices remind the faithful that Christ is still suffering with his people, and still urging his disciples toward merciful action. Complete healing of all ills and the renewal of creation will come only on the last day; but hope and the joyous good news of Easter contribute to perseverance through present trials.

Fortunately, the isolation and stigmatizing effect of suffering can be alleviated when it is recognized and responded to with empathy and charity. A sensitive analyst of the harsh isolation that many Holocaust survivors endured observes, "It may be that suffering shared, suffering respected, is suffering endurable. Suffering that is misunderstood or dishonored can turn on the self in unendurable pain."[10] Christians especially should find it impossible to look at victims and engage in what has been called "the production of distance," a distance which deadens empathy and stifles action. Those who empathize with victims can openly join in collective mourning. Sharing suffering counteracts the silence and stigma that increase pain. Shared lamentation can help to heal the insult of having been humiliated and helpless. In human life the gift of language acts against the numbing and muting effects of affliction. Without shared speech and empathy, sufferers can succumb to despair. When we lament and protest, energy is released for the struggle to end the sufferings of this world. Such an insight may be the key to Pope John Paul II's claim that "suffering unleashes hope."[11] Hope inspires action. The church does well to hold up the cross as a perennial reminder that repeated crucifixions are being suffered, but that they are neither meaningless nor the end of the story.

Jesus Prince of Peace

The sustained gaze at Jesus suffering not only heals the stigma of vulnerable victims, but also induces a judgment of the injustice meted out by powerful authorities of this world. When Jesus, an innocent man, is tortured and executed by order of rulers, it becomes clear that violent injustice often governs political power, in ancient Palestine or in the twenty-first century. Christians can never again mindlessly accept the governing powers' claims. The cruel execution of Jesus on the cross, followed by his resurrection, initiated an ongoing conflict between Christians and the secular powers that dominate the world. If Jesus is acknowledged as Messiah bringing in the Kingdom, then conflict with oppressive unjust rulers is inevitable. The imperial claims of Rome will be challenged. Christians could not offer the required ritual sacrifices to the emperor as divine. For this civil disobedience they were persecuted and often martyred. Despite such conflicts and the erratic persecutions that ensued, Christianity continued to spread rapidly. Because of the heroic witness of the martyrs, the charity practiced to the needy and the ill, and the dignity given to women and slaves, the faith flourished. The church slowly began to turn the world upside down. Or so it appeared to Pliny the Younger, an aristocratic Roman official disturbed by the defiance of this odd new sect of believers. He was particularly offended that mere slaves, and women at that, would, despite torture, defy the Roman authorities and die for their faith.

In modern times liberation theology and nonviolent resistance movements have developed within Christianity in attempts to effect justice and social reform. These struggles are mounted against secular oppression and against intrachurch defenders of the status quo. As at the beginning of Christianity, protests against secular and religious establishments are inspired by the words and life of the crucified Jesus, victim of injustice.

Thinking on the larger forces and powers that led to the crucifixion of Jesus results in sophisticated new analyses of "social sin" in Christian thought. Since the great twentieth-century reforming council of Vatican II, the understanding has grown that sins can be embedded in social structures as in racism, sexism, ethnic prejudice, or colonialism, which grind down God's children in misery. The suffering that arose from chattel slavery is an example of the power of structural social sin that transcended individual agency. War is another example of the way that large forces impose cruel suffering upon multitudes of innocent victims. Individuals, even good individuals, can be caught up in collective movements beyond their control. Since the structures of social sin are often supported by law, custom, elites, and greed, they are difficult to oppose, but they must be opposed to relieve the suffering of whole groups of people.

Christians who have known God's power in reversing the suffering Christ's death on the cross through resurrection have been inspired to counter the world's oppressive operations. It took generations of Christians and others to win the struggle against the entrenched slave trade. It was thought to be impossible to challenge profits, racism, economic systems, and apathy toward the suffering fate of those in bondage. People engaged in this liberation movement often had to endure ridicule and persecution. This Christian suffering endured to end suffering could be offered up to the Lord, who suffered to end human death and despair.

Christian movements to change the political structures of the world take the nonviolent teachings and life of Jesus to heart. Disciples who work in resistance movements inspired by the love and spirit of the cross foreswear violence and rely upon the active power of love and truth as the way to effect lasting change. The loving nonviolent practice and teaching of Jesus are recognized as God's way to transform hearts and minds. Christian peace and justice movements have understood that they must act as God in Christ acts. The followers of the crucified Lord assert that God in the incarnation models and endorses nonviolent means of love to overcome the world's evil and disorder. Gandhi said that "means are ends in the making"; thus those aiming for peace and justice must use peaceful and just means. This does not mean that conflict will not be necessary, but violent aggression and harming of others is rejected. Christ did not call down fire on enemies or engage in a messianic war for his kingdom. Violence begets violent reactions, hate breeds hate, and those who take the sword perish by the sword.

Christians acknowledge the continuing existence of evil and suffering, but as they encounter the resurrected Jesus they accept his teachings that God's love and truth will overcome the world as Jesus overcomes death and sin. Love of enemies is accepted as God's saving word. Enemies and persecutors too must be recognized as children of God who have been saved by Jesus Christ. What I do to another I do to Christ, and this forbids injuring my neighbor. Early Christians refused to bear arms. The gospel proclaims the faith that Christ's resurrection has won the victory. Death cannot hold the Lord. God's love and dynamic energy that broke the power of death will be invincible in the long run. A greater power than violence had been unbound in creation. Love forgives rather than take vengeance or do harm. If need be, it is better to suffer and be killed for loving God and neighbor than to inflict torture or suffering on one's fellow human being.

Only later in Christian history did the ideal of the crusading warrior become incorporated into Christianity. Pagan myths and pagan gods have always glorified heroic violence and fighting prowess. Christians too became accepting of war in the centuries after Constantine's conversion. Later, Christian armies and crusaders marched beneath the sign of the cross. Wading through the blood of infidel or heretic, Christians saw themselves as serving the Lord by violently subduing God's enemies. Pogroms, genocides, and massacres were carried out in Christ's name, supported by images from Old Testament Scriptures and New Testament apocalyptic texts. Scriptural scholars today would protest these narrow and literal readings of Scripture, but selective interpretations of texts justified military ventures abroad and violent methods of governance at home.

Today a resurgence of Christian nonviolent resistance movements against injustice has emerged led by great individuals like Dorothy Day, Gandhi, Martin Luther King Jr., Cesar Chavez, and others. Modern peace and justice movements point out that love and truth are more dynamic and effective than violence. Gandhi named the force of truth and love "soulforce" or "truthforce." Christians speak of the work of the Holy Spirit. Suffering and justice have been alleviated by struggles that refuse to hate. But the world still does not accept the gospel message. *After* a horrendous conflict in some countries, truth and reconciliation commissions are set up, but nonviolent strategies need to be employed before.

Always and everywhere the powers-that-be still use coercive force, torture, and execution to eliminate troublemakers and quell dissent. The ritual killing of scapegoats still serves the purposes of ruling regimes. Punishment of an offender in a slow trial provides a cathartic event that distracts the populace and discourages resistance. Surely, no one outdid the Romans at providing blood-soaked spectacles to entertain the populace. Christians faced a regime in which cruel gladiatorial games entertained citizens. Rome meted out cruel punishments to any who challenged imperial authority. Mass crucifixions followed the defeat of the slave rebellion of Spartacus. When a Roman army was defeated or defected from the field, it would be subjected to decimation, or the killing by lot of one in ten soldiers. The execution would be carried out by members of the victim's own cohort. Kill or be killed is the law of the jungle, the mob, and the dictatorial regime.

From ancient times humans have killed their enemies; it is now known that certain primate groups of chimpanzees, formerly thought to be pacific, practice ambush and aggression. Dominance hierarchies in man and other primates employ aggressive force. The logic of domination requires coercion and violence — often through preemptive strikes.

But in the resurrection the last will be first and the first will be last and the meek will inherit the earth. The good news proclaims that in Jesus a new creation and new order of life is born. The yoke of oppression is broken.

Through the gift of God as Holy Spirit, disciples are enabled to work with God in co-creating a new world. And here again in understanding God's nonviolent way the words of Jesus make sense; he is working, and his disciples are to work and do even greater things than Jesus.

Prudent persons can differ over what God's work will require of them. Some disciples have remained in dangerous situations and encountered suffering while others have departed. Judging for another can be a perilous project. St. Thomas More did not condemn those of his peers who swore Henry VIII's oath and thereby saved their lives. In this he imitated many of the earliest martyrs, who did not condemn those who could not follow their heroic example. Many martyrs testified to the presence of joy amid their sufferings. They experience intense love and hope that produces a joy that can coexist with suffering. How can such invincible joy be accomplished? If ecstatic joy and empathetic suffering coexist in the richness and plenitude of Christ's risen life, then disciples can seek to live in their Lord in the same way. Christians who are still subject to the contingencies of the human condition may suffer intensely but they can seek to possess Christ's joy.

One strategy of living with a double sensibility is found in the liturgy of the church. Sequences of both mourning and soaring joy are celebrated, with different times and seasons given over to both. Lent is followed by Easter. Prayers of sorrow alternate with prayers expressing the joy of rescue and deliverance. I once heard a priest complain that the Mass seemed to him to be manic depressive in its ups and downs of mood. I think he wanted to include only the celebratory themes of victory and good news. But this inclusion of mementos of sin and suffering may be an accurate reflection of the complex reality of the lived Christian condition. The reality of God's saving love is that the good news is eternally true, but that suffering still exists in the struggle against sin and evil. Joy and suffering exist in the liturgies and celebrations of the church year, just as they do in individual and group lives. The crucifix is displayed as reminder of the costs of Christ's mercy and for encouragement and consolation. Christians know that Jesus understands.

Rejoice Always

Ultimately, joy is the ground and primary reality of the good news, so Christ's joy must be cherished and celebrated. Death is no more. All human suffering and torment is passing away, but the joy of God's love will last forever. Accepting the glad tidings of great joy makes it fitting for Christians to delight in the goodness and happiness of creation. We need not feel guilty over being happy but rather grateful for God's gift. These moments of light must be welcomed. The psalms and praise songs of Scripture affirm this truth. And contemporary poet Jack Gilbert also understands as he writes: "We must have the stubbornness to accept our gladness in the ruthless furnace of this world. To make injustice the only measure of our attention is to praise the Devil." This is all the more important because "Sorrow everywhere . . . Slaughter everywhere. If babies are not starving someplace, they are starving somewhere else. With flies in their nostrils. But we enjoy our lives because that's what God wants." To refuse to risk delight in the world is to lessen the importance of the deprivations of "all the years of sorrow that are to come." Not to be happy or celebrate is to refuse the fullness of reality. "We must admit there will be music despite everything."[12] Christians must sing, dance, and play music. The beauty and delight of God's beloved world must be celebrated with laughter and joy. Liberation has come. Jesus saves, Christ is risen, God awaits. Life within the Trinity is full of unimaginable delight and good company. My joy I will give to you, says the Lord to his disciples. And so we must learn to understand joy.

– Seven –

JOY

⤷꧁꧂꧆

J OY HAS NEVER received as much attention as pain and
suffering, but having encountered Christ and received his
promise of joy, even in the midst of suffering, I need to understand the nature of joy more fully. Yet, joy is more difficult
to describe than suffering. The Israeli poet Yehuda Amichai
speaks of "the precision of pain and the blurriness of joy."
Pain, he says, can be categorized as "gnawing, throbbing, burning, sharp, or wrenching." But joy is described vaguely; it is
"great," "wonderful," "I have no words." "I was in seventh
heaven." Amichai wants to rise to this poetic challenge by attempting to "describe with a sharp pain's precision, happiness
and blurry joy." He feels up to the task since he has "learned
to speak among the pains."[1] But then again, hasn't everyone?
Don't we tend in our disordered world to focus more intently
on suffering? On the evening news, accounts of disasters and
crimes monopolize the hour. Catastrophes stand out in memory. All Americans can remember where they were when they
heard the news of September 11, but who can remember what
happened on the preceding day, or the happy times of the
previous month?

Another poetic testimony to the difficulty of describing
joy appears in the autobiography of the ex-slave Frederick
Douglass. After detailing his sufferings in bondage and his
flight to freedom, Douglass writes, "Anguish and grief, like
darkness and rain may be depicted; but gladness and joy, like
the rainbow, defy the skill of pen or pencil."[2] The rainbow is

147

a wonderfully apt image for joy. Like joy, the rainbow with its gorgeous bands of color and graceful arc arrives on the scene unpredictably. Its evanescent and elusive beauty lights the heart. In the Old Testament, Yahweh sets His bow in the clouds as a sign of hope for Noah and his descendants. Never again will God destroy the world by flood. (Fire next time say the pessimists, but that's another story.) Looking up above the clouds people can believe that over the rainbow bluebirds sing and joy reigns.

Despite the difficulty of describing surging feelings of joy, poets and writers have been undeterred. C. S. Lewis in his autobiography *Surprised by Joy* tells us that from childhood on into maturity he experienced unexpected moments of joy. In Lewis's case joy would well up accompanied by a yearning for he knew not what. James Joyce describes these unexpected flashes of radiance as "epiphanies," glimpses of the beauty, truth, and clarity that exist behind the veil of the everyday world. Or as Gerard Manley Hopkins, another literary genius also toiling away in Dublin's dull city, puts it, there are moments when we see that "the world is charged with the grandeur of God."[3] This Jesuit poet suffered much but also rejoiced in "the dearest freshness deep down things,"[4] and gave voice to the mystics' certainty that blissful moments of heightened consciousness are "consolations" sent by God.

Indeed, rapturous joy appears without warning. The great poet and Nobel prize winner Czeslaw Milosz describes such a moment: "In advanced age, my health worsening, I woke up in the middle of the night, and experienced a feeling of happiness so intense and perfect that in all my life I had only felt its premonition. And there was no reason for it."[5] The fact that joy comes "for no reason" points toward the "mystery of joy" that can be as challenging as the "mystery of suffering." Contemporary novelist and playwright Michael Frayn describes this feeling of intense happiness as "a direct and unanalyzable emotion, as irreducible as the experience of whiteness or saltiness."

The joy "may strike even in the midst of unhappiness, as freely as a stab of pain." The happiness is filled with "tenderness and delight," as in the transporting gaze of a beloved child.[6] Part of the puzzle of joy is the way it can be felt amid times of bleak and painful suffering. Viktor Frankl, the psychiatrist imprisoned by the Nazis in a death camp, describes how he could suddenly feel joy viewing a beautiful sunset, or in the glimpse of a candle shining in the darkness, or in the sound of a melody played by a distant violin. At other times Frankl felt immersed in consoling joy as he imagined conversations with his adored young wife — alas already sent to the gas chamber. Such intriguing descriptions of joy long voiced by poets, writers, and mystics has begun in the past few decades to receive consistent attention from psychology.

In a pioneering study, the humanistic psychologist Abraham Maslow explored the intensely positive moments of heightened consciousness and joy that persons report. Maslow named these moments "peak experiences," because individuals felt such an elevated sense of joyful union with a good and beneficent universe.[7] These "highs" brought with them an intrinsic assurance of the universe's meaningfulness. Peak experiences can be induced by natural grandeur (rainbows, stars, mountains, and oceans), by art, music, love, sport, achievement, and, in the religiously oriented, prayerful meditation. Expressions of joy and praise fill the psalms and inspired Scriptures. What William James called experiences of "immediate luminosity" mark religious life.[8] In fact, states of joy and exaltation, both secular and religious, have been described throughout history and across cultures; ecstasy appears to be an equal opportunity occurrence.

In response to the challenge of emotions such as joy and sorrow, which play such a large part in life, a new sub-discipline of psychology has emerged. The evolving psychology of emotion makes use of research findings from lab experiments, brain imaging, evolutionary biology, neurological medicine, and clinical interviews. These findings provide rich resources for Christians seeking to ground their theological understandings of emotional experiences. Interdisciplinary research upon consciousness and human feeling throws light on the meaning of God's creation. My own project devoted to a religious understanding of suffering and joy has been informed by years of study as a psychologist with a special interest in the interactions of mind, emotion, and moral development. The following reflections on the rediscovered terrain of the psychology of emotion are intended to help in understanding the experience of joy.

Sketching a Map of Joy

Oddly enough, conscious experiences of joy and happiness were until recently more or less ignored by scientific inquiry, and in fact all emotions were considered inappropriate areas of study. In the heyday of "hard" scientific behaviorism, or materialist naturalism, all subjective experiences were seen as off-limits to research. After all, how could one objectively quantify and empirically measure vague qualitative feelings? Only objective or operationally defined evidence could be studied by strictly scientific methods. In this hard-nosed approach, human consciousness was seen as nothing more than an "epiphenomenon," signifying nothing of importance in understanding human behavior. Then came the "cognitive revolution" in psychology followed by an explosion of interest in emotions. Suddenly the mind and thinking were respectable topics of research aided by the advent of computers, informational science, linguistics, and new techniques of brain imaging. This cognitive revolution renewed and validated an exploration of the mind's subjective processes that had once been of interest to the founders of psychology like William James. What he had called "the stream of consciousness" was an important focus of inquiry.

When paying attention to an individual's stream of consciousness and information processing, it quickly becomes clear that more is going on in the mind than abstract processes of problem solving or decision making. Qualitatively distinct emotional feelings and experiences (the so-called *qualia*) surge into subjective consciousness and then subside or give way to other mental activities, and such qualitative feelings interact dynamically with other systems and functioning operations.

Furthermore, emotions are marked by personal investments of feeling charged with positive or negative energy, and so have been called "hot cognitions," or "vital signs." The closer the thought or image is to personal desire, aversion, self-interest, or self-evaluation, the hotter the cognition. Mind, body, imagination, reason, and emotions interact in dynamic ways. Clearly, worrying about the results of your child's cancer operation tomorrow or remembering your mother's love for you are conscious experiences qualitatively different from planning how to balance your checkbook or how to solve an equation.

Emotions move humans toward or away from things, activities, situations, and people in actual or imagined environments. Emotions motivate and predispose to action. The emotional system appears to be an innate, pan-specific, and universal system that emerges in all human beings. Always and everywhere, certain innate and distinct core human emotions can be recognized as constituted by specific facial, postural, physiological, and conscious responses with recognizable patterns. Indeed brain imaging consistently confirms the existence of different activated patterns for different emotions. The evidence appears to show that the positive emotions and the negative emotions emerge from different systems, different parts of the brain with different pathways and different characteristics, as well as qualitative feelings.

Prior to such brain researches, investigators had established that a picture of a joyful or sad human face could, however, be equally recognized by natives of both New Guinea and New

York City. The emotional system resulting from evolutionary processes provides human beings with a common universal communication system or proto-language. Mimes and silent movies have employed to good effect the universal patterns of face, gesture, and rhythmic expression that convey meaning, and everyday social living makes use of this universal emotional language as people read each other's faces and expressions.

So it appears that human beings share an emotional common language. Every normal child develops a potential to read these emotional signals of others, and the skill becomes fine tuned in the course of early social interaction. Newly discovered "mirror neuron systems" show how infants and children can imitate, identify, and feel empathy for others. All social life and culture are built upon these capacities. The common mastery of this universal language of emotion and empathy allows Americans to watch documentaries of a remote stone age Amazon tribe and recognize the ways the children are playing and teasing one another; and most of the expressed emotions of the adults are also familiar — even though their language is incomprehensible and their tribal worldviews may be foreign.

In every human group face-to-face emotional communication is powerful, in fact so powerful that emotion is usually regulated by "display rules" in different cultural groups. Children learn the norms for expressing emotions, along with other lessons about what is appropriate and admirable behavior. Grief has its proper display and so does joy. Among Anglo-Saxon types, for example, those who mourn do not wail or tear their hair, and winners of a contested race don't gloat too openly. So too different displays of joyful religious ecstasy and enthusiasm are encouraged in different religious or cultural groups. The underlying core emotions may be the same cross culturally, but triggers for them and shadings and mixtures of expression can vary. Most importantly, unimpaired humans through their innate capacity of empathy can instantly and intuitively feel the emotions of others and respond. Infants cry when other infants cry, fear produces fear, anger breeds anger, and the other's joy and suffering are instantly felt. One person's joy and laughter elicits joy in others before they even get the joke. Obviously, the basic human ability to identify with others and feel what they feel is central to human moral and social life. No understanding of religious truth can avoid reflections upon what is an appropriate spiritual and emotional ideal. When we affirm that God is Love, much is implied about this emotion.

But within the field of emotional research positive emotions came to be studied only after negative emotions.[9] At first psychology, psychiatry, and evolutionary sociobiology focused upon negative emotional behavior rather than positive psychological experiences. This was in part because fear, sadness, anger, guilt, shame, disgust, and contempt create distress. The primary positive emotions are joy, interest, and love, though some theorists see love as an innate basic emotion while others view love as arising in the infant from a fusion of joy and interest. The recent explosion of interest in positive and optimal experiences has initiated a new "positive psychology," and the earlier "negativity bias" in the field has largely been corrected.[10] Yet all attention paid to negative emotions previously can be explained by the fact that these emotions when disordered or extreme produce depression, panic attacks, anxieties, phobias, and destructive outbursts of aggression and hostility. In addition, it seems that the basic negative emotions are more numerous and are felt more intensely than positive emotions.

While the evidence for a theory of an innate emotional response system built on primary emotions is convincing, it does not explain the complexity and dynamic quality of everyday emotional experience. Because so many subtle and complex combinations of emotions exist, the language of emotions is vast, as basic emotions are experienced in different degrees of intensity, in different combinations with other emotions, and in different linked associations with thoughts and images.

Certain patterns of thought and feeling may be experienced together so habitually that they are stored together in memory and will be triggered together. In a sad mood I remember sad events or, when pondering sad memories, I begin to feel sad in the present. By contrast, the sight of babies and puppies may induce joy along with other memories of happy events. While the American flag being raised at the Olympics to the strains of the "Star Spangled Banner" elicits goose bumps and a surge of patriotic feeling, surely the American response to the stars and stripes is not innate or universal. Some emotions are learned through cultural experience and social conditioning, and these secondary emotions tend to contain more cognitive components and are more nuanced and elaborated. Other basic emotions seem to have been innately programmed for survival such as fear of snakes, large animals, and heights; these fears are more spontaneous, intense, and hardwired with an intuitive meaning built in. Furthermore, there also exist background, diffuse, emotionally toned feelings called "moods," which do not become intense or articulated enough to count as a full-blown "emotion." In general, different individuals and different cultures and subcultures evince variations in their habitual emotional landscapes, even though a universal pan-psychic emotional system appears to have developed to ensure survival and social functioning.

Universally, emotions serve to provide tacit or implicit information about the internal or external environment of organisms. Varying emotional responses are necessary for living because they intuitively keep us in touch with our inner states and our relationships with other people and circumstances. Emotions are usually conscious signals, but at times a person's emotions may remain outside of awareness, although others might recognize the signs of anger, for instance. The presence of emotions signal heightened self-investment and convey a sense of conviction about reality: "Yes, this is really the way the world is." This quality of reality-reinforcement helps to motivate us to respond more effectively and instantaneously than would more abstract reasoned perceptions or conclusions. Such intuitive intensity may be related to the fact that our emotional system is evolutionarily older than our ability to engage in explicit, conscious reasoning and so operates more intuitively.[11] This nonconscious response system can be adoptive for survival. On the other hand, emotions can be so powerful that when they generate distorted or inaccurate appraisals of a situation or a person, it is hard for reasoning to counter them. An abstract thought does not have the vivid power of an intense emotion — at least while the emotion lasts. But emotions come and go, rise and fall, since their functioning serves to give tacit information about an ever changing environment. Waiting for an emotional surge to subside is one tried and true way of self-regulation or strategy for not being misled or overwhelmed.

Different emotions have different patterns of onset and dissipation. As already noted, moods or background emotional dispositions do not become intense enough to count as an articulated emotional signal, although a negatively toned mood of depression may make the world seem dark. Yet "feeling down" is different from pangs of suffering, just as a mood of calm contentment is different from a surge of joy. Less intense emotionally toned states may influence our views of the world but not with the power of a more intense emotion.

One theory offered to explain the fact that negative emotions are felt so vividly and often have a rapid onset is that humans need a rapid and decisive response to threatening information. In a dangerous environment, negative signals of danger that produce fight-or-flight responses have to be immediate and compelling. For 80 percent of human history small hunter-gatherer groups had to adapt to difficult environments filled with predators, so early humans had to be vigilant, ready to recognize danger, and take immediate action to survive.

Acute intense fear responses to any suspicious stimuli enable a rapid adaptive response. If you see what looks like a snake on the path, you need to act immediately, because taking time to find out whether what you see is actually a vine or a stick could be fatal. If cornered by a predator, instant rage mobilizes attack behavior.

More complex negative emotions that require social awareness, such as sadness, guilt, shame, disgust, and contempt, also have ensured human survival. When threatened with the loss or opposition of those upon whose help you depend for survival, realistic distress ensues, and this socially aversive state of feeling lasts until the disruption is resolved. To avoid the dangers of abandonment and social punishment, members of the group will conform to the rules; thus emotional bonds of attachment increase conformity and help hold groups together. The human species is relentlessly social, and humans are prepared from birth to imitate, empathize, attach, and conform. From infancy to old age individuals depend upon and flourish in relationships with others. To be shunned or abandoned brings despair, and, in primitive groups, actual death. Humans living in social groups become adept in reading emotional social signals and modifying their behavior accordingly. In fact, humans may have developed their unique abilities for conscious self-awareness mainly from the necessity of figuring out what other group members are feeling or thinking. Reading the cues that reveal another person's inner emotions and motivation will give important information to predictions that allow for adaptive responses. Empathy and intelligent reading of other persons increase the capacity for self-awareness and self-consciousness. Awareness of self and others develops together and keeps interpersonal relationships in good working order. So while evolutionary needs for defense can explain the selection of negative emotions rather easily, what role do joy and positive emotions play?

The Role of Positive Emotions

Because no survival needs are met by delight, the information that an emotion like joy provides is less clear. Nevertheless new research on positive emotions points to the huge influence they have. Whatever actions produce joy and pleasure tend to be rewarding and so are repeated. Feelings of joy lead to perseverance and continuity of practices. Individuals seek to return again and again to those persons, things, and activities that give satisfaction, pleasure, and delight. There seems to be an innate joy simply in the human capacity to make things happen, a motivation that has been named "self-effectance," and which is seen as related to curiosity and interest.

Another positive feeling state newly recognized has been that of "flow,"[12] which refers to immersion in ongoing activities involving an optimal exercise and engagement of human capacities with the environment. In "flow," the activity is neither overwhelming nor boring and is of high interest and meaning to the agent — climbing a mountain, solving a problem, creating a work of art. These satisfying forms of absorbing activity carry the person along and induce self-forgetfulness, but, at the same time, during and after the activity there emerges a sense of joy and self-enhancement. A person loses one's sense of self but also ultimately recovers it in the course of the creative challenge. Jesus' words about losing the self in order to find it can be applied to "flow" and the joy that it gives. Similarly, interest and joy are linked, especially in love, and can produce peak experiences as well. Curiosity and intellectual challenge give intrinsic satisfaction to the human effort of seeking and finding solutions, those "aha" experiences that are a form of intellectual ecstasy. Novelty and challenge that are not overwhelming or threatening are a source of joy and pleasure.

At the same time familiarity can induce positive feelings. Human beings like things, places, and people they see often and recognize. Taking joy in familiar people, places, and things serves to maintain and strengthen social bonds. This is my land; these are my people. Thus, familiarity does not breed contempt but instead feelings of comfort and affection. One particular expression of familiarity, that of mutual sexual joy with a long-term mate, is especially crucial to ensure the survival of the social group. The comfort and joy of frequent sex increases the bonds of union and interdependency between a mated pair. Although other animals mate and form pair bonds, the sensual pleasure of sex in big-brained human beings expands into mutual joy, love, and friendship. Sexual bonds sustain human mates in the arduous and prolonged tasks of caregiving to offspring. Such bonds also engender kinship and family relations, which provide the social foundation and survival of every known culture. The long evolutionary history of family bonding has shaped present human emotional responses. In every modern study of human happiness, the primary source of joy reported is that of family life; and over and over, the birth of a child is reported as a peak life experience.[13] Sexual joy, ecstasy, and love are accessible everyday experiences of positive heightened consciousness. Thus it is not surprising that mystics and poets have used sexual images of marital bonding to describe religious experiences; the joyful, fruitful love of family is seen as an apt image for divine love.

When people share joy, their nonverbal sense of empathy and identification increases. Families and all other groups are strengthened by participating in positive common activities. Sharing rituals, especially rituals of celebration, produces bonding. Shared joy sustains an orientation toward others; smiles beget more smiles. A mother and baby share joy in face-to-face, eye-to-eye communion. What has been called "emotional attunement" in recent infant studies is a wordless but powerful means of responding and adapting to another.[14] Empathy, attachment, and sharing relationships are programmed into the human organism. These processes of bonding produce patterns that last throughout life. New interest in what has been called "emotional intelligence" sees the beginnings of competence in the recognizing and regulating of emotions that appear between infants and caretakers. Those persons who are emotionally attuned to others and read others competently will be able to identify with, and weep or rejoice with others. Friendships that ensure cooperation and help in all of life's struggles are based upon shared joys as well as upon enduring negative ordeals together.

Shared humor and laughter make working together more efficient and less burdensome. Playfulness and playing have marked human groups and provided rewarding emotional experiences. Throughout human history hunters, farmers, and women harvesting, cooking, and sewing together have enjoyed sharing their work. Good work produces joy, and joy makes work more interesting and effective. Current research shows that positive emotions increase creative and intuitive forms of thinking, building, and broadening a person's resources of attention and life experiences.[15] Negative emotions, by contrast, are focused on correcting the organism's course or on surviving dangers; positive emotions turn outward and expand, enhancing and interacting with others and the environment. As positive emotions broaden and build upon one another, interest and joy, love and playfulness interact and spur engagement with tasks and other people. "Flow" enhances creativity. Moreover, aesthetic joy arises from the appreciation and creation of beauty. Those mysterious peak experiences that surprise people often happen as persons are transported by love and the beauty of persons, nature, art, and music. Audiences and readers can lose themselves in enjoying the narrative of a story. The dancer becomes the dance. Persons interacting with symbolic forms, rhythms, and patterns experience joy, which enhances and affirms their sense of self-in-union with others.

Today we are sure that our aesthetic responses are intrinsic to the human species because discoveries of the earliest

archeological remains of human groups always include arti-
facts that have been decorated. The magnificent cave art of
our immediate homo sapiens ancestors in different locations
around the globe testifies to a universal human sensitivity to
beauty in the world. Artistic achievements of every time and
place demonstrate how humans revel in aesthetic delight. The
joy of art and music is intrinsic to humankind. Indeed, many
new theories of music have surmised that communal rituals
of music and dance were central and formative experiences of
early humans. Hunting and gathering groups may have met
for celebrations, thereby spreading cultural discoveries, finding mates, and ensuring peaceful relations. Early musical rituals
may have reduced tensions and become early forms of worship.
Humankind may have been danced and sung into being. Other
than musical instruments there are no archeological remains of
musical practices, but the human brain seems to have amazing
musical capacities, or musical intelligence, which gives evidence
of lengthy evolutionary development. Scientific evidence of
the brain's musical abilities points to the crucial positive role
of music and joy in human development.

The joy that emerges early in infancy quickly fuses with interest to become love, and love shapes the mutual relationships
of giving and receiving that build up and produce ever more
joy. Sensations of pleasure are wonderfully present also, but joy
consists of much more than physiological relief or satisfying
sensation. In the same way that pain may, or may not, be identical with suffering (we know human suffering can be acute
without physical pain), so physical pleasure does not automatically produce joy, and joy can be felt without physical pleasure.
Some further engagement and psychological enhancement of
self must be involved for the existence of joy.

In summary joy springs from a heightened psychological
self-awareness and expansive affirmation of the well-being of
a whole person. Ideally, the most amplified experience of joy
includes physical closeness, the enhancement of self in mutual

love and interest: an infant nursing in a loving mother's arms, the enduring symbol of Madonna and child, the lovers of the Song of Songs — all are potent images of joy.

Surely, too, homo sapiens has always played and laughed with joy, even though laughter, like song and dance, leaves no archeological traces. Laughter, play, and humor also appear to be innate to the human species. Laughter in infancy is elicited by unplanned, unexpected stimuli that occur during innately patterned play between babies and caretakers. Peekaboo with a parent brings peals of laughter, since such play provides a baby with surprise and interest embedded in the mutual emotional relationship of love and affection. Thus, when theologians speak of a God who surprises us with delight, they tread on firm psychosocial ground. And humans, of course, continue to play right into adulthood. Surprise, incongruity, or disruption of existing patterns produce laughter as a form of transcendence beyond routine. However, direct efforts to give one's self joy and induce laughter in solitude are usually less successful, just as tickling oneself does not work. It is engagement with others that produces laughter and happiness.

Humor, laughter, and joking affirm the freedom of one's self in the face of the challenge of necessity. "Help me up to the block, I can come down by myself," quips Thomas More before his beheading. "Turn me over, I am done on this side," says the St. Lawrence of legend, as he is being roasted to death on the torturer's grid. Laughter manifests the joy, of a self, consciously observing and rising above the imposed circumstances. Indeed, all of the positive emotions of joy, interest, and love arise from healing broadening and elevating encounters with the world and others. One of the most important new findings in psychology and medicine is that positive emotions can counter and undo the harmful effects of negative stressful emotions.[16] Joy, love, and laughter have healing properties that affect the psyche and the body. The immune system is influenced by positive emotions, and those who grieve or have suffered traumas and disease can be helped to heal by experiences of positive emotions.

All the different manifestations of joy bring a sense of self-transcendence. And surprisingly, gladness, joy, and happiness may come for no reason. Peak experiences are not the product of control or effort, but drop down like the dew as gift. The rhythms of giving and receiving love intensify joy. Musical duets express this ascending delight. People in love become receptive to new realities and bloom expansively. Lovers are physically transformed. The physiological effects of joy positively tune and energize. Sensory perception becomes more acute, roses seem redder, the sun brighter, the body more buoyant. The expansive reverberating buoyancy of joy may account for its blurriness or luminous quality. In the movies joyful lovers bound toward one another, floating in slow motion, slightly out of focus to the sound of music. Lovers in tune soar with the music. In joy time slows down. Mystics have always claimed that when lost in the rapturous encounter with God (the ultimate "flow" experience?) they lose track of the minutes that pass. Many holy and joyful saints have been famed not only for their ecstasies but also for their floating or levitating in their lighthearted joy.

When joyful, time slows down because no change is desired. The present moment expands with the desire that the consummation may last forever. In psychological research happiness has been observed to slow down certain cognitive processes and enhance others. Taking time and being absorbed can be an intellectual advantage for creative kinds of thinking and problem solving. While anxiety and fear quicken and sharpen some kinds of focused information processing, joy slows down other cognitive processes that further the kind of knowledge that comes from prolonged attentive appreciation. Mothers who love their children take joy in gazing at them intimately. Mothers can spot an illness or discern talents and gifts that others have not taken the time to observe. Artists and workers who love their work make new discoveries and find more inventive ways to be creative. Love's joyful attention produces heartfelt understanding as well as delight. The added dimension to love's knowledge arises from the sustained attention that joy brings over time.

Joy and Altruism

Just as the role of joy, happiness, and positive emotions had been scanted in the study of human evolutionary development, so too only belatedly have studies of altruism come into their own.[17] In the past altruism or helping behavior has been explained away as self-interest, as an indirect way to get one's own genes reproduced in the next generation. If an individual helps or sacrifices his life for his children, siblings, or cousins, then his own genes, which he shares with his kin, will be perpetuated. Or if an individual sacrifices for others who are not related, the future favors he receives will favor his or her reproductive success. Ergo, say the pessimists, altruistic behaviors always can be reduced to subtle forms of self-interest.

However, such reductive approaches to altruism are currently being challenged by evolutionary theorists who see altruism as an independently evolving human response. Yes, humans have evolved to be selfish, competitive, and aggressive in seeking reproductive success, but they have also evolved to be altruistic, joyful, and intrinsically attached to others. Cooperation in nature and society may be as dominant, or even more dominant, than competition, selfishness, and aggression.

Further analyses of the independent and potent influence of human capacities for joy, love, and empathy give weight to theories of the existence of altruism in human history; an understanding of the potency of human empathy, love, and joy is key. If altruism has puzzled some evolutionary theorists, it may be because they ignored the innate and intrinsic joy that arise when one person gives joy and shares joy with another.

Since empathy exists as a kind of intuitive identification with another, a person can be "infected" with positive emotions as easily as with negative. I fear with your fear, I hurt with your pain, but I also rejoice in your joy. One simple anecdote illustrating this truth appears in Abraham Maslow's account of feeding strawberries to his son. "If I love strawberries and my adored child loves strawberries, then when I feed my strawberries to him I get more joy from his joy than if I ate them myself." Such instances of the way joy and altruism are linked can be multiplied, starting with maternal nurturing. Even when the cost of altruism is higher than forgoing strawberries, humans can take joy in producing and sharing the happiness and well-being of others just for its own sake. What have been described as "together goods" — often ignored positive mutual activities that you can experience only *with* and *through* shared relationships — have to be recognized as central motivations for human life.[18] Altruistic acts can be intrinsically rewarding; it is more blessed to give than receive.

More extensive research on human origins and development supports this more complex approach to human evolution; an increase in cooperation has been consistently discerned throughout the development of human life and culture. Our nature appears to be made up of innate selfish drives for survival as well as predispositions to unselfish, helping behavior. Negative aversive emotions and positive emotions *both* develop, but on independent paths. The existence of diverse capacities and pathways have received more confirmation from new studies of the brain. It appears that the location, operation, pathways, and sources of positive and negative emotional systems in the brain are different, and these different systems allow for the possibility of experiencing positive and negative emotions at the same time.[19] In short, suffering and joy do not necessarily exclude one another, nor need one emotion or motivation be subsumed, fused, dependent upon, or reduced to the other.

Other clinical and experimental accounts appear to confirm this complexity or parallel processing of emotional operations. Persons can report feeling both sorrow and joy at the same time, along with an I who observes the feelings. Czeslaw Milosz says of his joy that "it didn't obliterate consciousness; the past which I carried was there, together with my grief." Other experiences of simultaneous joy and sorrow are attested to in literature and in psychological research. For example, in one study widows interviewed about their late husbands reported feeling both sadness and joy while thinking of their husband's love and of his loss. The fact that the women were older, with access to more memories and life experience, may also have been a factor in their more complex emotional responses. A firmer sense of self-consciousness that can transcend the present may give access to different memories and trigger simultaneous emotions.

There may be limiting conditions to emotional regulation or to the coexisting of joy and suffering in consciousness. The joy must be of a certain kind, and the suffering must not be self-inflicted or blameworthy. The suffering that can coexist with joy could hardly be the self-inflicted suffering that is filled with intense self-obsessed negative or hostile emotions. Pure joy would surely be impossible to feel if at the same time a person's consciousness is fixated and suffused with aroused anger, hatred, contempt, disgust, envy, lust, or desire for revenge. Such negative emotions are usually linked with thoughts and desires that exalt the self over others or at the cost of others. Certain hostile negative emotions tend to be highly intense, fevered, or frenzied — the so-called emotional wildfires. Most spiritual paths and disciplines have seen the incompatibility of such emotions with feelings of joyous beneficence and lovingkindness. Negative emotions bent on flight or fight can hardly coexist with the joy that desires to bask, savor, enjoy, and continue in celebration. Blameworthy negative emotions of agitated distress and pain push for change and control. In the obsessive grip of aroused self-will, there is no energy for receptive openness to love and delight. And without love and openness, joy cannot enter consciousness to give comfort, peace, and consolation. Unfortunately self-inflicted, self-initiated blameworthy forms of suffering arise from rebelliously embracing harm-doing and self-willed rebellion against the good. But innocent suffering that arises especially from empathy or from the consequence of loving actions undertaken to end another's suffering — these can coexist with joy because they are open to others and to the goodness. They offer no obstacle to joy.

If joy and suffering may coexist in consciousness, they may also alternate with quicksilver speed. Different threads of a tapestry may be interwoven, or different notes in music may alternate. As we have noted, literature, poetry, music, and religious accounts reflect these rich emotional complexities. Those familiar with religious and devotional writing can attest to these subtle patterns of alternating surges of feeling. Judeo-Christian Scriptures, in particular the psalms, show many passages of alternating positive and negative emotional responses. The prophecies, the Gospel hymns, St. Paul's letters, and later Christian writings all demonstrate near-symphonic patterns of ascending and descending emotional responses. One striking example can be found in the great medieval mystic Julian of Norwich, who describes her alternating feelings as "joy and delight — then feeling was reversed, oppressed, weary of my life, and disgusted by no comfort...only faith hope and love in reality but I could not feel them in my heart, then again spiritual rest and comfort, with certainty and pleasure, no bodily pain distressed me. And then the sorrow again first one, then the other about twenty times." She concludes her account with a fundamental insight: "Hold on to bliss for bliss lasts eternally, and pain passes and shall vanish completely. And therefore it is not God's will that we should be guided by feelings of pain, grieving, and mourning over them but should

quickly pass beyond them and remain in eternal joy."[20] This testimony of Dame Julian that "all will be well" reveals not only
the complexity of emotional consciousness but also confidence
in the essential triumph of joy in God's creation. It is the Christian faith that suffering will be overcome and that liberating
joy will prevail. She confirms the good news that negative emotions can be overcome and finally wither away when God is all
in all.

Indeed, many saints and holy persons demonstrate in this
life their capacities for joyful living in God's presence. But how
does this happen? Before moving to a further consideration of
a theology of joy, it is well to reflect briefly on how persons
can differ so much in their consciousness of positive emotions.

Individual Differences

As in all capacities of human beings, the playing field is
never equal. Different individuals, families, and cultures will
differ, and this is especially true in the experience and expression of positive and negative emotions. Various innate
temperaments exist and provide the basis for different emotional predispositions. Though joy may be an innate universal
emotion, some persons are born more ready to feel positive emotions than others, with brains constructed so that
the positive responses centered in the left side of the brain
dominate. In psychological research on personality, characteristics such as "agreeableness" and "openness to experience"
exist as two of the five basic variables that differentiate individuals, along with "conscientiousness," "neuroticism," and
"introvert-extroversion." Children can be born innately shy and
introverted, or more reactive to stimuli and fearful than extroverts. Other children may be easily aroused to irritability,
aggression, and anger. "Easy to rear" children are born with
extroverted agreeable dispositions and readily adapt to life and

so elicit positive responses in their caretakers. Agreeable extroverts open to experience will more easily seek, accept, and enjoy novel experiences. If they also are conscientious and have fewer neurotic qualities, they are all the more ready to be socialized. Sunday's child is full of grace.

Fortunately, while innate, temperamental differences exist, they need not determine the final outcome of a person's life. Genetic predispositions always interact with the surrounding social and physical environment and with the normal individual's own efforts to pursue ideals through self-regulation. A person's individual responses are shaped by their inherited qualities and their choices, but also by their immediate family, their peer group, their larger culture, and a host of other contingent circumstances. On the negative side, abusive families or natural disasters such as famine and plagues can stunt and skew human development. Living in a totalitarian society can decrease the amount of reported happiness in a population, whereas governments with political freedom increase positive responses. It is also the case that individual parents can work to help their children overcome vulnerabilities; shy children can learn to cope with their anxieties or fears. Human beings, blessed with intelligence and free will, can work to shape their own character and emotional responses. In ordinary circumstances unimpaired adults can make choices and exercise efforts to shape their own emotional reactions.[21]

Still it appears to be easier for some people to find more joy in the world than their slightly depressed, pessimistic, or temperamentally irritable counterparts. It's no accident that among the seven dwarfs we meet "Grumpy" and "Bashful," along with "Happy." In the same way, Christian disciples and saints display different temperaments and predispositions, some displaying more cheerful temperaments than others. Christ's joy will always be proclaimed and be present in those affirming and living the Good News, but its expression and emphases may vary. Exuberant spirits from extroverted expressive families, societies, and eras will display a different style of holiness than cooler, more inhibited individuals in more reserved cultures. Apparently Baron von Hügel worried about the sanctity of his great friend John Henry Newman, because Newman was so often sad. Could expressions of Christian joy and love be more inhibited in cold, gloomy climates filled with rain?

Naturally, given individual differences, varied environments, and unique past experiences no one can ever be joyful for another, any more than one can profess religious faith for another or be moral for someone else. Moreover, happiness, like virtue, often comes as a by-product from individual efforts toward other goals. Individual acts of agents build up over time to create life narratives. Joy and happiness have a head start, however, if an individual is born with an agreeable temperament into a loving family, in a religious moral community that cherishes neighbors and engages in celebrations. Also it is becoming increasingly obvious that the mind-body unity of human beings ensures that positive emotions affect health in positive ways. The jawbreaking label "psychoneuroimmunology" is given to the new field of scientific investigation of the effect of emotions on the immune system. Happiness, joy, and love lower stress and predispose persons to healthy behavior and social support. But can there by any distortions in positive emotions?

Distortions and Abuses of Joy

Having seen the ways that suffering in and out of religion has been skewed and abused, it may come as no surprise that joy too can be distorted. A realistic attitude must admit that *all* human capacities can be open to misuse. Clearly negative emotions become destructive when they overwhelm a person's control or moral standards of worth and so-called stop rules fail. So what about joy? Spontaneously surging moments of

unalloyed joy may not be easily deformed, but joy can become toxic when linked with aggressive thoughts and aroused
violent behavior. Warriors have felt joy in battle and combat,
taking pleasure in killing. Joy has been displayed along with
the hate and aggression of lynch mobs and genocidal murders,
and in gladiatorial games. Equally dangerous perversions of
joy come when pride and self-exaltation induce joy in feeling
superior to others and indulging contempt for others. Sadistic cruelty inflicted upon others can be experienced as a joy in
exercising domination. Hitler espoused "power through joy"
and exulted in the triumph of the will for his master race.
The Führer's delight in conquest impelled his happy little jig
at the surrender of Paris. He laughed with joy over the successful persecution of the Jews. Malicious joy is stimulated by
the misfortune of others, especially in their moral failures and
humiliations. Cynical laughter and a cruel humor can be aimed
at the vulnerable and the weak. At the opposite pole of per-
version is the masochistic joy that takes pleasure in the pain of
being humiliated or hurt as a victim.

Joy is distorted not only when linked with malevolence but
also when disconnected or disassociated from positive sources
of authentic joy. A perverted joy is not based in the transcendence of love, beauty, truth, and goodness but is narrowed to
self-centered pleasure. Instead of being ready to receive gifts,
a person strives for more control in a quest for more self-
centered power, status, sex, novelty, and distraction. When
joy is skewed and disengaged from its sources in love, then
addictions arise. Various intoxicating "highs" are obsessively
sought, from drugs, sex, gambling, risk-taking, or violence.
Ironically such false and compulsive quests for pleasure give
testimony to the human need for joy. The heart is restless until
it finds its rest in the joys of loving. Unfortunately the pleasures of self-administered artificial intoxicants short-circuit the
processes that are necessary to receive the gifts of unalloyed
joy. More and more artificial stimuli are required to obtain less

and less pleasure. In a diminishing cycle on a hedonic treadmill, fevered efforts to procure and control pleasure backfire. False and artificially induced highs cannot be sustained because they are disconnected from the natural environment, and most of all from positive moral relationships with other people. Persons become ensnared and in the end can only hope to avoid the pains of withdrawal and destructive consequences. Seeking the addictive substance or activity becomes so all-encompassing that it leaves no energy for moral commitments to family, work, or mental and physical health. Even strong maternal drives can be overcome in cocaine addictions. Babies born to addicts lie abandoned in hospitals.

The intense pleasures of cocaine and other addictions may be the result of the activation of the same pleasure pathways in the brain as in experiences of authentic joy. But there is an all-important difference. True joy is integrated and related to a person's whole life and values. Human beings are "hardwired for joy," but in authentic joy they receive pleasures, highs, and peak experiences as gifts from interpersonal commitments, exercises of reason, bonds of love, and altruism. True joy and delight are not severed from engagements of love and moral standards of worth.

Another instructive pathological example of pseudo-joy can be seen in the physiologically caused mood disorders of manic euphoria. As diagnosed in clinical psychology, highly aroused manic states of exhilaration can appear alone or as one pole of bipolar depression. In manic highs an individual is physiologically hyper-aroused and exhibits an intense isolating flight of positive mood and grandiosity. "Flight" is the right descriptive word because mania is dangerously unresponsive to the realities of the environment or the responses and needs of other people. An inner speeded-up, biochemically frenzied flood of arousal results in failures of perception and judgment. Mania is manifested in irritability toward others who cannot keep up, or who may get in the way of the manic self's imperial will.

Manic states lead people to take foolish risks, engage in immoral behavior, and irritably discount reasonable arguments. It is far removed from love's joy and care — or the powers of rational thinking. Reasoning with someone with mania is like reasoning with a four-year-old. Euphoric intoxication can swamp the mind's self-critical functions or concern for others and is an example of false joy.

While clinical mood disorders are extreme forms of a failure of emotional self-regulation, such deficiencies can also appear in immature or immoral persons. Even normal individuals can regress under abnormal conditions of stress. We have all seen people (or been the person ourselves) who fall apart or melt down as self-control is overwhelmed by a flood of emotion. Those who study emotional intelligence describe this loss of self-regulation as an "emotional highjacking." Surely such out-of-control emotional states have created the traditional suspicion moralists have felt toward emotions of all kinds. All emotional reactions were thought to be bodily irrational negative impulses surging up from the animal nature of humans. Emotions, according to this view, should be strictly controlled by the higher faculty of conscious reason, if not completely suppressed. All involuntary reactions of human functioning were dangerous, or as Augustine thought, the involuntary aspects of human beings were the effect of original sin's destruction of integrity and complete self-control. Even today when the phrase "Don't be emotional" is used, it generally means "Don't be stupid" or "Don't be wrong." The emotions of joy, love, and interest are ignored or not seen as necessary for life.

Admittedly, the moral rehabilitation of emotional responses has been slowed by their lack of controlled reliability or predictability. Yet, normal, unimpaired, well-socialized persons are rarely totally overwhelmed, emotionally highjacked, or helplessly gripped by extreme maladaptive emotional responses. Only when there is some serious impairment of the normal "stop rules" that regulate emotions does one find persons subject to destructive depressions, anxieties, or manias.

Thus, I would contend that moralists must remember that we need our positive emotional responses in order to survive, function, and flourish in society. The presence of emotions or "hot cognitions" marks self-investment in a process of thinking and provides the impetus and energy for work and love. Normally, emotions are adaptive because they motivate action and help persons become tacitly informed about their inner and external environment. Abstract reason is not enough. Without love, joy, and desire, persons would not want to live, much less nurture others. Emotions are core requirements for moral thought and behavior. Positive emotions of love and attachment make us desire to be good.

God and Joy

Christians who believe in God as Love and Creator of all that is good need not be surprised by joy when it arrives. The mystery of joy does not disturb the faithful in the same way that the presence of suffering in creation does. God can easily be thanked as the source of all joy because God's being and perfection engender joy and love. God in three persons is constantly giving and receiving love in divine joy, which overflows in creation. In Christian belief this world and humankind are created in joyful love, through love, and for love, and they reflect God's goodness. All of the sources of joy — loving communion, good work, beauty, truth, the physical world, and creativity in all its forms — come as God's gifts. Faith and gratitude impel worship of God with shouts of joy and praise, song, timbrels, cymbals, and dance. All the isles and forests and mountains bless the Lord. Hearts and minds celebrate God's lovingkindness in creating us as beings made in God's image. What a joy it is to be alive, to be conscious: to think, to know, and to love.

Joy is the center of the gospel message. As the wise old curé says in *Diary of a Country Priest,* "Joy is in the gift of the Church, whatever joy is possible for this sad world to share." He goes on to assure his young priest friend that joy is given for nothing. "You have only to ask.... The opposite of a Christian people is a people grown sad and old." If worshipers in the pews are yawning through Mass on Sundays, there's a reason. "You don't expect the Church to teach them joy in one wretched half-hour a week, do you?" This fundamental message of Christian joy is finally accepted by the tormented and dying young priest, as he thinks at the end of his life. "Joy! A kind of pride, a gaiety, an absurd hope, entirely carnal, the carnal form of hope, I think, is what they call joy."[22]

Paul says that joy is the fruit of the Holy Spirit. Perhaps it is this divine origin and diffusion of omnipresent joy that makes it seem more mysterious and harder to describe than suffering and pain. In authentic joy persons become open to a reality that is always present and sustaining creation. It does not seem true, as certain spiritual masters have claimed, that God purposely withdraws and hides from those who suffer — for their own good, of course. In this view God sends darkness and aridity in order to test or strengthen faith so that when the consolations of joy and love are received they will not be mistaken as merited human achievements. But this is to misunderstand the fact that joy and love always come as unearned gifts.

A more accurate approach understands that God's love and joy are always and everywhere present. Only the sin, chaos, and disorder of the evolving incomplete resisting world obscure God's blessings. Moreover, in an evolving world human emotions and consciousness have to be ever changing in order to respond to needs. The disciples must come down from the awesome radiance of the mount of transfiguration to engage in works of mercy. Mary Magdalene cannot hold on to her risen Rabboni but must go to tell the disciples the incredible news. God does not hide or abandon creation but has given it freedom to become. And development through time and space necessitates some veiling from the overwhelming Light that could blind with its power. Moses wore his veil when his face shone with the Light of God's presence. Paul had to take time to recover from being struck blind by Christ's call. The radiant cloud that so often accompanies divine revelation in time and history exists as a protective filter for the fire and grandeur of an ineffable God. Yet since the graciousness and mercy of God has intimately bonded with humanity in Jesus Christ, love and joy can become present to every heart that seeks. Those who seek find. Those who knock will have the door opened to them. And this door no one can close. Of course, the seeker does not earn, or merit, or deserve the divine gift. The thirsty will be freely given the living water and the hungry will be filled. A good mother does not turn away, or abandon, or impose suffering upon her nursing infant. A good father does not give a stone to the child who asks for a fish. When suffering or aridity come, the darkness and pain do not come from the God of love, light, and joy.

In the New Testament Paul teaches that the final fullness of joy may be so intense that it is beyond our imaginative grasp: "What no eye has seen, nor ear heard, nor the human heart conceived . . . God has prepared for those who love him" (1 Cor. 2:9). Despite the suffering that exists Christians will strive to pray to be for others what God is for them.

– Eight –

PRAYER, JOY,
AND SUFFERING

❦

C HRISTIANS PRAY for the end of suffering and the recep-
tion of God's gift of joy. While we are grateful when our
prayers for rescue, healing, and relief are answered, many of
our fervent pleas are not granted. On the way to the hospital
my infant dies, or the tidal wave comes, the cancer spreads,
the torturer remains undeterred, and the secret police ferret
out the victim's hiding place. When ardent prayers do not deliver us from evil, faith is challenged. In the midst of suffering,
the promise of joy can seem hollow and doubt arises with its
perennial question: How can our prayers be effective in alleviating the suffering of this world? Or is it only that prayer
transforms Christians so that we can be joyful no matter what
we suffer?

If I focus on the power of prayer to change concrete circumstances here on earth — or not — one immediate query is "Why
would any believer pray for rescue in the first place?" Those
who assert that God is omnipotently controlling our world according to a detailed predestined plan must assume that each
event is unfolding according to that providential blueprint, in
which case, human prayers could make no concrete difference
in what happens. Praying can only serve to help believers accept whatever God has ordained. Karl Rahner objects to this
approach in that it reduces prayer to serving a merely tranquil-
izing function,[1] a placebo effect. Yet at the same time, those
who believe in God's absolute control of every event have, in a

176

confusing move, celebrated divine interventions and miracles as the result of the prayers of the faithful. The Turks are turned back from Vienna through prayers to Our Lady of Czestochowa. Plagues are averted. Miraculous cures are granted in response to pilgrimage and prayer.

However, when prayers fail to effect any visible change, believers have been told that while an omnipotent God has heard their prayers, He has refused their petitions. Although God *could* effect a divine rescue, in this case that option is not in the divine plan; believers must accept that God's answer to their specific plea is "no." Although we cannot understand it now, in the long run, any suffering or disaster not averted is said to be "all for the good" in accordance with God's will. If every prayer includes the proviso of "thy will be done," then whatever happens must be assumed to be God's will. Trust God, we are told to submit; whatever the outcome, a true believer is ready to accept suffering as sent by God for his or her own good and the good of others. Thus both unanswered and answered prayers are direct exercises of God's omnipotence.

Within this view, the notion that God rejects specific petitions is softened by asserting another (undeniable) spiritual truth. While we may receive "no" as an answer to what we ask for, in another sense God answers every prayer because all prayers further our intimacy with God. Growth in holiness counts as a positive good even if no concrete external circumstance is changed. Since "prayer is a constant reeducation of desire,"[2] prayers including praise and adoration, thanksgiving and petition all increase one's union with God. Indeed even prayers of complaint, argument, and lamentation in the prophetic mode of Moses or Job deepen the divine-human friendship. Those who pray to God constantly will speak whatever is on their mind with frankness and forthrightness. Often, these prayers also will include expressions of contrition, and these will work to further feelings of forgiveness, gratitude, and inner peace. Petition and supplication are not the only forms of prayer.

Some who hold prayers of petition as suspect will argue that they should actually be seen as prayers of adoration. Prayer puts one in the presence of God and provides consolation, encouragement, and serenity, whether or not a specific petition is granted. Isn't it enough of a grace that prayer can heal the heartbroken and transform those who pray? Why focus so intently on changing the world with the risk of reducing prayer to superstitious magic? To pray for rain or even to pray for a cure of my cancer is, from this perspective, a primitive form of prayer. The faithful who defend prayers of petition have to argue their case. When Karl Rahner begins such a defense, he provocatively asserts that prayers of petition should be seen as the highest form of prayer. Why? Because petitions combine both a boldness in addressing God and a humility in praying for help. Obviously, lively debates continue over the nature and meaning of prayer. What is prayer and what should I pray for, with what expectations?

What Is Prayer?

Because such a plethora of perspectives exist concerning different forms of prayer, the first step is to recognize the obvious, that praying is a uniquely human activity. Only those with a measure of developed consciousness and awareness can pray. While newborn babies, lilies of the field, and birds of the air all give glory to God, they do not pray, for prayer, like work, involves some measure of focused intention or directed consciousness. Only with awareness can a self focus attention upon God as the ultimate transcendent spiritual reality and immanent ground of being and becoming. One traditional definition of prayer, given in the Roman Catholic *Catechism*, quotes John Damascene, "Prayer is when an individual or group lifts the heart and mind to God." This definition uses age-old vertical images of going "up" to God. Other definitions of prayer use imagery that describes prayer as turning "in" or "centering" on God within.[3] But, in addition to "up" and "in," why not also see prayer as turning "outward" to adore and contemplate God in the beauty of the world? Regardless of direction all forms of prayer can be viewed as "a movement of the heart" toward a God who is present everywhere.

It is also important that prayer not be narrowly defined as a unilateral, unidirectional act of human beings, since prayer presumes a mutual inter-relatedness between God and humans created in God's image. Prayer is a form of communion, a conversation, a mutual indwelling. God loves us and draws us toward God's self through stirrings of our hearts, and in praying we respond. With God, to seek is to find, and God engenders the seeking. Christians have been assured that the Spirit helps human beings to pray and to find the right words. Many of the greatest Christian prayers have first been given in Scripture as the word of God. In the Gospel accounts, for instance, Jesus taught his disciples to pray the Our Father. Those who love the Rosary attribute its appeal and power to the fact that so many of its invocations are derived from the words of angels and holy persons found in the Bible.

Another apt description of prayer is to see it as "soul breathing."[4] The breathing of prayers Godward requires active initiative, but prayers are drawn forth and repeated with the rhythm of respiration, so that those who pray can enjoy resting in the Lord. Silent contemplation and heartfelt listening are potent forms of praying. Nevertheless, easy as it sounds, meditative centering prayers of quiet in which the mind is emptied in a receptive waiting upon God are not effortless. This form of prayer takes practice and discipline. Those who attempt meditation quickly learn that nothing is harder to focus than the skittering "chattering monkey" of the mind. Christians can be grateful for those spiritual guides who advise, "Pray as you can, not as you can't." A plethora of ways exist to give praise, thanks, and glory to God.

Formally structured prayers with prescribed words can be read and recited, either alone or in groups. Informal spontaneous prayers can be offered aloud or as inward silent ejaculations, such as my own simple standbys, "Help! Help!" or "Thank you! Thank you!" Daily reading of Scripture and receptive listening to the Word are other tried and true ways of combining structured and unstructured prayer. The alternations of different forms and kinds of prayers characterize Christian liturgy and rites. In particular, the celebration of the Eucharist is an intensely powerful form of worship that contains many different modes of prayer and activity.

As a form of human expression, prayer ranges in emotional temperature from cool to emotionally hot. In heightened states of consciousness those inspired to "speak in tongues" erupt in spontaneous, nonconceptual sounds to pray to God, but such rapturous outpourings of joyful noise need interpretation to be understood by others. In a cooler, more formal mode, liturgical prayer consists of directed gestures, ordered movements, and preordered postures offered in worship. In liturgical prayer, the movements of our hearts toward God are also embodied in acts of singing, dancing, music making, incensing, sprinkling, washing, and lighting fires — all ways of praying and giving reverence. Penitents bow, prostrate themselves, or kneel with arms outstretched; in the past sinners have donned sackcloth and ashes, or flogged themselves. In times of great travail and suffering, praying can consist of wailing, laments, cries, tears, sighs, and groans wrung from the soul's depths. "My God, my God, why have you forsaken me?"

Of course, informal internal prayers of sorrow or joy, being uniquely personal, can be offered anywhere and at any time — in one's closet, in sickrooms, on deathbeds, at births, feasts, or celebrations, or while working in the field, desert, library, or kitchen. Brother Lawrence famously disciplined himself to practice the continual presence of God amid the pots and pans of his monastery kitchen.

Different forms of Christian prayer, whether formal or informal, public or private, hot or cool, reflect varying ethnic traditions and individual temperaments. Simon Stylites and other ascetic devotees in the ancient world prayed continually while residing for years on the top of pillars. Other hermitages for prayer have been constructed in caves or in church walls and outside monasteries. In prayerful activities the ascetic fasts, the scholar studies, the juggler juggles before the altar of Our Lady while the pilgrim crawls up the holy mountain or plods along reciting the Jesus prayer. In ecstasy King David danced naked before the Ark to glorify the Lord. Today, Sufi devotees continue to dance and spin in order to reach states of tranced worship. Other enthusiastic worshipers are swept away into unconscious swoons called being "slain in the Spirit."

Today in America, different cultural groups cultivate different aspects of their common Christian heritage. Arguments over liturgical celebrations abound, but ideally every member of the faith should be able to find within its rich tradition the spiritual food they need for the journey. In the broad rainbow of Christian worship — from calm, cool, restrained formality to fiery, uninhibited exuberance — I find the most joy, solace, and inspiration in the formal structured liturgical tradition of the Roman Mass. Rites of ordered worship with a great deal of silence hold power for me in their controlled expressions of passionate adoration and petition. Reverent formal responses, measured gestures, and processions help bring me into God's presence. Prayers that included speaking in tongues or dancing spontaneously, much less losing consciousness in a trance, would be much too threatening.

Yet all Christians, whatever their practice of prayer and worship, hope that when God speaks to them, the message will be received with a willing heart: "Here am I, Lord, send me."

Prayers of Petition

Giving thanks and praise in prayer is one thing; praying for concrete help for myself or those I love is another. So many of my prayers, like those of most ordinary believers, consist of petitions. Some supplications can be desperately focused on an immediate crisis, while other petitions center on chronic problems; but almost all such prayers seek relief from suffering.

Prayers of petition have always played a central role in Christian life. "Lord, please heal my son, my ill daughter, my mother-in-law." Or, closer to the bone, "God, let this cup pass from me." In the midst of human distress, we cry out to God for rescue, relief, and healing. A whole array of needs are fervently prayed for. But lately, as noted above, prayers to God for concrete things have not found approval. This may be because of the danger of lapsing into the business of bargaining with God or futile unsavory attempts to coerce God's hand. There may be a fine line between a promise to fulfill a vowed action in response to an answered prayer and a less than admirable magic power play.

However, when one's case becomes desperate, even the most disapproving believer can ask God for what he or she needed. As Karl Rahner has written, even academe elites will resort to prayers of petition when their backs are against the wall. After the emergency is over, such believers may reassert their opinion that it is spiritually acceptable only to pray that God's will be done. Specific requests are judged to be too close to "crass supernaturalism." Negative attitudes toward petitions may reflect other doubts that God ever could or ever should intervene in the natural operations of this world. The belief that God influences natural events can seem especially unacceptable to adherents of garden-variety materialism, with its reductive assertions that the universe is a closed and determined system. Christians in an age of secular unbelief can be intimidated by the skepticism of many academic authorities. Believers may retreat to safer concepts of God as the ground of all being who only works at a far distance, if at all. The old conviction that there is a split between mind and matter still holds sway in much of Western culture and is matched by older religious beliefs in the strict separation of nature and the supernatural.

Another hesitation in regard to prayers of petition comes from the feeling that it is presumptuous to ask God to grant one's own self-interested pleas. Who am I to bother the ineffable transcendent Holy One, who dwells in unapproachable Light, with my petty concerns? Lingering vestiges of the religious traditions that valorize suffering can support such a notion. Is it not unworthy to beg for relief, or to pray for the fulfillment of a desired dream? Besides, say many who decline to join in the "primitive" petitions of "folk Catholicism," no limited human being could possibly know what is best in any specific situation or discern what God's will is. The whole tapestry being woven by God is obscure; humans living in darkness can only be seeing the underside of the design. A resigned detachment is encouraged by the traditional belief that God sends suffering or employs it for the greater good of His providential plan.

Yet scripture itself tells a different story. At the very beginning of Jesus' mission, Mary asks Jesus to help with the concrete difficulty of too little wine at the wedding feast of Cana. Thereafter in the rest of his ministry, Jesus prays to God in petitions for various things, receives answers to his requests, and in turn answers the many pleas of others directed toward him. When he teaches his disciples how to pray, they are instructed to ask for what they need. In fact, the Lord's Prayer is filled with requests, including a petition for daily bread and deliverance from evil. The followers of Jesus are to pray without ceasing and with confidence that petitions will be answered. Praying privately in secret, the disciples can know that God will hear and respond to their requests. As opposed to attitudes that discourage petitionary prayer, Jesus reveals a God who is more generously giving and attentive to petitions than any human parent. If a father on earth will not give his child a stone when he asks for a fish, will God refuse good things to those who ask? Jesus tells his disciples that if they have faith the size of a tiny mustard seed, they have only to ask in order to move mountains. With God nothing is impossible. The faithful will be able to heal and do great works in Christ's name.

Thus, prayers for healing and liberation from suffering will be one major way Jesus' disciples can carry on his work. Beyond the circle of his disciples, many others in the Gospels are praised by Jesus for their persistence in seeking God's help. Jesus welcomes the Gentile woman with the flow of blood who persevered in her faith, and Jesus gives his approval to those who noisily importune him. A mother determined to receive healing for her daughter won't take no for an answer and eventually gets what she begs for. He even tells a parable that recounts the success of a persistent woman who wears down a judge with her ceaseless begging. The lesson given by Jesus is that asking, knocking, pleading, and praying for relief are praiseworthy actions and that the requests will be answered. Two or three gathered together in prayer in Christ's name will receive what they pray for; God cares for the beloved people and responds to their cries.

In his teachings on the efficacy of prayers of petition, Jesus is being true to Israel's confidence in God's interventions in history that relieve suffering. While Christ refuses to use violence and destructive force to coerce people or events, he acts as a prophet to accomplish a saving mission with great deeds. The new Moses will save his people through his intercession and responses to their pleas. The assumption is that Yahweh answers prayers and intervenes in the natural world as well as in human hearts and minds. A new living heart will replace hearts of stone, but the story of Israel includes an account of the ways God's power accomplishes wondrous interventions on earth. When the prophet Elijah intends to prove God's ascendancy by besting the priests of Baal, he confidently calls upon God to send down fire from heaven. Exactly on cue, the miraculous fire descends and crushes the ineffectual pagan claims. The Jewish prophetic tradition of God's saving acts in history in response to prayer is brought into Christianity. Christians adopt the psalms' pleas for deliverance from danger, and for good things. "May God grant your heart's desire." It is right and good to have heartfelt desires and to have them fulfilled. So, those who continue in their constant "childlike" pleas for help are being true to the gospel teaching. Disciples ask for blessings and gifts, as well as deliverance from evil.

Unanswered Prayers of Petition

So when our prayers of petition go unanswered, what should we conclude? Do we doubt Christ's promises? One approach to unanswered prayers has been to claim that they failed because they did not fulfill the requirements for requests that Christ taught were necessary: either the prayers were not made "in Christ's name" or according to his will, or those who pray did not have sufficient faith, or the two or three gathered together did not truly agree with one another. These explanations view God as rejecting specific petitions because something is flawed in those offering the prayer or in the prayers themselves. But can we believe that God, Christ, Mary, or the saints would actually hold flawed prayers against us? If God is full of maternal love, then God wants to answer our every prayer for help, for no mother would deny her child's cry because he didn't say "please" or "thank you" in the proper way. Moreover, God has promised to give the Holy Spirit's help in our inadequate efforts to pray.

The issue of unanswered prayers thus has to be understood as part of the larger story of God's nature and the divine relationship with an evolving open creation. God has created the universe and granted it free and independent powers for evolving self-organization. Humans made in God's image are granted freedom and power as created co-creators. The different kinds of sufferings that mar and stunt our lives do not arise from God, but rather from what is "not God," the otherness that has been granted to the evolving creation. In the process of cosmic evolution, open systems of various kinds can create novelty as well as disorder and conflict. As discussed in previous chapters, chance conditions interact with lawful order, and both interact with free intentional human actions. While wondrous evolutionary developments occur, so do resistances and obstacles to God's beneficence.

Human error and sinful intentions produce harmful events that create horrible suffering and distortions of the good, but such sufferings are not sent, or desired by a good God. Instead, God continually seeks to draw creation Godward. God desires to heal all wounds, overcome all evils, and bring the best outcomes possible in every event at every moment. But God, being God as made fully visible to us in Christ, will act only through the nonviolent power of creative love and the magnetic persuasive attractions that induce co-creativity in freedom. When God influences history or actors and events, it is to save and renew the world, not to judge, condemn, or inflict suffering. The incarnation and resurrection of Jesus Christ have effected the great healing from inside creation; he is the decisive beginning of the end of all suffering. Since then, a universal childbirth into joy is taking place with great labor.

Prayers, and prayers of petition, play a central role in this birthing just as other human actions do. In this interim time of struggle before the final fulfillment, prayer sustains righteous and merciful friends of God in their work of love and service to neighbor. Prayers made in the light of faith, the cross, and resurrection assure disciples that when evil and suffering come to us, God in Christ suffers *with* us and within him we shall rise to new life. Our every anguished pang is felt by God in divine empathy; God, unlike human beings, never experiences "compassion fatigue." God's empathy is not fragile nor subject to a "narrative of numbness." God in Jesus understands the horror and heartbreak humans undergo. For this reason, the cross is our symbol that God in Jesus is with us, loves us, and saves us.

But for all God's empathy, Christ who hears our prayer and suffers with us does not intervene with coercive power to forcefully reverse each ongoing horror of the world — no matter how hard and fervently we pray. Christ did not come down from the cross and wreak revenge upon the wicked evildoers around him. Rather, he suffers to reveal the nonviolent way God's love operates to bring to birth this new creation. While certain scriptural passages echo the old innate human lust for violent retribution, the cross at the end of Jesus' earthly life points to God's deeper truth. God's victory over evil will be won through loving nonviolence.[5] Love and truth ultimately overcome resistance. Gandhi named this truthful power of love "soulforce." God does not retract the freedom once granted to co-operators in the great renewal of the heavenly Jerusalem, so time is necessary for the new Jerusalem to be built up through prayer and work.

Our perception of time is at the heart of the issue, it seems. God is the Eternal Present, yet our created universe is an evolving historical narrative; certainly our prayers of petition are based within our own linear frame of a past moving toward the future. But what if the universe is actually infinitely evolving, a creative gift that keeps being given forever?[6] A few theologians have even speculated that God may have emptied Godself into time just as God became fully human in the incarnation.[7] Such a *kenosis* into time seems improbable to those who believe in a transcendent, infinite God. More likely the traditional Christian approach is correct in holding that time as we experience it will have but a limited run. What kind of existence will come in God's "fullness of time" remains unimaginable for limited human minds mired in twenty-first-century ignorance. When I read in a respected physicist's book of "quantum erasures" or possible reversals of time's events I am flummoxed.[8] These ideas of time seem as odd to me as the reports of cloistered nuns praying to change past historical events. Whether time really exists or will exist forever or will exist in some more complex form as dimensions is beyond our present ken. But it does seems clear that even if our present experience of linear time is not the last word, the framework of narrative serves as a base for Christian prayer for future hope. Perhaps the next generations of theologians will have more to say when they can work with the next generation of physicists now probing the nature of matter, space-time, and the fate of the universe.

Within our present understanding it seems safe to say that the universe is the result of a big bang that initiated an ongoing evolution in time that is still proceeding. The opening chords of a great unfinished symphony have rung forth. Themes enter and new movements are orchestrated in varying unfolding tempos and resolutions. With the advent of humankind, new players with new instruments join in the music making. Those scientists who advocate "anthropic reasoning" see the universe as once awaiting on the advent of human observers. At least, it can be admitted by all, that earlier movements of the symphony make the present parts of the composition possible. Also self-conscious intentional choices of humankind have entered the performance. Or to use another favored analogy, an event-packed theodrama is in progress, although no one knows exactly which act or turn of the plot is in process. Christians do affirm, however, that the drama is not an illusory shadow play on a cave wall, nor the strategic deception of some world demon out to mislead humankind. The unfolding story to date can be partially comprehended by human beings, and they are assigned major roles in the drama.

Theologically, God is believed to be bent on tactful courtship and Self-disclosure that does not overwhelm or coerce human freedom. God invites and woos humankind into participation in God's family life. The magnetic Christ drawing us onward has been poetically named the Omega point. "I am the Alpha and Omega, proclaims the risen One." The past seems to lie behind us, but the present and the future lie all before us, open to change and the struggle for fulfillment.

So when my specific prayer of petition appears ineffective in immediately relieving suffering or obtaining some good, I should not necessarily conclude that this failure is due to my flawed performance, or to God's direct refusal of an unworthy request that is counter to the divine plan. Rather, I can recognize that my request may be good and worthy and completely in accord with God's loving desire. God wants the infant to live, the young mother to be rescued, and every natural disaster averted. But blockages and resistance can exist due to time and inertia in creation. Independent and autonomous forces, evolving out of God's original gift of freedom to the created world, mean that much incoherence and evil remain.

The diseases that humans suffer and, indeed, death itself are grim reminders of the disorder of the evolving narrative. Death, diseases, parasites, plagues, and natural disasters such as earthquakes are present consequences of developments and systems that served a purpose in the past evolution and functioning of earth. The openness that produces novelty and development includes side effects that cause human suffering, just as some scientific theorists hypothesize that the same genes that make growth and reproduction possible at the beginning of life eventually produce aging and death. Certainly, the death and extinction of earlier species opened the way for succeeding species in earth's narrative. Would it not now be foolish for persons to hope and pray that the extinction of the dinosaurs be reversed, or that human life should return to the sea?

Once events have happened, the way forward to greater fulfillment is through creative novelty. God works to bring the best outcome possible out of every circumstance — and human beings are commanded to imitate God. With our reason, creativity, and capacity to love, we are specifically commanded "to play God." Imitate God's mercy: eradicate smallpox, fight leprosy, outwit the AIDS virus, lower the infant mortality rate, control ecological disasters, eradicate the misery of poverty, and provide for human flourishing. Yet for all of this, time and space (or space-time) are required. Christ in his earthly ministry did not cure all ills instantly. Lazarus was resuscitated but had to die again. Jesus tells his disciples that sins against the little ones will continue, and that future wars will come before God's end time. The Roman oppressors were not aggressively and definitively routed as the Zealots demanded. The poor and needy remain among us because the rich and greedy have not been violently destroyed.

Unanswered prayers or failed petitions can be accepted as part of the process of transformation taking place in an immature, still developing resistant universe. Prayers can be thwarted and blocked in the present visible world by the obstacles inherent in free development. But hope for the invisible effects of prayer endures since faith is the hope in things unseen, for a future still being born. Tennyson's famous words ring true. "More things are wrought by prayer than this world dreams of." Indeed, in dramatic cases, visibly answered prayers confirm belief in the Gospel affirmations of the powers of prayerful petition.

Answered Prayers of Petition

Answered prayers of petition induce joy and gratitude, but they present their own puzzles. If the freedom granted to an evolving world can block God's help for those who pray, then how do positive interventions in response to prayer take place?

Why here, and why now? An individual prays for help and is rescued. At the same time others caught in the same disaster, who are praying with equal desperation, are lost in the flood, airplane crash, or epidemic. Did they not pray hard enough, or not have enough people praying for them with enough faith and persistence? Also other forms of spiritual question appear when certain individuals are found able to exert extraordinary influence in their spiritual efforts and prayers. Saints, prophets, gurus, or holy hermits are regularly praised for the effectiveness of their prayers and guidance. Certain persons demonstrate the power to heal illnesses or give others comfort, counsel, and guidance. The suspicion of partiality in God's actions arises. Resentment over not being equally accepted or acceptable to God is a long-standing reaction in religious life, as demonstrated in the stories of the Hebrew Scriptures. The dramatic case of Cain and Abel is placed prominently at the start of history. Even to this day worrisome problems arise over whether God particularly loves and elects certain chosen ones. This apparent selectivity affronts believers because it appears to contradict other core revelations of the God who is impartial in bestowing love and wills equal justice for all. Christian Scriptures emphatically testify to God's universal inclusive love and desire that all be saved; God longs to shower good things upon all the beloved creation. Christ's saving love and teaching reveal God as the loving parent who desires union with each of God's children. Should not this impartial, infinite, and universal love mean equality in having petitions answered?

Skeptics, of course, brush away questions raised by answered prayers as one more characteristic of our "illusions of control," or false attributions of causality. Persons see cause and effect operating where none really exists. The illusion is sustained because when persons see positive results after some prayer they forget the many times when they prayed and nothing happened. Evidence that contradicts any cherished expectations tends to be discounted. People need to find meaning, a sense of control, and order in their lives, so they tend to focus upon events, that confirm their expectations and ignore disconfirming facts. Praying, like other superstitions or the gambler's belief in luck, remains part of a person's repertoire because positive "hits" are remembered and "misses" are not noticed. Admittedly the fact that a prayer was answered can never be proven without a doubt. After all, it is hard to sustain a claim that any single cause produces any specific effect even within a controlled laboratory environment. In real life there is always too much distracting "noise" to be able to establish convincing causal efficacy for anything such as prayer. Yet the faithful continue to testify that their prayers and petitions are answered, and produce concrete positive results in this world.

Certainly, the Hebrew Scriptures, the New Testament, and the subsequent history of the church give repeated witness to the power of prayerful petitions. How can believers understand the real power of prayer? Here reflections on failed petitions have relevance to the possibility of successful prayers as well. In an evolving open world there are times when God's universal beneficent desire to rescue and save is not blocked or resisted. When a prayer is answered, God's creativity has been able to operate through novelty, chance, and co-creators to out-maneuver negative conditions. Dynamic and loving creativity finds a new path or a new energy to remedy and change a situation. In between necessary invariant ordered laws and open, contingent "chance" events the continually emerging story of the universe can offer room or occasions for novelty and converging probabilities. The same freedom that brings the human capacity to choose sin or that can result in disordered natural systems can also produce the probability of beneficent outcomes. Whereas in popular parlance these positive effects are described as upward turns of the wheel of fortune, or gifts from Lady luck, Christians instead see these events as examples of God's continuing creation and active influence in a dynamic open universe. While God gives freedom to what is "not God" and respect to what has been created in the past, God also creates continually, sustaining and acting within all things moving to the future. Human hearts and minds that God has made in God's own image are particularly open to God's magnetic attraction. Human prayers for one another draw upon humanity's common shared nature and consciousness, as well as the Spirit of God within those praying and those prayed for. Humans are innately entangled with one another through love, reason, and emotional contagion. Since prayer is a personal act it may influence another person, especially a beloved person, more easily than moving mountains. The human nature and the indwelling Spirit that all humans share can provide a common milieu within which spiritual influence can operate. When I pray for someone my exercise of love and good intention cannot coerce their freedom, but it may increase the frequencies or the volume of the still small voice that stirs our common consciousness.

Answered prayers can be understood as the result of movement toward the complete rescue and communion that a God of Love is bringing about in the future, when *all* tears will be wiped away. In the cosmic narrative, conversions, change, discoveries, and surprises appear. The magnetic nonviolent workings of God's loving creativity may be either slow and subtle, or sudden and dramatic. Here too, cosmic evolution has been observed to show patterns of slow gradual change punctuated by larger shifts. A new species can be one kind of positive surprise. Positive spiritual surprises also occur against a background of stable growth. Different spiritual developments can be poetically described as the quiet gradual growth of seeds beneath the ground, or as rainbows that suddenly manifest divine epiphanies. Answered prayers that come about through convergences of contingencies and human action can be either small, gradual, and ordinary, or rare dramatic events that we call miracles because they astound. Whether small or large,

slow or sudden, answered prayers and miracles may only appear to be at odds with the ordinary ongoing lawful structures
that give stability and order to the universe. An older reading and theological interpretation of miracles overemphasized
their violent character as dramatic interventions and upheavals.
Miracles were thought to be manifestations of "supernatural"
interventions of the sovereign divinity acting from above the
clouds. This divine ruler was one who could, and would, arbitrarily disrupt creation in order to instill awe and compel
obedience. The more arbitrary and violent the event, the more
holy and divine it would be. But this reading of God's miracles and answered prayers scents those Hebrew Scriptures that
present images of God as the still small voice or a tender maternal caregiver. God is like the mother eagle protectively teaching
her chicks to fly; God is a nursing mother who will never abandon or forget her infant; God carries the people as ewes and
lambs are carried to safety over rough places.

Christians who have known Christ as God made visible in
humble service will affirm the nurturing images of Hebrew
tradition. Answered prayers and miracles will manifest God's
noncoercive cooperation and loving friendship with humankind. The greatest of all miracles is that God arrives as an
infant to pin humankind. God does not compel obedience
from afar but works through, in, and with the beloved creation. The Light comes into the world. God's power draws
others to participate in God's work of healing and renewal.
In one perspective miracles in the present draw upon dimensions and resources of the ever fruitful universe that are not
yet understood or not yet discovered. In a dynamic ongoing
cosmic narrative many potentials exist (especially in the brain
and consciousness) that are not yet explicitly known. A miracle
or answered prayer can be seen as an instance of what God and
humanity will co-create in the future. Present human abilities
to tap electrical energy to produce light or to use biochemical
drugs to regulate disordered organs are no longer viewed as

miracles. This view helps account for the fact that "miracles" of healing are found in many different religions by spiritual practitioners. Positive interventions are performed by shamans, gurus, and enlightened ones. Christians for their part will affirm that answered petitions and miracles are God working through, with, and in a dynamic natural creation.

In Christianity as in many other faiths answered prayers and miracles also have meaning as sign values.[9] Positive beneficent effects in response to prayer point to ultimate invisible reality beyond the visible. Whether slow and ordinary, or sudden and dramatic, answered prayers witness to the continuity of our everyday reality with the life of God upholding and grounding the present visible world. There is More to Reality than what we can see. The More may be interpreted in different ways, as it is in different religions, but it is the foundation of all that can be seen and known. Why is there something rather than nothing? Why have the wondrous universe and human awareness come into being? For those who have eyes to see, answered prayers and miracles testify that humans are related to the More that exists. Rescue, healing, and miracles large and small, mundane or dramatic, inform humankind of the good news.

In the Christian tradition we find an abundance of miracles and answered prayers. After all, Jesus Christ comes to reveal the good news that a loving personal God creates, intervenes, and saves this concrete everyday world beginning here and now. This saving action is taking place in world history and within each unique and specific individual life. The prophets of Judaism always understood that while God was transcendent and beyond all imagining, God was deeply concerned and intimately involved with His specific (and stiff-necked) people. Every thought and deed is important to God. Christians received this heritage and understand that history in its particular details is the means of carrying out the divine work. The understanding of the church as the continuation of Christ's body and life in the world expands the role of being chosen to do God's work. Everyone is uniquely called in a specific time and place.

Such understandings of the historically embedded process of receiving the gospel gives a further counterargument against the accusation of God's partiality and favoritism. All are equally loved, all are equally called, but each and every creature is different and has uniquely evolved in ongoing historical time and in a specific location. God works through these circumstances, which come about evolved partly through chance. A complicated evolved process affects the way great servants of God emerge in history. Those who are "chosen" and perform great spiritual works of mercy are not preferred in the way that a sovereign chooses court favorites for far greater access to power and influence. But different unique individuals will have different formative experiences in their different social and physical environments. Degree of readiness to hear God's word is an outcome of many convergent historical occurrences. Those who are ready have the God-given freedom to respond, ignore, or reject God's call. Those who assent are imbued with the power of God's Spirit; they are willing to say, "Yes, Lord, Here I am. Send me." Every free response to God produces an increased capacity to make a further response. Great saints become good friends with God because they keep saying yes and moving further along the path of prayer and love. Those who continually love and respond become transformed. As they deepen their union with God's love and truth they manifest God's power of loving and healing. Persons become tuned to God's reality and gain confidence to pray and work. Great saints always see themselves as instruments of God's love and healing power. And instruments, as in an orchestra, differ.

All human beings become children of God in their own specific way. There is always a family resemblance, but each member is unique. Instead of thinking in categories of greater, higher, lesser, or more powerful, the friends of God think of themselves as recipients of unique gifts and unique roles. The prayers of each will be equally pleasing to God. The hesitant humble prayer of the sinner or the child's innocent prayer is invited and welcomed. Those who have spiritual power in prayer gain it because they are humble and receptive to God. Friends of God grow to be like God as they become more themselves. At the same time those loving God and others intensely will ask for more — as lovers are emboldened to do. Disciples will persist in their petitions. Growing union with God gives persons a confidence in the Spirit's power. Love inspires persons to pay attention to the Spirit's presence in this very moment in this person, place, or event.

Trust in God's action in the world is strengthened through the understanding that when God becomes flesh, no chasm or split between matter and spirit can exist. This world and the next have been joined. In an interconnected dynamic universe groaning toward the fulfillment of new birth, conscious prayers, both individually and collectively offered, can be seen to infuse creation with the positive energy of loving intention, order, and meaningfulness. Today's science reveals the dynamic entangled processes of the universe operating at different levels and over distance. The famous butterfly effect in which the flutter of wings can influence the weather a continent away is a modern cliche. The interconnectedness of reality in interacting complicated systems is accepted in modern culture. Matter and energy are now known as equivalent, and new findings in physics of "action at a distance" point to the ways that information can be causally effective. Human beings are particularly entwined and entangled with one another and react powerfully to social influence. It is true, as the Gospels claim, that we are members of one another, and the life, death, and prayers of each one affects all.

A simplistic but suggestive analogy for the power of prayer is that of the magnifying glass, which can focus the sun's energy and light. Those who pray for God's loving intervention are like those who hold up a glass to the sun in order to focus and intensify the light that pervades the world. Light magnified and focused for a sufficient length of time can kindle fires upon the earth. The more glasses deployed and the longer the focus is held, the more enkindling. Scriptural commands to persist in prayer and pray without ceasing seem to acknowledge that spiritual energy and influence also accrue over time. But of course. Those who practice "folk Catholicism" have always championed repetition; novenas to St. Jude and other saints presume that persistence counts! Along with numbers! When one or two, or millions, pray together over time, more should be expected. The other point to be remembered is that prayers, or the deployment of magnifying glasses, are free acts of human initiative and stewardship. Humans exercise their co-creative roles in prayerful offering, ordering, and enacting God's love within the world.

Christians see a plenitude of positive influences shaping the history of the universe as well as influencing their own individual stories. Believers reflecting on their own past journeys experience an interesting phenomenon. A new event or new information gained in the present can transform the significance of the past. As a perceptive literary and cultural critic notes while writing about her family as Holocaust survivors, a novel occurrence can act "like some newly introduced bit of code that travels backwards through an entire text." The new event seems "to insert itself into the past and add its own information to my reading of my generations' story, and history."[10] The present thus decodes or transforms the meaning of the past. Similarly, disciples of Jesus who experienced the resurrection event read the Hebrew Scriptures in new ways and gave new significance to their past encounters with Jesus. Those who pray to the risen Lord can also discover anew how their prayers are answered slowly and unexpectedly.

God becomes acknowledged as a God of complicated surprises, both large and small. And here it is important to also note the tiny and humorous ways that prayers and pleas of daily life are answered. Every believer who prays has had experiences in which micro events surprised them, or benefited them, or provided flashes of insight. God seems to respond to certain petitions through the workings of our nonconscious minds. No one understands the multidimensioned operations of memory or intuition, but spontaneous ideas arrive, or elusive solutions pop into the mind. For example, while attempting to write the above lines describing the way present events decode the meaning of the past I was groping to remember where I had seen the reference. Where, oh where, dear God, was it? Suddenly, I had an impulse to cast my eye on a bookshelf and to pull down a book that opened to the very page and paragraph I had been seeking. No wonder the poets and artists of the ancient world envisioned the nine muses directly inspiring them. In such moments I give thanks to the God of small things who can work through the nonconscious mind. How fortunate that evolutionary processes have provided human brains with capacities for implicit thinking and remembering that can process more information than open to explicit self-awareness. When I pray to St. Anthony to help find my lost car keys and then find them, I give thanks for God's gift and merciful activation of implicit memory. Such tiny answered petitions are saved from being magic, I maintain, because I am not seeking domination over things, but humbly asking for help.

When it comes to large and desperate needs the prayers grow ever more humble and persistent. We pray without ceasing because we believe even unanswered prayers can have invisible results in the long, entangled, evolving movement of the Spirit toward God's fulfillment. Yet we are more emboldened by experiences of God doing novel, creative deeds in the here and now. Christians believe in answered prayer because we have already received so many gifts and been rescued so many times.

And yet for everyone the end game of old age and death approaches. As Montaigne wrote about dying, "Now we will see what is at the bottom of the pot." The last things approach. Prayers can now be focusing on the need to die in joyful hope. With death, remaining questions about suffering and joy in the afterlife loom large.

– Nine –

THE LIFE TO COME

⬥⬥⬥

I NTEREST IN LIFE after death is eternal. Anxiety over dying
is a perennial concern of human beings, and today there
is a virtual explosion of afterlife themes and scenarios to be
found in movies, television, novels, and theology. One source
of this interest may well be the spread into popular Western
culture of Eastern religious ideas of reincarnation. The view
that the soul progresses through many lifetimes has spread.
What happens in one incarnation determines what happens in
the next. The general assumption is that one lifetime is too
brief a period for a soul to learn all that it needs to learn on
the road to spiritual perfection. One short sprint around the
track is not long enough to achieve union with ultimate reality.

Another source of Western culture's resurging emphasis on
the afterlife may come from the growing awareness of modern
scientific and evolutionary concepts of time and matter. In the
light of billions of years of cosmic development, a single life
span, even of a hundred years, appears as a mere flicker. And
since the fate of the universe is subject to debate, no one knows
how many eons of time are yet to come. Moreover, spiritual
realities seem easier to consider when the universe appears so
mysterious, with multitudes of unsolved questions about the
nature of matter, time, and the number of dimensions in string
theory. Is there perhaps a parallel universe interacting with our
own? Scientists now deal with invisible realities and uncer-
tainties that cannot yet be proven by empirical evidence but
can only be reasoned and argued about. Religious arguments

employ reason in the same way and so can be given a hearing. When the confident certainty of reductionist materialism falters, societies become more open to spiritual concepts of continuing existence beyond the dissolution of the physical body. Moral questions, however, remain as obscure and difficult as ever. Christians who believe in the life to come differ in their beliefs and expectations.

Suffering, Joy, and the Life to Come

If and when a second act of existence begins, what hope can there be for just restitution? Can there be joy for the billions of innocent victims, including children, who have suffered and had their lives destroyed? And what is in store for the wicked who have inflicted cruel pain and misery upon others? Traditionally the Christian view of the afterlife has included a belief in God's just judgment, followed by the imposition of eternal punishment for sin. The sufferings imposed for sin would be either temporary, as in purgatory, or forever, as in hell. The hopelessly wicked are damned to suffer for all eternity; the imperfect are purified of their sins by suffering in purgatory. Good persons who have been forgiven their sins immediately enter into the joy of paradise. These views of life after death satisfied the requirements of God's justice.

A newer Christian view of judgment, suffering, and joy can contain many of the same traditional affirmations but reinterpret them in the light of God's maternal love and evolutionary thinking. Older hopes for universal salvation can be revived when God is known as ever patient, ever merciful, ever nurturing, and ever able to creatively draw new potential goods from evolving events over cosmic time. Since God's desire for the salvation of all has been proclaimed, it follows that God's loving invitation to each person could stand firm forever. Christ promises that the door that he has opened will never be shut. God, however, never coerces, so free human beings must give real assent to the loving relationship with God. With God-given freedom, humans retain the capacity to reject God's love and turn away from the Light. Now that "hell" is defined as the absence of God, the choice of hell must be an option for free creatures. But, say those who believe in universal salvation, would a choice to refuse God have to be a one-time decision that lasts forever? Persons who have repudiated God and the good might come to see the light, accept love, repent, and be forgiven. Conversion could always be a possibility. Turning toward God's love and light might happen because of further experience after death.

The other great hope for universal salvation comes from the fact that limited human beings are always operating in ignorance. Choices to reject God and the good may not be made with full knowledge. Humans are free agents, but it is also the case that their choices can be constrained and distorted by prior conditioning and deformations that were beyond their control. Today's understanding of the complex ways that humans are influenced for good or ill by other people and socio-biological pressures they encounter casts a different light on moral failures and sin. Humans are so innately susceptible to errors of thinking and feeling that they may be less responsible for wrongdoing than has been previously claimed. Fear of death and anxiety over survival infect human relationships from the beginning of life. Since all individuals are emotionally entangled and dependent upon others for their formation, infants and children can be damaged and inducted into morally distorted lives through no fault of their own. The sins of the fathers are passed on to new generations who can hardly know any better. Morals responding to the good may be all but impossible for many who start life in poisoned families living in cruel and immoral conditions. Human populations include many stunted, impaired, and morally limited persons who cause endless suffering for themselves and those around them. Cycles of violence and evil can be perpetuated without full moral awareness. In addition to their inherited vulnerabilities, humans are conditioned by social forces that are flawed by greed and violent exploitations.

Evil and suffering abound in history because of the intractability of inherited socio-biological wounds, environmental deprivations, abusive customs, and toxic social environments. These baleful conditions are sometimes called the sin of the world, and they create obstacles for moral growth and conversion. Moreover, even some individuals born into good families or morally advanced social groups can be born with impaired abnormal brain structures; they lack the normal ability to experience empathy or emotional attachments. The brain's mirror neuron systems may not function well enough for them to acquire morality through socialization. A multitude of accidents, injuries, diseases, and destructive traumas corrupt and wound bodies, minds, and psyches. Resources for receiving the good news can be so minimal that persons hardly have a chance to develop or mature morally. (For that matter, infant and child mortality, along with abortion, ensure that millions of human lives are ended before any self-consciousness begins.) Could all these human lives be lost forever?

A view of God as Mother affirms that God alone can read hearts and feel empathy with the ills that beset humankind. Will not God be as merciful as a mother in forgiving the "poor banished children of Eve"? When Jesus tells his disciples to judge not, he may be referring not only to God's sole prerogative, but to the unknown ability of the hidden wounds and weaknesses of those who do evil. God as love has come to liberate and save the poor suffering, benighted, and sinful people of the world, not to condemn them. And the divine healing powers must never be underestimated. Jesus, in the quest to reach all his brothers and sisters, is believed in one tradition to have gone to preach to the dead on Holy Saturday so that they could have a chance to hear the good news. Steadfast love finds a way — and never gives up.

Those who did not hear, or could not fully understand, or fearfully rejected the good may be open to conversion after death. But are there not evildoers who act with full knowledge and freedom in their cruel infliction of sufferings upon others? What happens to torturers, serial killers, child abusers, dictators, and other moral monsters in the next life? Many who make others suffer seem to take a perverted sadistic joy in their depravity. Other calculating evildoers impose cruelty in order to grasp social and economic advantages. For instance, those committing genocide are often partially motivated by the chance to appropriate the goods and property of their victims. Nazi collaborators who betrayed Jews could be rewarded with their possessions. Inflicting suffering upon others can be profitable and pleasurable for many. Sins of commission and omission can pay well — at least in the short run.

Certainly, at times, the wicked receive punishment in this world; they find themselves cut off from inner and external resources of love, friendship, and joy. The callousness and indifference it takes to wantonly harm others hardens and corrupts both the personality and mind. Suppressing sympathy and rejecting moral reasoning narrows consciousness and diminishes the emotional and intellectual capacities to cope with frustration and adversity. Hateful persons become loathed; they are isolated and often betrayed in their turn. Those dictators who send others to their deaths suspect and distrust others. Moreover, truly hardened sinners can be filled with raging destructive emotions such as hate, anger, greed, and fear. King Herod is said to have burst open and died, a symbolically appropriate end. While some of the wicked may receive various kinds of retribution in their earthly lives, those who do not and who never repent challenge those who preach God's saving mercy for all. Could the wicked ever repent — and how?

Some hope arises from the many historical examples of great sinners who in the midst of sin turned their lives around. "Amazing Grace" is a song written by a sea captain who was a slave trader and experienced a conversion. He was blind and then could see. God does not cease invitations to slavers or other sinners. In the heart of darkness, God's light can still be discovered. The divine influence appears to work through memory, imagination, empathy, and relationships with other people. Jesus in his life, death, and teaching always demonstrates God's unconditional, merciful forgiveness. God made visible in Jesus proclaims love for enemies and commands his disciples to love others as God in Christ loves them.

Jesus, however, does refer to the fires that punish sinners after death in recorded accounts of his teaching. Certain evildoers are described as being cast into outer darkness where there is great wailing and gnashing of teeth. The rich man who ignored Lazarus as he lay begging on his doorstep burns in flames after his death because he has failed to relieve the suffering at his gate. The parable of the sheep and goats ends with a judgment and punishment of those who failed to meet the needs of others. At the end of time the tares that have grown up with the wheat will be gathered up and thrown into the fire, and those towns that reject Christ's teaching and the coming of the kingdom will suffer. As for those who abuse the little ones it will be better that a millstone should be around their necks. These teachings and other visions of a final decisive judgment and an apocalyptic end time were used by Christians to affirm that there will be a divine judgment of human lives after death, accompanied by appropriate punishment or reward. Indeed, every word and deed in life will count. Jesus teaches that the person who contemptuously calls his brother a fool is in danger of hellfire, but a cup of water given in his name or the temple offering of the widow's mite will receive its reward.

Today, however, it is possible to understand that these punishing fires do not have to be understood literally, nor need they burn forever. Hell and heaven are not concrete "places" but ways to describe the absence or presence of God. It also can be seen that sufferings and pain could be present after death but not be coming from God's condemnation or punishment. In a risen life with no more death, disease, natural disorder, or entrenched human cruelty, only self-imposed, blameworthy suffering could still exist. If consciousness and self-identity through memory continue, the consequences of resistance to God would not automatically go away. But if God as pure positivity does not condemn or punish, then self-imposed suffering could be understood as reversible or limited. There could continue to exist the potential for sinners to learn and change, to repent and turn to love of God and neighbor. With an infinite God who makes all things new, it should never be too late to start afresh.

The suffering that arises after death can be seen as like that described in the traditional teaching of purgatory. These pains are limited and linked to the need to prepare persons to experience the fully blessed state. The sufferings in purgatory have been understood as goal-oriented processes that come to an end when growth and change take place. This view of limited self-imposed suffering oriented to a future end state assumes that some form of time exists. There is before, during, and after. Those who have insisted that the suffering of the damned must last eternally have based their belief partly on the affirmation that after death, earth's space-time runs out and with it opportunities to change. In an unchanging eternity there could be no second chances. Sinners would have had their one and only shot at salvation while alive on earth.

The argument for a decisive, irreversible, eternal damnation based on the nonexistence of any continuing time is not convincing. The doctrine of purgatory alone contradicts the assumption. But there is another argument for the hopelessness and eternity condition of "hell" that is more plausible. This view would maintain that sinners have had sufficient freedom in their past lives to choose evil over and over again; by these acts that are never repented they destroy all of their potential to respond to the good. Persons voluntarily harden their hearts and close their minds and so choose to become morally deaf, dumb, and blind. Sinners can no longer see, hear, or respond to love and goodness. Consequently, when the wicked man dies and meets Christ he cannot see or recognize him. In his past actions the sinner has repeatedly turned away from Christ in his neighbor or within himself. This self-imposed blindness of heart cannot be undone.

This story challenges the ground of Christian hope. Other depictions of life after death are equally pessimistic. Persons, or souls, are described as entering the next life without any insight, perhaps not even recognizing that they are dead. These scenarios are the exact opposite of depictions in the popular near-death literature in which the dying enter a tunnel and then experience a loving light that welcomes them into paradise where their families and friends await. In more depressing accounts of life after dying, personal continuity of the self survives death but there is no encountering a loving light, no paradise, no dramatic meetings with the Lord, nor any confrontation with God's judgment. The self is shown as operating in a space and time that is relaxed and flexible but still oriented to earthbound concerns. In several recent best sellers of life after death, God and Christ are noticeably absent. A traditional heaven is at best only a distant rumor. As you learn wisdom from the five people you meet in heaven, or bask in your own particular heaven, surviving selves attend mostly to the people and concerns left behind. One recent novel begins with the narrator describing her own rape and murder; she lives in an oddly bland heaven, sans God, but she minutely participates in her family's search for her lovely bones hidden by her serial killer. In other grim depictions of life after death persons wander around aimlessly in boring bewilderment.

Occasionally, popular culture produces comic depictions of the afterlife — usually by way of Hollywood. These may feature romancing ghosts or tales of remedial learning, or some combination of both. In the movie *Groundhog Day* viewers watch the progress of a selfish, arrogant young man who after dying finds himself forced to live the same day over and over again until at last he grows wiser and more kindhearted. Each morning he awakes to the prospect of repeating the same episodes with the same people in the same settings. Gradually he begins to respond differently and manages to win the heart of the girl he loves. The movie uses flashbacks and identical replays of incidents to show the hero painfully and hilariously learning to get each encounter right. Eventually, after the young oaf has learned to love and be considerate of others, he gets his girl and is resurrected into the joy of a day in which he can have new life experiences.

Two points will spark the interest of moviegoers who are theologically inclined. First it takes a whole community of townspeople and friends to reeducate this rude and selfish young man. Friends and acquaintances correct and encourage his good behavior and just as important, allow him to help them in turn. Second, the personal transformation of the hero takes time and repeated opportunities for new experiences, humorous though some are. While this account of the afterlife is comic, many others present chilling landscapes that echo traditional depictions of the anterooms of hell, if not hell itself. If it is the case that many people who die do not discern the presence of a loving Lord offering them hope of salvation, would they be lost forever? Should all hope be abandoned? I think not.

Even if Christ is not met or cannot be recognized at the moment of death, surely *someone* could be encountered. No conscious self can cease relating or responding to others. Certainly any human person who has ever achieved self-awareness will have been socially embedded in personal relationships. Each self that is morally responsible enough to sin, or free enough to choose to reject the good, will have arrived at that condition through interaction with other selves. In order to survive at all, human beings from infancy onward have to be provided with food, shelter, and emotional attachments that make social learning possible. Even abandoned street children in the slums or orphaned concentration camp children have been able to bond with their peers.

The most depraved and darkened sinner could still possess the remains of the day. Everyone was once a baby before becoming a moral monster. Hitler seems to have loved his mother and Stalin his daughter. Often too, aesthetic sensibilities and abstract intelligence exist in corrupt persons. Intellectual abilities may be honed in lives where moral and emotional intelligence is stunted or distorted. While the capacity for positive feeling and love may become frozen, even hardened sinners remain human. Believers in universal salvation will affirm that no member of the human species made in the image of God can completely destroy the imprint of that gift. Love and life will always retain more resilient energies and resources for transformation than the forces of evil.

Surely, lingering positive involvement with other people and with the goods of creation can provide the opening for God's nurturing and tutorial work. And here once again Christians have to pay attention to their own mission of co-creation. If it takes a village to raise a child, it can take a communion of saints to enlighten and heal sinners — before and after death. A company of holy friends of God can embrace and befriend those who have lost their way. A person is going to meet more than five people in heaven. Surely, those who already enjoy life with God will be ardently ready to love and work to relieve suffering. The Catholic *Catechism* affirms that "in the glory of heaven the blessed continue joyfully to fulfill God's will in relation to other men and to all creation" (no. 1029). The God of loving surprises, who is ever new and a fountain of dynamic novelty, can provide friends and co-creators work to do. One of the greatest joys of human life is to heal, teach, befriend, and comfort others in need. The blessed workers in God's vineyard can be called to love and nurture their suffering brothers and sisters into their fulfillment. Instead of a heaven spent enjoying the "edifying" shrieks of the damned who suffer in hellfire, as Jonathan Edwards imagined, the blessed will feel empathy and love. They will be as intent as their physician, friend, and teacher to alleviate suffering and inspire new transformations.

I think we can now imagine an afterlife filled with many sojourners on the pilgrim path. Those further along in the way, the truth, and the life will delight in helping others into the Light, out of their gloom and misery. Of course, the great challenge for anyone engaged with resistant sinners is to break open the imprisoning chains of stubborn isolation. Breaching fortified defenses is never easy. Here the lessons of Helen Keller's journey come to mind. As a child Helen was struck irreversibly blind, deaf, and dumb, the result of an illness she had suffered as a toddler. In her misery she became violent and full of rage. When her teacher Annie Sullivan came to rescue this wild child, Helen's sense of touch was the only channel of communication open. With heroic persistence and creativity, Helen's teacher slowly brought her out of her isolation into the world of meaningful symbols, love, and joy. So Christ, our Teacher and physician, liberates us, but God's saving work is also done through "other Christs" in love of neighbor.

Hope affirms that hardened sinners can be brought out of their numbness or selfish rage but not easily. Hellish desolation has been aptly depicted by Dante as being paralyzed in ice. Hellish aggression and envious anger have been imagined as burning in fiery torment. Torture chambers and prison camps in this world feature fiery pain as well as icy boredom, impotence, and apathy. Dramatic visions of hell can now be complemented by understandings of evil persons as shallow, trivial, and boring. The "banality of evil" is a modern phrase that applies to many perpetrators of genocide and serial killers. Eichmann and Pol Pot are prime instances of the hollow men inhabiting the heart of darkness.

Other challenges for healers can be gleaned from the accounts of the mentally ill and those afflicted with brain dysfunctions and impairments. Patients describe dreadful experiences of being depersonalized, disembodied, fragmented, and numbed. Dreaded attacks of intense anxiety and panic threaten disintegration and dissolution of the self. The desolations of severe depressions are described as darkness made visible. Unlike the wicked, the mentally ill are not culpable or responsible for their sufferings, but their conditions cast light on the power of evil. How can such misery be alleviated? Those who are solidly frozen and entombed will, like Helen Keller, require the greatest efforts to rescue. At least the wicked who wail and gnash their teeth can have access to their inner pain. Those persons who have been expert in calculating and inflicting suffering upon their victims may learn to acknowledge their own deprived depravity as they experience new self-other communications. For instance, new victim education programs in prisons have been successful in enlarging the empathy awareness of predators. By talking and listening to their victims and their families, they learn what their cruelty caused. Other "miracles" of loving transformations are experienced in families who do not give up on their prodigal children.

After death there may exist expanded dimensions of reality that make loving strategies of change possible. This hope persists despite the admission that it is impossible to fully imagine such a future. If we image our present bodies as seeds being sown at death which will be raised to a new life, we get a good sense of the limitations our minds face. When physicists talk today of the existence of eleven dimensions of reality beyond our familiar four dimensions of space-time, it is another sign of the challenges of the completely new. When the curtain goes up on the next act, what might exist?

One guess is that human consciousness of time would be expanded so that all of a person's life experience could be simultaneously present. It makes no sense to think that a person who dies in a demented or diseased state would have their identity confined to their last seconds. Many people facing accidental deaths have spoken of an instantaneous life review flashing through the mind's eye. Even in ordinary conditions of life our memories have the power to move back and forth through time to produce vivid experiences of the past. After death an expanded time consciousness of past experiences that were formerly obscured could provide conditions for moral conversion. Encountering the unveiled reality of a life's embedded self-other relationships would be searing. To see clearly all the entangled human acts and events of one's life and realize all the suffering and harm that you have done to others (and to self) would be dreadful. To feel one's whole history, undimmed by the fog of denial or evasive defenses, would be a form of purgatorial suffering. No more questions would have to be asked such as, "When did we see you hungry?" For the first time, in the mirror, the image of one would not be obscured. In the Light all secrets stand revealed. An individual would not only know, but actually feel, the harm that he or she has done. Sins of omission could also become clear. Those sufferings that you might have relieved but did not would cause pain.

Such self-awareness would engender guilt, shame, and other forms of suffering. Only the most exceptional persons of the highest virtue and goodness could be spared the experiences of burning knowledge. Saints would fare well because they would already have practiced severely honest examinations of conscience; they would already have suffered contrition, repentance, and made confession with amends for harms they have done. The more ordinary Christian also could have sought forgiveness and attempted reparations. But even the best and the brightest might feel pangs of regret upon seeing what more they might have been, and what more achieved. The tolls of the road not taken may be paid in full. To know one's self as one has been known could be an agonizing confrontation. Once awakened and engaged, the sense or conscience imposes its own punishment. Conscience as the God-given sacred self-monitor can be diminished and denied, but not destroyed. Moral sufferings, arising in face-to-face encounters with the Light of Truth and Love, are self-imposed. No punitive God of wrath or torturing demons with pitchforks and fire are required for self-imposed retribution.

As sinners and other pilgrims expand their awareness and empathy, their desires for healing, growth, and progress on the path to love increase. Love begets joy — and more love. Perhaps even the saints keep growing in the friendship with an infinite God. The idea of a heaven of passive rest seems inadequate to the dynamic nature of God. Indeed, one important move toward wholeness within the family of God would be the reconciling of victims and their abusers. Understanding and repenting of the pain that one has given others would lead to actively seeking forgiveness from those one has injured. Such difficult acts of reconciliation can be imagined to occur in a future life because heroic acts of forgiveness happen here and now. Victims forgive those who tortured, them and parents forgive the criminals on death row who murdered their children. Riven societies have set up successful truth and reconciliation commissions after violent civic convulsions of guerrilla wars.

Extreme situations, however, are not the only occasions where forgiveness and peacemaking are expressed. Ordinary persons come to forgiveness in family life, in therapy groups, or in Twelve-Step programs such as AA. Healing comes from apologies and amends offered and usually accepted. In fact, if evolutionary psychologists are correct, conflict resolution and peacemaking may be an innately evolved human trait. Evidence from early human societies points to rituals of healing and reconciliation. If forgiveness can take place in less than ideal circumstances without the possibility of restitution, then surely in a risen renewed life victims can forgive their tormentors and oppressors. Joy and positive emotions have the power to undo negative emotions. When death is undone and all are reunited, then parents, children, abusers, and victims can start afresh. When persons have themselves been forgiven and loved by Christ within God's family, then healing and conversion should become easier. The knowledge that losses can be restored gives joy. Thomas More said to his betrayers before his beheading that he expected to meet them in heaven where they would be merry together. Infinite new possibilities and gifts of love can expand the heart to achieve miracles of mercy in God's peaceable kingdom. The lion can lie down with the lamb, and those whose children have been murdered and maimed in genocides and holocausts can return good for evil. Hope for the overcoming of suffering springs from faith in the power of joy.

Joy

In God's time all the damaged, impaired, distorted lives cut off without a chance can have their chance to bloom. The prophet Isaiah proclaims the good news that in God's holy presence there will be no death of infants or young mothers, or countless victims of lethal violence. The resurrection of Jesus ensures the fruition of many innocent lives whose time on earth was cut short and deformed. God can grant new life and love for all, including the most vulnerable and flickering of lives. The nurturing and caretaking, the gardening and watering of lives can be joyfully carried out by the strong and good. Those who have spent their earthly lives taking joy in all the different deeds of mercy will continue their work in gladness. It is not a new thought that human beings could delight in ministering to one another forever. Mothers and lovers understand.

Many who die in doubt and unbelief will be surprised by joy; they will feel amazed wonder at the love and truth they encounter. At last they will be able to see and understand the evolving world and their role in the drama of creation. To know and understand gives intellectual joy. All will see that a loving God does not send suffering but rather intends the joyful flourishing of creation. In the great unveiling it will be manifest why and how incompleteness, ignorance, and resistance to God causes so much harm. While God's subtle creative influence never coerces or violates human freedom, wickedness can be outwitted and wither away. Suffering and sin will never be forgotten or changed into a good thing, but they can be remembered as but temporary obstacles that God's love dissolves. In an infinite creative story, the horrors of suffering that have been endured can become an ever fainter thread woven in an unfolding tapestry of glory and joy. In every event whatever potential good that can be harvested will be gathered into the whole. The creative good work of humankind will also become manifest. Now it also will not be necessary to ask: When did we see you needy and give you comfort? Or speak that word of admonition or encouragement? All of the hidden sacrifices and efforts toward justice and charity will become known. The last will be first. The Light will shine on secret treasure and unsung gifts. The pangs of every birth will not be forgotten. Dame Julian, the great mystical visionary, foresees a radiant Christ meeting each new entrant into heaven with the words, "Thank you for your sufferings, especially when young." Julian of Norwich prophetically conveys God's maternal graciousness and tenderness.

Joy is the greatest mystery; the love of God is beyond human comprehension. Slowly growing up into Christ's fullness, human beings are infants who but dimly perceive the glory. Yet we see enough to trust that "all will be well, all will be very well."

NOTES

1. Suffering

1. Ann-Marie MacDonald, *The Way the Crow Flies* (New York: HarperCollins, 2003), 617.

2. John Paul II, *Apostolic Letter Salvifici Doloris: On the Christian Meaning of Human Suffering,* February 11, 1984, IV, 15.

3. Nicholas Wolterstorff, *Lament for a Son* (Grand Rapids: Eerdmans, 1987), 63.

4. See Gustavo Gutiérrez, *God-Talk and the Suffering of the Innocent* (Maryknoll, N.Y.: Orbis, 1988).

5. Wolterstorff, *Lament for a Son,* 89.

6. Nicholas Lash, *Believing Three Ways in One God: A Reading of the Apostles' Creed* (Notre Dame, Ind.: University of Notre Dame Press, 1992), 10.

7. See Ariel Glucklich, *Sacred Pain: Hurting the Body for the Sake of the Soul* (Oxford: Oxford University Press, 2001).

8. Daniel Harrington, S.J., *Why Do We Suffer? A Scriptural Approach to the Human Condition* (Franklin, Wisc.: Sheed & Ward, 2000), 1.

9. Jerome Miller, *The Way of Suffering: A Geography of Crisis* (Washington, D.C.: Georgetown University Press, 1988), 175.

10. Eric J. Cassell, *The Nature of Suffering: And the Goals of Medicine* (New York: Oxford University Press, 1991), 33.

11. Ibid., 36.

12. Glucklich, *Sacred Pain.*

13. See Arthur W. Frank, *At the Will of the Body* (New York: First Mariner Books Edition, 2002).

14. William Styron, *Darkness Visible: A Memoir of Madness* (New York: Vintage Books, 1990), 38, 50.

15. Scott Kiser, "An Existential Case Study of Madness: Encounters with Divine Affliction," *Journal of Humanistic Psychology* 44, no. 4 (Fall 2004): 441.

16. See Anne Applebaum, *Gulag: A History* (New York: Anchor Books, 2003).

17. Richard Rhodes, *Masters of Death: The SS Einsatzgruppen and the Invention of the Holocaust* (New York: Alfred A. Knopf, 2002), 22

18. Elaine Scarry, *The Body in Pain: The Making and Unmaking of the World* (New York: Oxford University Press, 1985).

19. Sister Diana Ortiz, with Patricia Davis, *The Blindfold's Eyes: My Journey from Torture to Truth* (Maryknoll, N.Y.: Orbis Books, 2002), 64.

20. See Susan Griffen, *A Chorus of Stones* (New York: Doubleday, 1992).

21. Edward Schillebeeckx, *Christ: The Experience of Jesus as Lord* (New York: Crossroad, 1989).

22. Simone Weil, *Waiting for God* (New York: Harper & Row, 1951), 121.

23. Dorothee Soelle, *Suffering* (Philadelphia: Fortress Press, 1975), 68.

24. Albert Camus, *The Plague* (New York: Vintage, 1991), 182.

25. Ibid., 181.

26. Elizabeth Robinson, *The True and Outstanding Adventures of the Hunt Sisters* (New York: Little Brown, 2004), 148.

27. Quentin Smith, "Big Bang Cosmology and Atheism," *Free Inquiry* 18, no. 2 (Spring 1998): 35.

2. The Plan?

1. St. Vincent de Paul, conferences quoted in *Magnificat* (September 2003): 353.

2. George H. Tavard, "The Mystery of Divine Providence," *Theological Studies* 64 (2003): 712.

3. Ariel Glucklich, *Sacred Pain: Hurting the Body for the Sake of the Soul* (Oxford: Oxford University Press, 2001), 153–78.

4. Robert A. Orsi, *Between Heaven and Earth: The Religious Worlds People Make and the Scholars Who Study Them* (Princeton, N.J.: Princeton University Press, 2005), 21

5. Marjorie Williams, *The Woman at the Washington Zoo: Writings on Politics, Family, and Fate* (New York: Public Affairs, 2005), 343; see also Harold S. Kushner, *When Bad Things Happen to Good People* (New York: Schocken, 1981).

6. A description of the debate and its philosophical implications are discussed in Susan Neiman, *Evil in Modern Thought: An Alternative History of Philosophy* (Princeton, N.J.: Princeton University Press, 2002).

7. Ibid., 249.

8. Ibid., 243.

9. Ibid., 287.

10. Ibid.

11. For a thorough discussion of these problems, see Marilyn McCord Adams, *Horrendous Evils and the Goodness of God* (Ithaca, N.Y.: Cornell University Press, 1999).

12. See George M. Marsden, *Jonathan Edwards: A Life* (New Haven, Conn.: Yale University Press, 2003).

13. Ibid., 187, 328.

14. Albert Camus, *The Plague* (New York: Vintage, 1991), 224–25.

15. Quoted in Jonathan Bennett, "The Conscience of Huckleberry Finn," *Philosophy* 49 (1974): 123–34.

16. David C. Toole, "Divine Ecology and the Apocalypse: A Theological Description of Natural Disasters and the Environmental Crisis," *Theology Today* 55, no. 4 (January 1999): 551.

3. God and Creation

1. C. S. Lewis, *A Grief Observed,* large print edition (London: Faber and Faber, 1961), 32.

2. Ibid., 40.

3. Ibid., 24.

4. J. M. Coetzee, *Elizabeth Costello* (London: Secker & Warburg, 2003), 205.

5. James Alison, "The Wild Ride," *The Tablet,* June 3, 2006, 5.

6. Edward Schillebeeckx as quoted in Lucien Richard, O.M.I., *What Are They Saying about the Theology of Suffering?* (Mahwah, N.J.: Paulist, 1992).

7. See John F. Haught, *God after Darwin: A Theology of Evolution* (Boulder, Colo.: Westview Press, 2000).

8. John Polkinghorne, ed., *The Work of Love: Creation as Kenosis* (Grand Rapids: Eerdmans, 2001), 94.

9. Ann Pedersen, *God, Creation, and All That Jazz* (St. Louis: Chalice Press, 2000); see also Elizabeth Johnson, "Does God Play Dice? Divine Providence and Chance," *Theological Studies* 57 (1996): 3–18.

10. Nicholas Lash, *Believing Three Ways in One God: A Reading of the Apostles' Creed* (Notre Dame, Ind.: University of Notre Dame Press, 1992), 53.

11. See Thomas G. Weinandy, *Does God Suffer?* (Notre Dame, Ind.: University of Notre Dame Press, 2000).

12. David Tracy, *Blessed Rage for Order* (San Francisco: Harper & Row, 1988), 179.

13. See Edward Farley, *Divine Empathy: A Theology of God* (Minneapolis: Fortress, 1996).

14. Tracy, *Blessed Rage for Order*, 183.

4. Jesus Saves

1. C. S. Lewis, *A Grief Observed,* large print edition (London: Faber and Faber, 1961), 25.

2. A clear and engaging description of historical theories of redemption can be found in Colleen Carpenter Cullinan, *Redeeming the Story: Women, Suffering, and Christ* (New York: Continuum, 2004).

3. James Wood, *The Book against God* (New York: Farrar, Straus & Giroux, 2003), 55.

4. See Robert J. Daly, S.J., "Sacrifice Unveiled or Sacrifice Revisited: Trinitarian and Liturgical Perspectives," *Theological Studies* 64, no. 1 (March 2003): 24–42.

5. Different models of salvation are described in Richard J. Clifford, S.J., and Khaled Anatoloios, "Christian Salvation: Biblical and Theological Perspectives," *Theological Studies* 66 (2005): 739–69.

6. Catherine Mowry LaCugna, *God for Us: The Trinity and Christian Life* (San Francisco: HarperSanFrancisco, 1991); see also Kathryn Tanner, *Jesus, Humanity, and the Trinity: A Brief Systematic Theology* (Minneapolis: Fortress, 2001).

7. See Lucien Richard, O.M.I., *Christ the Self-Emptying of God* (Mahwah, N.J.: Paulist, 1997).

8. Romanus Cessario, O.P., *Introduction to Moral Theology* (Washington, D.C.: Catholic University of America Press, 2001), 212.

9. See N. T. Wright, *The Resurrection of the Son of God* (Minneapolis: Fortress, 2003).

10. John Donne, "Holy Sonnet XV," in *Selections from Divine Poems, Sermons, Devotions, and Prayers* (New York: Paulist Press, 1990), 82.

11. Mary Grey, *Feminism, Redemption, and the Christian Tradition* (Mystic, Conn.: Twenty-Third Publications, 1990), 177; see also Elizabeth A. Johnson, *She Who Is: The Mystery of God in Feminist Theological Discourse* (New York: Crossroad, 1991).

12. Michael Albus, "Spirit and Fire: An Interview with Hans Urs von Balthasar," *Communio* 32 (Fall 2005): 592.

5. Jesus the Man of Sorrows

1. Jean-Pierre Batut, "Does the Father Suffer?" *Communio* 30 (Fall 2003): 386–405.

2. Mark Danner, "Abu Ghraib: The Hidden Story," *New York Review of Books*, October 7, 2004.

3. Elizabeth A. Johnson, C.S.J., *Consider Jesus: Waves of Renewal in Christology* (New York: Crossroad, 1993), 19–34.

4. See Robert Karris, *Prayer and the New Testament* (New York: Crossroad, 2000).

5. Johnson, *Consider Jesus,* 115–27.

6. Kevin Burke, S.J., *The Ground beneath the Cross: The Theology of Ignacio Ellacuría* (Washington, D.C.: Georgetown University Press, 2000), 180.

7. See Joseph A. Komonchak, "The Violence of the Cross: A Mystery, Not a Punishment." *Commonweal,* January 28, 2005, 19–22.

8. Karl Rahner, "Why Does God Allow Us to Suffer?" *Theological Investigations* 19 (New York: Crossroad, 1983), 203.

9. John Paul II, *Apostolic Letter Salvifici Doloris: On the Christian Meaning of Human Suffering,* February 11, 1984, vi, 27.

10. Baron Friedrich von Hügel, *Letters to a Niece,* quoted in Paul Elie, *The Life You Save May Be Your Own: An American Pilgrimage* (New York: Farrar, Straus & Giroux, 2003), 282.

11. Johnson, *Consider Jesus,* 60.

12. Images of Christ as a hero rescuing captives in hell are described in Alister E. McGrath, *A Brief History of Heaven* (Oxford: Blackwell Publishing, 2003), 88–94. This view is quite different from the concept of Christ's experience of being abandoned to sin and suffering during Holy Saturday. The activity of the medieval tradition of heroic harrowing, although violent, seems more accurate.

6. Suffering in Practice

1. Lucien Richard, O.M.I., *What Are They Saying about the Theology of Suffering?* (Mahwah, N.J.: Paulist, 1992), 54.

2. Sebastian Moore, "A Note on the Cult of Suffering," in *The Crucified Jesus Is No Stranger* (New York: Seabury Press, 1981), 23.

3. There are many feminist analyses of women's secondary roles in the world and the church which are encouraged by the valorization of suffering; see Elizabeth A. Johnson, C.S.J., *She Who Is: The Mystery of God in Feminist Theological Discourse* (New York: Crossroad, 1991).

4. Roy Schafer, "The Pursuit of Failure and the Idealization of Unhappiness,"*American Psychologist* 39, no. 4 (April 1984): 405–17.

5. Fyodor Dostoevsky, *Notes from Underground* (New York: Vintage Books, 1993), 34.

6. Norman Marcus, *The Hooligan's Return* (New York: Farrar, Straus & Giroux, 2003), 246.

7. Elizabeth V. Spelman, *Fruits of Sorrow: Framing Our Attention to Suffering* (Boston: Beacon Press, 1997), 127.

8. See Paul G. Crowley, S.J., *Unwanted Wisdom: Suffering, the Cross, and Hope* (New York: Continuum, 2005).

9. Kristine M. Rankka, *Women and the Value of Suffering* (Collegeville, Minn.: Liturgical Press, 1998), 232.

10. Eva Hoffman, *After Such Knowledge: Memory, History, and the Legacy of the Holocaust* (New York: Public Affairs, 2004), 49.

11. John Paul II, *Apostolic Letter Salvifici Doloris: On the Christian Meaning of Human Suffering,* February 11, 1984, v, 23.

12. Jack Gilbert, "A Brief for the Defense," in *New Yorker,* November 15, 2004, 86.

7. Joy

1. Yehuda Amichai, "The Precision of Pain and the Blurriness of Joy," *New York Review of Books,* February 18, 1999, 10.

2. Frederick Douglass, *The Life and Times of Frederick Douglass* (Ware, Hertfordshire: Wordsworth, 1996), 152.

3. Gerard Manley Hopkins, *Poems of Gerard Manley Hopkins,* 3rd ed. (Oxford: Oxford University Press, 1948), 70.

4. Ibid.

5. Czeslaw Milosz, *New and Collected Poems, 1931–2001* (New York: HarperCollins, 2003), 70.

6. Michael Frayn, *A Landing on the Sun* (New York: Viking, 1991), 195.

7. Abraham H. Maslow, *Motivation and Personality* (New York: Harper & Row, 1970).

8. William James, *The Varieties of Religious Experience* (New York: Modern Library, 1936), 16.

9. See Barbara L. Frederickson, "What Good Are Positive Emotions?" *Review of General Psychology* 2, no. 3 (September 1998): 300–319.

10. See Martin E. P. Seligman, *Authentic Happiness* (New York: Free Press, 2002).

11. See Timothy D. Wilson, *Strangers to Ourselves: Discovering the Adaptive Unconscious* (Cambridge, Mass.: Harvard University Press, 2002).

12. See Mihalyi Csikszentimihalyi, *Flow: The Psychology of Optimal Experience* (New York: Harper & Row, 1990).

13. See Mark Kingwell, *In Pursuit of Happiness: Better Living from Plato to Prozac* (New York: Crown Publishers, 1998).

14. See Daniel N. Stern, *The Interpersonal World of the Infant* (New York: Basic Books, 1985).

15. Barbara L. Frederickson and M. F. Losada, "Positive Affect and the Complex Dynamics of Human Flourishing," *American Psychologist* 60, no. 7 (October 2005): 678–86.

16. Barbara L. Frederickson, R. A. Mancuso, C. Branigan, and M. M. Tugade, "The Undoing Effect of Positive Emotions," *Motivation and Emotion* 24 (2000): 237–58.

17. See Stephen G. Post, Byron Johnson, and Michael E. McCullough, Jeffrey P. Schloss, eds., *Research on Altruism and Love* (Philadelphia: Templeton Foundation Press, 2003).

18. Charles Taylor, *A Catholic Modernity?* ed. James L. Heft (Oxford: Oxford University Press, 2003).

19. Jeff T. Larsen, Peter A. McGraw and John T. Cacioppo, "Can People Feel Happy and Sad at the Same Time?" *Journal of Personality and Social Psychology* 81, no. 4 (October 2001): 684–96.

20. Julian of Norwich, *Revelations of Divine Love* (New York: Penguin Books, 1998), 63, 64.

21. See Daniel Goleman, *Emotional Intelligence* (New York: W. W. Norton, 1995).

22. Georges Bernanos, *A Diary of a Country Priest* (New York: Macmillan, 1937), 236.

8. Prayer

1. Karl Rahner, "The Apostolate of Prayer," *Theological Investigations* 3 (London: Darton, Longman & Todd, 1963), 209–19.

2. James Alison, *The Joy of Being Wrong: Original Sin through Easter Eyes* (New York: Crossroad, 1998), 144.

3. See Patrick Collins, *Prayer in Practice* (Maryknoll, N.Y.: Orbis Books, 2001).

4. Ibid., 16.

5. See James W. Douglass, *The Nonviolent Coming of God* (Maryknoll, N.Y.: Orbis Books, 1991).

6. Illia Delio, O.S.F., "Is Creation Eternal?" *Theological Studies* 66, no. 2 (June 2005): 279–303.

7. John Polkinghorne, ed., "Kenotic Creation and Divine Action," in *The Work of Love: Creation as Kenosis* (Grand Rapids: Eerdmans, 2001), 102–3.

8. Brian Greene, *The Fabric of the Cosmos: Space, Time, and the Texture of Reality* (New York: Knopf, 2004), 194–99.

9. See Kenneth L. Woodward, *The Book of Miracles: The Meaning of the Miracle Stories in Christianity, Judaism, Buddhism, Hinduism, Islam* (New York: Simon & Schuster, 2000).

10. Eva Hoffman, *After Such Knowledge: Memory, History, and the Legacy of the Holocaust* (New York: Public Affairs, 2004), 241.

BIBLIOGRAPHY

Ackroyd, Peter. *The Life of Thomas More*. New York: Doubleday, 1998.

Adams, Marilyn McCord. *Horrendous Evils and the Goodness of God*. Ithaca, N.Y.: Cornell University Press, 1999.

Albus, Michael. "Spirit and Fire: An Interview with Hans Urs von Balthasar." *Communio* 32 (Fall 2005): 573–93.

Alison, James. *The Joy of Being Wrong: Original Sin through Easter Eyes*. New York: Crossroad, 1998.

———. "The Wild Ride." *The Tablet*, June 3, 2006, 5.

American Psychologist, special Issue on Happiness, Excellence and Optimal Human functioning, 55, no. 1 (January 2000).

Amichai, Yehuda. "The Precision of Pain and the Blurriness of Joy." *New York Review of Books,* February 18, 1999.

Applebaum, Anne. *Gulag: A History*. New York: Anchor Books, 2003.

Armstrong, Karen. *Buddha*. New York: Penguin Books, 2001.

Balthasar, Hans Urs von. "Joy and the Cross: Retrieving the Tradition." *Communio* 31 (Summer 2004): 332–44.

———. "Spirit and Fire: An Interview with Hans Urs von Balthasar." *Communio* 32 (Fall 2005): 573–93.

Barbour, Ian G. *Religion and Science: Historical and Contemporary Issues*. San Francisco: HarperSanFrancisco, 1997.

Barrett, Lisa Feldman, Paula M. Niedenthal, and Piotr Winkielman, eds. *Emotion and Consciousness*. New York: Guilford Press, 2005.

Barret, L. Feldman, and J. Russell. "Independence and Bipolarity in the Structure of Affect." *Journal of Personality and Social Psychology* 74 (1998): 967–84.

Batut, Jean-Pierre. "Does the Father Suffer?" *Communio* 30 (Fall 2003): 386–405.

Bennett, Jonathan. "The Conscience of Huckleberry Finn." *Philosophy* 49 (1974): 123–34.

Bernanos, Georges. *A Diary of a Country Priest*. New York: Macmillan, 1937.

Billy, Dennis J., and James F. Keating. *Conscience and Prayer*. Collegeville, Minn.: Liturgical Press, 2001.

Black, David M., ed. *Psychoanalysis and Religion in the 21st Century: Competitors or Collaborators?* London and New York: Routledge, 2006.

Borgmann, Albert. "Contingency and Grace in an Age of Science and Technology." *Theology Today* 59, no. 1 (April 2002): 6–20.

Bouchard, Charles E., O.P. "Recovering the Gifts of the Holy Spirit in Moral Theology." *Theological Studies* 63, no. 3 (September 2002): 539–58.

Bracken, Joseph A., S.J. *The One in the Many: A Contemporary Reconstruction of the God-World Relationship*. Grand Rapids: Eerdmans, 2001.

———. "Images of God within Systematic Theology." *Theological Studies* 63 (2002): 362–73.

Brown, Peter. *The Rise of Western Christendom*. 2nd ed. Oxford: Blackwell, 2003.

Burke, Kevin F., S.J. *The Ground beneath the Cross: The Theology of Ignacio Ellacuría*. Washington, D.C.: Georgetown University Press, 2000.

Bynum, Caroline Walker. *Jesus as Mother: Studies in the Spirituality of the High Middle Ages*. Berkeley: University of California Press, 1982.

Byrne, Patrick H. "Evolution, Randomness, and Divine Purpose: A Reply to Cardinal Schoenborn." *Theological Studies* 67, no. 3 (September 2006): 653–65.

Cacioppo, J. T., and W. L. Gardner. *Emotion: Annual Review of Psychology* 50 (1999): 191–214.

Cacioppo, J. T., W. L. Gardner, and G. G. Bernston. "The Affect System Has Parallel and Integrative Processing Component: Form Follows Function." *Journal of Personality and Social Psychology* 76, no. 5 (1999): 839–55.

Callahan, Sidney. *In Good Conscience: Reason and Emotion in Moral Decision Making*. San Francisco: HarperSanFrancisco, 1991.

———. "The Psychology of Emotion and the Ethics of Care." In *Medicine and the Ethics of Care,* ed. Diana Fritz Cates and Paul Lauritzen. Washington, D.C.: Georgetown University Press, 2001.

———. *Women Who Hear Voices: The Challenge of Religious Experience*. Mahwah, N.J.: Paulist Press, 2003.

Camus, Albert. *The Plague*. New York: Vintage, 1991.

Carstensen, L. L., H. L. Fung, and S. T. Charles. "Socioemotional Selectivity Theory and Emotion Regulation in the Second Half of Life." *Motivation and Emotion* 27 (2003): 103–23.

Cassell, Eric J. *The Nature of Suffering: And the Goals of Medicine*. New York: Oxford University Press, 1991.

Cavanaugh, William T. *Torture and Eucharist: Theology, Politics, and the Body of Christ*. Oxford: Blackwell, 1998.

Cessario, Romanus, O.P. *Introduction to Moral Theology*. Washington, D.C.: Catholic University of America Press, 2001.

Clifford, Richard J., S.J., and Khaled Anatoloios. "Christian Salvation: Biblical and Theological Perspectives." *Theological Studies* 66 (2005): 739–69.

Coetzee, J. M. *Elizabeth Costello*. London: Secker & Warburg, 2003.

Collins, Patrick. *Prayer in Practice*. Maryknoll, N.Y.: Orbis Books, 2001.

Congar, Yves. *I Believe in the Holy Spirit*. New York: Crossroad, 2000.

Coyne, George, S.J. "God's Chance Creation." *The Tablet*, August 6, 2005, 6–7.

Crowley, Paul G., S.J. *Unwanted Wisdom: Suffering, the Cross, and Hope*. New York: Continuum, 2005.

Crysdale, Cynthia S. W. *Embracing Travail: Retrieving the Cross Today*. New York: Continuum, 1999.

Csikszentimihalyi, Mihalyi. *Flow: The Psychology of Optimal Experience*. New York: Harper & Row, 1990.

Cullinan, Colleen Carpenter. *Redeeming the Story: Women, Suffering, and Christ*. New York: Continuum, 2004.

Custers, Ruud, and Henk Aarts. "Positive Affect as Implicit Motivator: On the Nonconscious Operation of Behavioral Goals." *Journal of Personality and Social Psychology* 89 no. 2 (August 2005): 129–42.

Dalai Lama and H. C. Cutler. *The Art of Happiness: A Handbook of Living*. New York: Riverhead Books, 1998.

Daly, Robert J., S.J. "Sacrifice Unveiled or Sacrifice Revisited: Trinitarian and Liturgical Perspectives." *Theological Studies* 64, no. 1 (March 2003): 24–42.

Damasio, Antonio. *Descartes' Error: Emotion, Reason, and the Human Brain*. New York: Putnam, 1994.

Danner, Mark. "Abu Ghraib: The Hidden Story." *New York Review of Books*, October 7, 2004.

Delbanco, Andrew. *The Death of Satan: How Americans Have Lost the Sense of Evil*. New York: Farrar, Straus & Giroux, 1995.

Delio, Illia, O.S.F. "Is Creation Eternal?" *Theological Studies* 66, no. 2 (June 2005): 279–303.

Diener, Ed, Richard E. Lucas, and Christie Napa Scollon. "Beyond the Hedonic Treadmill: Revising the Adaptation Theory of Well-Being." *American Psychologist* 61, no. 4 (2006): 305–14.

Dodds, Michael J., O.P. "Thomas Aquinas, Human Suffering, and the Unchanging God of Love." *Theological Studies* 52 (1991): 330–44.

Donne, John. *Selections from Divine Poems, Sermons, Devotions, and Prayers*. New York: Paulist Press, 1990.

Dostoevsky, Fyodor. *Notes from Underground*. New York: Vintage Books, 1993.

Douglass, Frederick. *The Life and Times of Frederick Douglass* (Ware, Hertfordshire: Wordsworth, 1996).

Douglass, James W. *The Nonviolent Coming of God*. Maryknoll, N.Y.: Orbis Books, 1991.

Duffy, Stephen. "Our Hearts of Darkness: Original Sin Revisited." *Theological Studies* 49 (1988): 597–622.

Dulles, Avery. "Faith and Revelation." In *Systematic Theology: Roman Catholic Perspectives,* vol. 1, ed. Francis Schüssler Fiorenza and John P. Galvin. Minneapolis: Fortress Press, 1991.

Ekman, Paul. "Facial Expression and Emotion." *American Psychologist* 48 (1993): 384–92.

Elie, Paul. *The Life You Save May Be Your Own: An American Pilgrimage*. New York: Farrar, Straus & Giroux, 2003.

Ellsberg, Robert. *The Saints' Guide to Happiness*. New York: Farrar, Straus & Giroux, 2003.

Erickson, Millard J. *What Does God Know and When Does He Know It?* Grand Rapids: Zondervan, 2003.

Farley, Edward. *Divine Empathy: A Theology of God*. Minneapolis: Fortress Press, 1996.

Figura, Michael. "The Suffering of God in Patristic Theology." *Communio* (Fall 2003): 366–85.

Frank, Arthur W. *At the Will of the Body*. New York: First Mariner Books Edition, 2002.

Frankl, Viktor. *Man's Search for Meaning: An Introduction to Logotherapy*. Boston: Beacon Press, 1962.

Frayn, Michael. *A Landing on the Sun: A Novel*. New York: Viking, 1991.

Fredrickson, Barbara L., R. A. Mancuso, C. Branigan, and M. M. Tugade. "The Undoing Effect of Positive Emotions." *Motivation and Emotion* 24 (2000): 237–58.

Fredrickson, Barbara L. "What Good Are Positive Emotions?" *Review of General Psychology* 2, no. 3 (September 1998): 300–319.

Fredrickson, Barbara L., and M. F. Losada. "Positive Affect and the Complex Dynamics of Human Flourishing," *American Psychologist* 60, no. 7 (October 2005): 678–86.

Frith, Christopher D., and Daniel M. Wolpert. *The Neuroscience of Social Interaction: Decoding, Imitating, and Influencing the Actions of Others*. Oxford: Oxford University Press, 2003.

Gelpi, Donald L. *The Turn to Experience in Contemporary Theology*. New York: Paulist Press, 1994.

Gilbert, Daniel. *Stumbling on Happiness*. New York: Alfred A. Knopf, 2006.

Gilbert, Jack. "A Brief for the Defense." In *New Yorker*, November 15, 2004, 86.

Gladwell, Malcolm. *Blink: The Power of Thinking without Thinking*. New York: Little, Brown, 2005.

Glover, Jonathan. *Humanity: A Moral History of the Twentieth Century*. New Haven, Conn.: Yale University Press, 1999.

Glucklich, Ariel. *Sacred Pain: Hurting the Body for the Sake of the Soul*. Oxford: Oxford University Press, 2001.

Goleman, Daniel. *Emotional Intelligence*. New York: W. W. Norton, 1995.

Gonzaga, Gian C., Rebecca A. Turner, Dacher Keltner, Belinda Campos, and Margaret Altemus. "Romantic Love and Sexual Desire in Close Relationships." *Emotion* 6, no. 2 (May 2006): 163–79.

Greene, Brian. *The Fabric of the Cosmos: Space, Time, and the Texture of Reality*. New York: Knopf, 2004.

Grey, Mary. *Feminism, Redemption, and the Christian Tradition*. Mystic, Conn.: Twenty-Third Publications, 1990.

Griffen, Susan. *A Chorus of Stones*. New York: Doubleday, 1992.

Gross, J. J. "The Emerging Field of Emotion Regulation: An Integrative Review." *Review of General Psychology* 2 (1998): 271–99.

Guroian, Vigen. "Salvation: Divine Therapy." *Theology Today* 61 (2004): 309–21.

Gutiérrez, Gustavo. *God-Talk and the Suffering of the Innocent*. Maryknoll, N.Y.: Orbis, 1988.

Hanby, Michael. "The Culture of Death, the Ontology of Boredom, and the Resistance of Joy." *Communio* 31 (Summer 2004): 199.

Harrington, Daniel, S.J. *Why Do We Suffer? A Scriptural Approach to the Human Condition* (Franklin, Wisc.: Sheed & Ward, 2000).

Hassin, Ran R., James S. Uleman, and John A. Bargh. *The New Unconscious*. Oxford: Oxford University Press, 2005.

Hatfield, E., and R. Rapson. "Love and Attachment Processes." In *Handbook of Emotions,* ed. M. Lewis and J. M. Haviland, 595–604. New York: Guilford Press, 1993.

Haught, John F. "Darwin, Design and the Promise of Nature." The Boyle Lecture 2004. St. Mary-le-Bow, London.

———. *God after Darwin: A Theology of Evolution*. Boulder, Colo.: Westview Press, 2000.

Heft, James L. *A Catholic Modernity: Charles Taylor's Marianist Award Lecture*. New York: Oxford University Press, 1999.

Hellwig, Monika. *The Christian Creeds: A Faith to Live By.* Dayton, Ohio: Pflaum, 1973.

Hick, John. "Soul-Making and Suffering." In *The Problem of Evil,* ed. Marilyn McCord Adams and Robert Merrihew Adams, 168–88. Oxford: Oxford University Press, 1990.

Himes, Michael J., and Kenneth R. Himes, O.F.M. *Fullness of Faith: The Public Significance of Theology*. Mahwah, N.J.: Paulist Press, 1993.

Hoffman, Eva. *After Such Knowledge: Memory, History, and the Legacy of the Holocaust*. New York: Public Affairs, 2004.

Hopkins, Gerard Manley. *Poems of Gerard Manley Hopkins*. 3rd ed. Oxford: Oxford University Press, 1948.

Howard, Evan B. *Affirming the Touch of God: A Psychological and Philosophical Exploration of Christian Discernment*. New York: University Press of America, 2000.

Hubble, Mark A., Barry L. Duncan, and Scott Miller. *The Heart and Soul of Change: What Works in Therapy*. Washington, D.C.: American Psychological Association, 2002.

Izard, Carroll E. "Basic Emotions, Relations amongst Emotions, and Emotion-Cognition Relations." *Psychological Review* 99 (1992): 561–65.

James, William. *The Varieties of Religious Experience*. New York: Modern Library, 1936.

Jamison, Kay Refield. *Exuberance: The Passion for Life*. New York: Vintage Books, 2005.

John Paul II. *Apostolic Letter Salvifici Doloris: On the Christian Meaning of Human Suffering*. February 11, 1984.

Johnson, Elizabeth A., C.S.J. *Consider Jesus: Waves of Renewal in Christology*. New York: Crossroad, 1993.

———. "Does God Play Dice? Divine Providence and Chance." *Theological Studies* 57 (1996): 3–18.

———. *She Who Is: The Mystery of God in Feminist Theological Discourse*. New York: Crossroad, 1991.

Jones, James W. *Contemporary Psychoanalysis and Religion*. New Haven, Conn.: Yale University Press, 1991.

Julian of Norwich. *Revelations of Divine Love (Short Text and Long Text)*. Trans. Elizabeth Spearing. New York: Penguin Books, 1998.

Karris, Robert J. *Prayer and the New Testament*. New York: Crossroad, 2000.

Katz, Claire Elise. "Raising Cain: The Problem of Evil and the Question of Responsibility." *CrossCurrents* (Summer 2005): 215–33.

Keck, David. *Forgetting Whose We Are: Alzheimer's Disease and the Love of God*. Nashville: Abingdon Press, 1996.

Kingwell, Mark. *In Pursuit of Happiness: Better Living from Plato to Prozac*. New York: Crown Publishers, 1998.

Kiser, Scott. "An Existential Case Study of Madness: Encounters with Divine Affliction." *Journal of Humanistic Psychology* 44, no. 4 (Fall 2004): 431–54.

Komonchak, Joseph A. "The Violence of the Cross: A Mystery, Not a Punishment." *Commonweal*, January 28, 2005, 19–22.

Korsmeyer, Jerry D. *Evolution and Eden: Balancing Original Sin and Contemporary Science*. Mahwah, N.J.: Paulist Press, 1998.

Kuschel, Karl-Josef. *Laughter: A Theological Reflection*. New York: Continuum, 1994.

Kushner, Harold S. *When Bad Things Happen to Good People*. New York: Schocken, 1981.

LaCugna, Catherine Mowry. *God for Us: The Trinity and Christian Life*. San Francisco: HarperSanFrancisco, 1991.

Larsen, Jeff T., A. Peter McGraw, and John T. Cacioppo. "Can People Feel Happy and Sad at the Same Time?" *Journal of Personality and Social Psychology* 81, no. 4 (October 2001): 684–96.

Lash, Nicholas. *Believing Three Ways in One God: A Reading of the Apostles' Creed*. Notre Dame, Ind.: University of Notre Dame Press, 1992.

Laughlin, Robert B. *A Different Universe: Reinventing Physics from the Bottom Down*. New York: Basic Books, 2005.

LeDoux, J. E. "Emotions: Clues from the Brain." *Annual Review of Psychology* 46 (1995): 209–33.

Lewis, C. S. *A Grief Observed*. London: Faber and Faber, 1961.
———. *The Problem of Pain*. New York: Macmillan, 1962.

Lynch, William. *Images of Hope: Imagination as Healer of the Hopeless*. Notre Dame, Ind.: University of Notre Dame Press, 1965.

MacDonald, Ann-Marie. *The Way the Crow Flies*. New York: Harper-Collins, 2003.

Magill, Arthur C. *Suffering: A Test of Theological Method.* Philadelphia: Westminster Press, 1982 (1968).

Marcus, Norman. *The Hooligan's Return.* New York: Farrar, Straus & Giroux, 2003.

Marsden, George M. *Jonathan Edwards: A Life.* New Haven, Conn.: Yale University Press, 2003.

Maslow, Abraham H. *Motivation and Personality.* New York: Harper & Row, 1970.

Matera, Frank J. "Christ in the Theologies of Paul and John: A Study in the Diverse Unity of New Testament Theology." *Theological Studies* 67 (2006): 237–56.

May, Gerald G., M.D. *The Dark Night of the Soul.* San Francisco: HarperSanFrancisco, 2004.

McGrath, Alister E. *A Brief History of Heaven.* Oxford: Blackwell Publishing, 2003.

McKenna, Megan. *The New Stations of the Cross: The Way of the Cross According to Scripture.* New York: Doubleday Image Books, 2003.

McMahon, Darrin M. *Happiness: A History.* New York: Atlantic Monthly Press, 2006.

McManus, Kathleen, O.P. "Suffering in the Theology of Edward Schillebeeckx." *Theological Studies* 60 (1999): 476–91.

Miller, Jerome. *The Way of Suffering: A Geography of Crisis.* Washington, D.C.: Georgetown University Press, 1988.

———. "The Way of Suffering: A Reasoning of the Heart." *Second Opinion* 17, no. 4 (April 1992): 21–33.

Milosz, Czeslaw. *New and Collected Poems, 1931–2001.* New York: HarperCollins, 2003.

Moore, Sebastian. *The Crucified Jesus Is No Stranger.* New York: Seabury Press, 1981.

Murphy, Nancey. *Bodies and Souls, or Spirited Bodies?* Cambridge: Cambridge University Press, 2006.

Murray, Fr. Paul, O.P. "The Task of Happiness: A Reflection on Human Suffering and Christian Joy." The Second Annual Joseph and Edith Habiger Lecture in Catholic Studies, University of St. Thomas and St. John's University, *Logos: A Journal of Catholic Thought and Culture* 4, no. 4 (Fall 2001): 11–32.

Myers, David G. *The Pursuit of Happiness: Discovering the Pathway to Fulfillment, Well-Being, and Enduring Personal Joy.* New York: HarperCollins, 1992.

Neiman, Susan. *Evil in Modern Thought: An Alternative History of Philosophy.* Princeton, N.J.: Princeton University Press, 2002.

O'Connell, Timothy E. *Making Disciples: A Handbook of Christian Moral Formation*. New York: Crossroad, 1998.

O'Keefe, Mark, O.S.B. *Becoming Good, Becoming Holy: On the Relationship of Christian Ethics and Spirituality.* New York: Paulist Press, 1995.

———. *What Are They Saying about Social Sin?* Mahwah, N.J.: Paulist Press, 1990.

Orsi, Robert A. *Between Heaven and Earth: The Religious Worlds People Make and the Scholars Who Study Them*. Princeton, N.J.: Princeton University Press, 2005.

Ortiz, Sister Diana, with Patricia Davis. *The Blindfold's Eyes: My Journey from Torture to Truth*. Maryknoll, N.Y.: Orbis Books, 2002.

Pedersen, Ann. *God, Creation, and All That Jazz*. St. Louis: Chalice Press, 2000.

Pinker, Stephen. *How the Mind Works*. New York: W. W. Norton, 1997.

Polkinghorne, John. *The Faith of a Physicist: Reflections of a Bottom-Up Thinker.* Minneapolis: Fortress Press, 1996.

———. *Faith, Science and Understanding*. New Haven, Conn.: Yale University Press, 2001.

———, ed. *The Work of Love: Creation as Kenosis*. Grand Rapids: Eerdmans, 2001.

Post, Stephen G., Byron Johnson, Michael E. McCullough, and Jeffrey P. Schloss, eds. *Research on Altruism and Love*. Philadelphia: Templeton Foundation Press, 2003.

Rahner, Karl. "The Apostolate of Prayer." *Theological Investigations* 3. London: Darton, Longman & Todd, 1963, 209–19.

———. "The Eucharist and Suffering." *Theological Investigations* 3. London: Darton, Longman & Todd, 1963, 161–70.

———. *The Practice of Faith: A Handbook of Contemporary Spirituality*. New York: Crossroad, 1986.

———. "Reflections on the Unity of the Love of Neighbour and the Love of God." *Theological Investigations* 6. London: Darton, Longman & Todd, 1963, 231–49.

———. "The Theological Concept of Concupiscentia." *Theological Investigations* 1. London: Darton, Longman & Todd, 1963, 347–82.

———. "Why Does God Allow Us to Suffer?" *Theological Investigations* 19. New York: Crossroad, 1983, 194–208.

Rankka, Kristine M. *Women and the Value of Suffering*. Collegeville, Minn.: Liturgical Press, 1998.

Rhodes, Richard. *Masters of Death: The SS Einsatzgruppen and the Invention of the Holocaust*. New York: Alfred A. Knopf, 2002.

Richard, Lucien, O.M.I. *Christ: The Self-Emptying of God*. Mahwah, N.J.: Paulist Press, 1997.

———. *What Are They Saying about the Theology of Suffering?* Mahwah, N.J.: Paulist, 1992.

Robinson, Elizabeth. *The True and Outstanding Adventures of the Hunt Sisters*. New York: Little, Brown, 2004.

Roy, Louis, O.P. *Transcendent Experiences: Phenomenology and Critique*. Toronto: University of Toronto Press, 2001.

Rychalk, Joseph E. *In Defense of Human Consciousness*. Washington, D.C.: American Psychological Association, 1997.

Salzman, Mark. *Lying Awake*. New York: Alfred A. Knopf, 2000.

Scarry, Elaine. *The Body in Pain: The Making and Unmaking of the World*. New York: Oxford University Press, 1985.

Schacter, Daniel L. *Searching for Memory: The Brain, the Mind, and the Past*. New York: Basic Books, 1996.

Schafer, Roy. "The Pursuit of Failure and the Idealization of Unhappiness." *American Psychologist* 39, no. 4 (April 1984): 405–17.

Schillebeeckx, Edward. *Christ: The Experience of Jesus as Lord*. New York: Crossroad, 1989.

Schneiders, Sandra M. *Written That You May Believe: Encountering Jesus in the Fourth Gospel*. New York: Crossroad, 2003.

Schner, George. "The Appeal to Experience." *Theological Studies* 53 (1992): 40–59.

Schwebel, Lisa J. *Apparitions, Healings, and Weeping Madonnas: Christianity and the Paranormal*. Mahwah, N.J.: Paulist Press, 2004.

Seligman, Martin E. P. *Authentic Happiness: Using the New Positive Psychology to Realize Your Potential for Lasting Fulfillment*. New York: Free Press, 2002.

Sloyan, Gerard S. *Jesus in Focus: A Life in Its Setting*. Rev. ed. Mystic, Conn.: Twenty-Third Publications, 1994.

———. *Why Jesus Died*. Minneapolis: Fortress Press, 2004.

Smith, Quentin. "Big Bang Cosmology and Atheism." *Free Inquiry* 18, no. 2 (Spring 1998): 35.

Soelle, Dorothee. *Suffering*. Philadelphia: Fortress Press, 1975.

Spelman, Elizabeth V. *Fruits of Sorrow: Framing Our Attention to Suffering*. Boston: Beacon Press, 1997.

Stark, Rodney. *The Rise of Christianity: A Sociologist Reconsiders History*. Princeton, N.J.: Princeton University Press, 1996.

———. *The Victory of Reason: How Christianity Led to Freedom, Capitalism, and Western Success*. New York: Random House, 2005.

Stern, Daniel N. *The Interpersonal World of the Infant*. New York: Basic Books, 1985.

Stoeger, William R. S.J. "God and Time: The Action and Life of the Triune God in the World." *Theology Today* 55, no. 3 (October 1998).

Styron, William. *Darkness Visible: A Memoir of Madness*. New York: Vintage Books, 1990.

Tanner, Kathryn. *Jesus, Humanity, and the Trinity: A Brief Systematic Theology*. Minneapolis: Fortress Press, 2001.

Tavard, George H. "The Mystery of Divine Providence." *Theological Studies* 64 (2003): 707–18.

Taylor, Charles. *A Catholic Modernity?* Edited by James L. Heft. Oxford: Oxford University Press, 2003.

Thiel, John. *God, Evil, and Innocent Suffering*. New York: Crossroad, 2002.

———. *Senses of Tradition: Continuity and Development in Catholic Faith*. New York: Oxford University Press, 2000.

Toner, Jules. *Love and Friendship*. Milwaukee: Marquette University Press, 2003.

Toole, David C. "Divine Ecology and the Apocalypse: A Theological Description of Natural Disasters and the Environmental Crisis." *Theology Today* 55, no. 4 (January 1999): 547–61.

Tracy, David. *Blessed Rage for Order*. San Francisco: Harper & Row, 1988.

Walker, Adrian J. "'Rejoice Always.' How Everyday Joy Responds to the Problem of Evil." *Communio* 31 (Summer 2004): 200–235.

Weil, Simone. *Waiting for God*. New York: Harper & Row, 1951.

Weinandy, Thomas G. *Does God Suffer?* Notre Dame, Ind.: University of Notre Dame Press, 2000.

———. "Does God Suffer?" *First Things* (November 2001): 35–41.

White, Nicholas. *A Brief History of Happiness*. Oxford: Blackwell, 2006.

Wiley, Tatha. *Original Sin: Origins, Developments, Contemporary Meanings*. Mahwah, N.J.: Paulist Press, 2002.

Wilkin, Robert Louis. *The Spirit of Early Christian Thought*. New Haven, Conn.: Yale University Press, 2003.

Williams, Marjorie. *The Woman at the Washington Zoo: Writings on Politics, Family, and Fate*. New York: Public Affairs, 2005.

Wilson, David Sloan. *Darwin's Cathedral: Evolution, Religion and the Nature of Society*. Chicago: University of Chicago Press, 2002.

Wilson, Ian. *Murder at Golgotha: Revisiting the Most Famous Crime Scene in History.* New York: St. Martin's Press, 2006.

Wilson, Timothy D. *Strangers to Ourselves: Discovering the Adaptive Unconscious.* Cambridge, Mass.: Harvard University Press, 2002.

Witherup, Ronald D. *Conversion in the New Testament.* Collegeville, Minn.: Liturgical Press, 1994.

Wolterstorff, Nicholas. *Lament for a Son.* Grand Rapids: Eerdmans, 1987.

Wood, James. *The Book against God.* New York: Farrar, Straus & Giroux, 2003.

Woodward, Kenneth L. *The Book of Miracles: The Meaning of the Miracle Stories in Christianity, Judaism, Buddhism, Hinduism, Islam.* New York: Simon & Schuster, 2000.

Wright, N. T. *The Resurrection of the Son of God.* Minneapolis: Fortress Press, 2003.

Young, Pamela Dickey. "Beyond Moral Influence to an Atoning Life." *Theology Today* 52, no. 3 (October 1995): 344–55.

INDEX

Of Related Interest

John E. Thiel
GOD, EVIL, AND INNOCENT SUFFERING
A Theological Reflection

"Many current books on evil see human suffering mainly as a conceptual problem to be solved by philosophical analysis, while others see suffering as a compelling reason to reject Christian belief. John Thiel offers an arresting theological alternative to such views. Belief in the omnipotence of divine love, he argues, is a faithful and coherent response to the innocent suffering we see all around us — and to our deep sense that God is in no way the cause of evil. Whether or not they agree with his conclusions, Thiel's readers will be challenged to look at an ancient problem afresh by this welcome and thought-provoking book."
— BRUCE MARSHALL, Perkins School of Theology

"John Thiel's book provides the most compendious mapping and critical evaluation of the theological responses to the problem of innocent suffering that I know. Moreover, it does so with great economy, and in a style that is clear, fresh, and engaging. Its critique of tendencies in classical and modern theology to evade the scandal of innocent suffering is especially compelling. Yet this book also offers a constructive and original alternative to traditional and modern accounts. It argues that the issue of innocent suffering properly belongs within the parameter of a doctrine of God, indeed that the problem illuminates in a powerful way God's involvement in the world on the side of human beings who are vulnerable to all kinds of evil, not the least of which is death. The book is prophetic in the strict sense. It speaks to the God of promise, who announces the truth of God's being with us, nothing less than the end of what divides, rends, and annihilates us."
— CYRIL O'REGAN, University of Notre Dame

0-8245-1928-0, paperback

crossroad

Of Related Interest

Paula D'Arcy
WHEN PEOPLE GRIEVE
The Power of Love in the Midst of Pain

An internationally renowned expert on the issues of pain, loss, and bereavement helps us cope with the process of grief and reach out to others with loving kindness. Now revised and updated, this classic manual is full of practical advice. Paula covers a whole range of issues and topics including: Loss, Grief, and Love, Depression, Shock, Anger, Moodiness, The Body's Response to Grief, Tips on Visiting, Honest Conversation, Things Not to Say, Feelings of Guilt, God's Will? The Power of Prayer, Specific Ways to Help, The Gift of Touch, The Holidays, Ways You Can Help, The First Two Years, The Pattern of Grief, and many others.

PAULA D'ARCY, bestselling author, is a former psychotherapist and president of the Red Bird Foundation. A frequent speaker in Europe, Asia, and the United States, she lives in northern California.

0-8245-2339-3, paperback

crossroad